BABYLON

BABYLON

EDITED BY

I.L. FINKEL AND M.J. SEYMOUR

with contributions from
J.E. Curtis, A.R. George, J. Marzahn, J.E. Reade and J.J. Taylor

OXFORD
UNIVERSITY PRESS

Exhibition organised by the British Museum, the Musée du Louvre and
the Réunion des Musées Nationaux, Paris and the Staatliche Museen zu Berlin.

   S M
B Staatliche Museen
zu Berlin

Oxford University Press

Oxford University Press, Inc., publishes works that further
Oxford University's objective of excellence
in research, scholarship, and education.

Oxford New York
Auckland Cape Town Dar es Salaam Hong Kong Karachi
Kuala Lumpur Madrid Melbourne Mexico City Nairobi
New Delhi Shanghai Taipei Toronto

With offices in
Argentina Austria Brazil Chile Czech Republic France Greece
Guatemala Hungary Italy Japan Poland Portugal Singapore
South Korea Switzerland Thailand Turkey Ukraine Vietnam

First published in 2008 by British Museum Press
A division of The British Museum Company Ltd
38 Russell Square, London WC1B 3QQ

Published in North America in 2009 by
Oxford University Press, Inc.
198 Madison Avenue
New York, New York 10016

www.oup.com

Oxford is a registered trademark of Oxford University Press

Babylon / edited by I.L. Finkel and M.J. Seymour.
   p. cm.
 Originally published: London : British Museum Press, 2008.
 ISBN 978-0-19-538540-3
 1. Babylon (Extinct city) I. Finkel, Irving L. II. Seymour, M. J. (Michael J.)
 DS70.5.B3B33 2009
 935--dc22

2008031942

ISBN-13: 9780195385403

Printing number: 9 8 7 6 5 4 3 2 1

Printed in Italy

Contents

Sponsor's Foreword

On behalf of the Blavatnik Family Foundation, I congratulate Neil MacGregor and all his team at the British Museum most warmly for organising this unique and historic exhibition.

The saga of Babylon should demand the attention of us all, wherever we live and work, and the world's current focus on the region adds greatly to the interest – historical, political and strategic – which the exhibition will arouse.

My own personal and business connections to the Middle East are just some of the reasons I am delighted that the Blavatnik Family Foundation is supporting this event.

I look forward keenly, together with my own family, to enjoying and learning from this experience and I am confident that the Museum's many visitors will feel the same.

Len Blavatnik

Director's Foreword

For two thousand years, Babylon has haunted the European imagination like no other city. Its historical reality obscured by distance and decay, the myth of Babylon has flourished, fascinating poets and film-makers, painters and moralists. For classical authors, its Hanging Gardens and city walls were Wonders of the World, miracles of sophisticated engineering. Babylon in the Bible – and it is present from Genesis to Revelation – embodies pretty well every human shortcoming: the Tower of Babel the supreme example of overweening vanity justly punished, the city itself a byword for every metropolis mired in greed and self-indulgence.

But for the last two hundred years, there has also been a different Babylon: the 'real' Babylon. First slowly, then spectacularly, British, French and German scholars and archaeologists uncovered and pieced together the fragments of the historical city, sometimes confirming, sometimes contradicting the Biblical and classical narratives, revealing a great imperial capital, a centre of intellectual, scientific and political importance over many centuries. That continuing dialogue between the myth and the reality of Babylon is the subject of this exhibition. The three museums which, outside Iraq, have the deepest Mesopotamian collections – the Staatliche Museen zu Berlin, the Louvre and the British Museum – have worked together as never before to produce a cycle of three major exhibitions, of which this in London is the third. I owe a great debt of gratitude to Peter-Klaus Schuster, General Director of the Staatliche Museen zu Berlin and to Henri Loyette, Director of the Louvre. We all hope this will be the first of many projects between Berlin, Paris and London.

This happy collaboration between colleagues has led to three very different exhibitions, each with its own range of emphasis, and with three independent catalogues, although some contributions have been shared between them. In the British Museum we decided to concentrate on a very short period of Babylonian history, epitomised by Nebuchadnezzar II (605-562 BC), visionary builder and ruler of a vast empire. We have focussed on what in biblical terms were the Last Days of Babylon, before the arrival of the Persian army under Cyrus II in 539 BC ended native rule and heralded an altogether new age in the ancient Middle East. The process of Babylon's transformation into myth begins at this point, the voices of the Greek authors vying with those of the Hebrew prophets for centre stage. Nebuchadnezzar himself emerges as a beast, but at least with the compensation that he was to inspire William Blake. Here we have a unique opportunity to present the complex relationship between a remote ancient capital and later tradition and invention in a story that stretches from Antiquity to the present day.

It seemed compelling for us to focus too on the very latest phase in Babylon's extraordinary history. Since the outbreak of war in 2003, with its grave consequences for the archaeology of Mesopotamia, the British Museum has at all points been committed to help our Iraqi colleagues in every way possible and to publicise the challenges that they face. The damage to Babylon itself has shocked the world, but here we have the opportunity to do more than lament; we can look at this great culture in its heyday, celebrate a central icon of world culture in all its manifestations, and consider how it is now to be protected and preserved.

Neil MacGregor, Director

Editors' Acknowledgements

It is a pleasure for the editors to acknowledge here assistance and help received from many quarters in the preparation of the *Babylon: Myth and Reality* exhibition. Crucial from the outset has been our collaboration with colleagues in Paris and Berlin, and we would, therefore, particularly like to thank Béatrice André-Salvini, Sébastien Allard and Marianne Cotty of the Musée du Louvre, and Joachim Marzahn, Bernd Müller-Neuhof, Moritz Wullen and Hanna Strzoda of the Staatliche Museen zu Berlin. The exhibition, which has appeared in different forms in Paris and Berlin, is the result of an unprecedented close cooperation between the Réunion des Musées Nationaux, the Staatliche Museen zu Berlin and the British Museum, and is based on material drawn from these and other world collections. We gratefully acknowledge the generosity, assistance and support of all the lenders to the exhibition, who are listed on page 8.

Closer to home come the core team who have worked with us and with our departmental colleague and fellow exhibition curator, Jon Taylor, to produce the exhibition: Emma Kelly, Jill Maggs, Rebecca Richards, Hannah Payne and Paul Goodhead, all of whom contributed important ideas as well as professional expertise. We are also grateful to Michael Wilson for a fruitful period of early consultation on the exhibition's narrative and content. Many other members of the Museum have contributed to the project, and we wish to thank particularly our colleagues in the departments of Exhibitions, Communications, Marketing, and Conservation and Science. From within our own Middle East department we have received a great deal of assistance, and here we would like to express our gratitude to Dean Baylis, Angela Smith, Claire Burton, Rupert Chapman, Sarah Price, Jerry Baker, Theodora Georgiou, Jane Newson, Sarah Collins, Paul Collins, Venetia Porter, Nigel Tallis and our Keeper, John Curtis.

We are deeply indebted to the authors who have contributed chapters to this volume. We owe to Andrew George the specially written sections entitled *A Tour of Nebuchadnezzar's Babylon* and *The Truth about Etemenanki, the Ziggurat of Babylon*, as well as his *Ancient Descriptions: the Babylonian Topographical Texts* which was earlier published in French (in the exhibition catalogue *Babylone*) and in German (in the catalogue *Babylon: Wahrheit*). Joachim Marzahn allowed us to translate and adapt his contribution here entitled *Koldewey's Babylon*, which was first published in German in the same exhibition catalogue. Julian Reade produced major original contributions for this book in his *Disappearance and Rediscovery*, *Nineteenth-Century Exploration and Interpretation*, *Tablets at Babylon and the British Museum*, *Early Travellers on the Wonders: Suggested Sites* and *The Search for the Ziggurat*. Christopher Walker, as well as advising on aspects of Babylonian astronomy and mathematics, authored the text on Babylonian chronology shown on page 146. Jon Taylor, in addition to writing *Neo-Babylonian Kings at Babylon* and *Babylon, Jerusalem and the Jewish Exile*, has helped us in many ways with editing problems. Finally, John Curtis has written an important conclusion to the book from the unique vantage point of his own experience, *The Site of Babylon Today*. The remaining sections have been singly or jointly authored by the editors.

As well as the contributing authors, our thanks are also owed to many specialists for advice and information on particular topics. For generously sharing their expertise we are grateful to our British Museum colleagues Silke Ackermann, Catherine Eagleton, Philip Attwood, Sheila O'Connell, Giulia Bartrum, Martin Royalton-Kisch, Joseph Sharples, Sam Moorhead and Amelia

Dowler, as well as to those from other institutions, among whom we would particularly like to mention Michael O'Keefe and Colin Baker (British Library), Annie Vernay-Nouri and Valérie Sueur-Hermel (Bibliothèque nationale de France), Colin Wakefield (Bodleian Library), Francesca Rochberg (University of California Riverside) and Mark Geller (UCL).

Valentina Talian, Axelle Russo and James Perry researched and obtained images for this volume, production was handled by Melanie Hall and the copy-editor was Jenny Knight. Our final thanks must go to our designer, Carla Turchini, and our editor, Carolyn Jones, without whom this catalogue would never have been possible.

List of Lenders

Bibliothèque nationale de France

The Bodleian Library, University of Oxford

The British Library

Broelmuseum, Kortrijk

Conner Contemporary Art, Washington DC

The De Morgan Centre for the Study of 19th Century Art and Society, London

Deputy Ministry of Antiquities and Museums, Ministry of Education, Kingdom of Saudi Arabia

Edinburgh University Library

Hart Gallery, London

Kupferstichkabinett, Staatliche Museen zu Berlin

Laing Art Gallery, Tyne and Wear Museums, Newcastle City Council

M.C. Escher Foundation,The Netherlands

Mr Michael Lassel, Germany

Musée du Louvre, Paris

Mittelrhein-Museum, Koblenz

Musée d'Orsay, Paris

Pinacoteca Nazionale di Siena

Private collection

Private collection

Private collection

Tate

The Whitworth Art Gallery, University of Manchester

Victoria and Albert Museum

Vorderasiatisches Museum, Staatliche Museen zu Berlin

Walker Art Gallery, National Museums Liverpool

Babylon

Babylon
INTRODUCTION

Irving Finkel and Michael Seymour

Babylon, in all its manifestations, is at once remote to us and all around us. Like no other city, its history has become bound up with legend, and it is this remarkable phenomenon that is the subject of the present book. Babylon, the greatest city of ancient Iraq, sprawling by the great Euphrates river, famed for the Tower of Babel and the Hanging Gardens, was one of the great capital cities of Antiquity. Its very name is possessed of an enduring resonance that has made it a symbol and an inspiration ever since the days of Nebuchadnezzar II, its greatest king and most indefatigable builder.

This book, which accompanies the British Museum exhibition entitled *Babylon: Myth and Reality* (November 2008 to March 2009), has undertaken to create some tangible impression of this immense but shadowy entity. All the exhibited objects are illustrated in this book (indicated by **ⓔ**), together with much additional and related material. Both exhibition and book are devoted to the Babylon of the late seventh and sixth centuries BC, the period after the Fall of Nineveh when the kings of the Neo-Babylonian dynasty such as Nebuchadnezzar and Nabonidus ruled the

ⓔ FIG. 1
Glazed brick relief from Babylon showing a lion

Reign of Nebuchadnezzar (605–562 BC)
Baked and glazed clay
H 119 cm, W 241 cm
From Babylon
Staatliche Museen zu Berlin, Vorderasiatisches Museum,
VA Bab 4765
Marzahn et al. 1992: 112-7; Marzahn 1994

Throughout this book, the symbol **ⓔ** indicates that the object illustrated is on show in the British Museum exhibition BABYLON: MYTH AND REALITY.

world. The time span, indeed, is remarkably short given the profound historical significance of what actually took place: in less than a century, Babylon was to pass from its highest imperial peak to subjection to outside rulers, never to regain its true independence.

A gallery of remarkable individuals meets us on the way besides Nebuchadnezzar and Nabonidus: the Greek historians Herodotus and Ctesias, pioneering investigators of the site Claudius Rich and Robert Koldewey, as well as the Jesuit polymath Athanasius Kircher and the painter Rembrandt van Rijn all provide perspectives on Babylon and its legends stretching from Antiquity to the present. Other valued authorities remain anonymous: the dedicated and highly trained scribes of the ancient city of Babylon, who painstakingly recorded history as it unfolded and turned their cuneiform tablets to record royal inscriptions and political propaganda alike. It is from these contemporary tablets that confirmation comes for narratives that have long been known, as well as quite unexpected new insights into Mesopotamian belief and practice. With all this help we are able to examine ancient Babylon from twin perspectives: the archaeology that has come out of the ground, and the great panoply of legend and art that Babylon's name and accomplishments have inspired.

The way in which this vanished metropolis has retained its hold on the creative imagination is owed to the Old Testament on the one hand, and the collected testimony of the ancient Greek historians on the other. Its functions as model, parable, scapegoat and symbol of all that is wicked have combined to make it endlessly fascinating. It is remarkable, for example, how the simple didactic narrative of the Tower of Babel in Genesis has given rise to hundreds of towers in paint or ink. These, when viewed as a whole, would make a book in themselves in their mixture of interdependence and originality, and their endless reference to other worlds and other times.

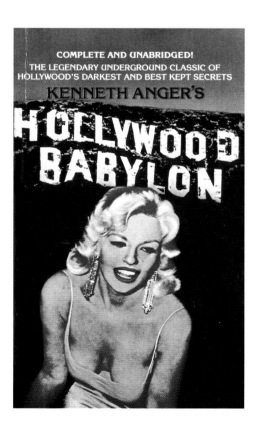

FIG. 2
Hollywood Babylon

Babylon lives on. The iconic cover of Kenneth Anger's *Hollywood Babylon*, first published by Straight Arrow Books, New York in 1975.

These paintings are iconic, but their origins in a real ancient structure, Nebuchadnezzar's temple tower, or ziggurat, are far less well known. This massive tower has all but vanished from sight, largely because his state-of-the-art building bricks were mostly removed and reused by later builders. Archaeology, undeterred, has reconstructed the ziggurat's ground plan and elevation by a mixture of spadework and textual decipherment, so that we know enough now to model the original in more or less accurate proportions. At the same time Babylon's Hanging Gardens still flourish in people's minds, notwithstanding the engineering problem of irrigation in an upward direction, or the conundrum of what might have been planted in them. Indeed, despite voluminous testimony in ancient Greek, we still cannot locate this paradise at the site of Babylon, while some have denied that it ever existed.

Babylon certainly had its share of World Wonders. Many lists included both the Gardens and the Walls, meaning that the city was unique in offering posterity two out of the seven. To the ancient Greeks, collecting and sifting their fable-like stories, Babylon was distant, exotic and incredible, and so it has remained to us.

Babylon's role in the Bible was not limited to the lesson from the Tower of Babel. The eventual sack of Jerusalem by Nebuchadnezzar in 587 BC which saw both the end of the temple and the beginning of the Judaean Exile in Babylon must, by any criterion, be viewed as one of the most significant episodes in world history, although this would hardly have been Nebuchadnezzar's own view of the affair. It was at this time, a period of complex social and religious development, that monotheistic thinking came to the fore, and perhaps it had its part to play in crystallizing the theologies that came later. At the same time Nebuchadnezzar's fateful conquest earned him a permanently blackened reputation in history, and Babylon, in the eyes of the Old Testament prophets, became a stark symbol of sin and wickedness.

It was Babylon that saw the Writing on the Wall, when the last native king learned from a mysterious inscription that his kingdom was about to be lost to the Medes and Persians. Belshazzar's Feast is supposed to have heralded a dramatic Fall, and although this is not borne out by contemporary documents nothing will dislodge the idea of cataclysmic destruction that overwhelmed Babylon at the end.

This doomed and wicked Babylon has borne remarkable fruit in later culture. Vice and sin have proven a potent mixture in art, both in the portrayal of Nebuchadnezzar as tyrant, beast and madman and in Babylon's central role in the Last Judgement and Apocalypse. The language of the prophets' tirades against Babylon has echoed so powerfully that no other place has ever surpassed it as the quintessential City of Sin.

Babylon's second legacy is less transparent, for it concerns inherited knowledge of a different kind, spin-offs from the mathematics, astronomy, astrology, magic and medicine of the ancient Mesopotamian academies. Survivals within these disciplines can be traced; the most immediate in our terms is the use of sixtieths to subdivide the minute and the hour, a phenomenon whose roots can be traced back in ancient Iraq to around 3000 BC, a time as distant from Nebuchadnezzar himself as his epoch is from us.

And Babylon today? On the one hand, enduring life in a bewildering profusion of images: film and music, slang and poetry, fine art and graffiti …

On the other, once again, destruction. The great city of Babylon is still no stranger to conflict. The concluding chapter of the book looks at Babylon in very recent times and considers the condition of the site and its monuments today.

Disappearance and rediscovery

Julian E. Reade

The ancient city which we know as Babylon was located on the Euphrates river in what is now central Iraq; *Babel*, *Babil* and *Babilu* are other forms of the same name. Babylon lay at the heart of a rich agricultural region that drew its water from the Euphrates, and sometimes from the Tigris, by extensive systems of canals. The region had been important since prehistoric times and was intersected by trade routes connecting Iran, Syria, Turkey, Arabia and the Gulf. Babylon began its own rise to prominence around 2000 BC and for much of the following 2,000 years, with periodic interruptions, it was the most powerful political and economic centre in the region. Its final period of greatness was as capital of the Neo-Babylonian Empire, when – as we shall see below – it was largely rebuilt by Nebuchadnezzar II (605–562 BC). The city continued as an important imperial capital under the Achaemenid Persians and – briefly – Alexander. Babylon also became a cultural centre whose influence extended far beyond the territories that were under direct Babylonian control. Later the city faded from the historical record, not going out in a blaze of glory but superseded by a succession of other cities, Seleucia, Ctesiphon, Kufa, Baghdad and Samarra, that were located elsewhere within the same region; these all had names that were illustrious in their time but the most famous of them was and remains Baghdad. A few hundred miles away, the Babylon neighbourhood was still a convenient site for a market town and local centre; this function is filled today by the nearby town of Hillah, said to have been founded in AD 1101. By that date Babylon was merely the name of a great city that had effectively disappeared. Its location, represented by ruins on the east bank of the Euphrates, was still known but it was no longer important. At one stage part of the city had been converted into a royal hunting reserve. Over the centuries the fine palaces and temples collapsed and were transformed into massive mounds of earth and rubble. The busy streets and residential quarters became a landscape of modest villages, palm-groves, vegetable gardens, fields of grain, and stretches of salty marshland and barren desert.

These features were set among a bewildering tangle of earthworks, some of which were the remains of the ancient fortifications while others were lines of spoil flanking successive irrigation canals, some dry, some still in use. At the same time, as is explored in this volume, the name of the city of Babylon – because of its time-honoured status – had acquired a second life in popular belief. Legends about its glorious past, amalgamating fact and fantasy, were widely disseminated among people living throughout the Middle East and around the Mediterranean Sea. Some of the stories lived on through the Middle Ages into our own time, and were responsible in Europe for many exotic pieces of orientalizing art and literature from the seventeenth to the nineteenth centuries. Over the ages the name of Babylon has been applied to places as far removed from one another as imperial Rome and modern New York.

Some of the earliest stories about a legendary Babylon are those that were told among the Jewish communities of the region, from the sixth century BC onwards. Such stories survive in the Bible, a book which itself owed much to Babylonian influence, and they consequently became familiar among both Jewish and Christian communities wherever these existed in later times.

One story concerned the Tower of Babel. The Book of Genesis recounted how, in some remote past, people had come together to build a city and a tower aiming for the sky, namely the Tower of Babel, and how God had dispersed them all, babbling in different languages, to the far corners of the earth. This provided an explanation for the existence of different languages, and even led

BLACK SEA

ANATOLIA

Ankara □

Halys

TAURUS MOUNTAINS

Harran •

Carchemish •

Balih

Hab

Aleppo •

Ugarit •

Orontes

Athens □

□ Beirut

Sidon •

□ Damascus

Tyre •

*SEA OF
GALILEE*

MEDITERRANEAN SEA

Jordan

□ Amman

JUDAH ISRAEL

Jerusalem •

*DEAD
SEA*

□ Cairo

EGYPT

Teima •

○ Cities in modern Iraq

□ Modern capital cities

▢ Neo Babylonian Empire 6th century BC

N
↑

Nile

RED
SEA

0   500 miles

0   800 kilometres

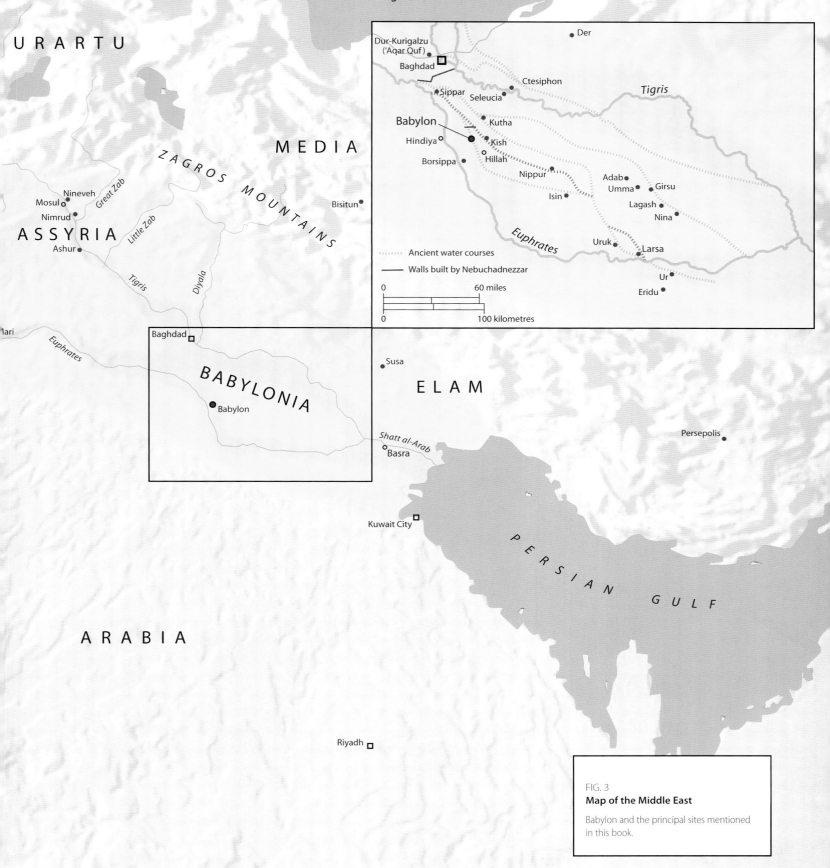

CASPIAN SEA

URARTU

MEDIA

ZAGROS MOUNTAINS

Nineveh
Mosul
Nimrud
Great Zab
Little Zab
ASSYRIA
Ashur
Tigris
Diyala
Bisitun

Der
Dur-Kurigalzu
('Aqar Quf)
Baghdad
Sippar
Ctesiphon
Seleucia
Tigris
Babylon
Kutha
Hindiya
Kish
Hillah
Borsippa
Nippur
Adab
Umma
Girsu
Isin
Lagash
Nina
Uruk
Larsa
Euphrates
Ur
Eridu

Ancient water courses
Walls built by Nebuchadnezzar

0   60 miles
0   100 kilometres

Mari
Euphrates
Baghdad
BABYLONIA
Babylon

Susa
ELAM
Persepolis

Shatt al-Arab
Basra

Kuwait City

PERSIAN GULF

ARABIA

Riyadh

FIG. 3
Map of the Middle East

Babylon and the principal sites mentioned
in this book.

ⓔ FIG. 4

The Babylonian Map of the World, or the *Mappa Mundi*

Probably 6th century BC
From Sippar, excavated by Hormuzd Rassam and acquired
by the British Museum in 1882
Clay
H 12.2 cm, W 8.2 cm
British Museum, BM 92687
Horowitz 1998: 20–42

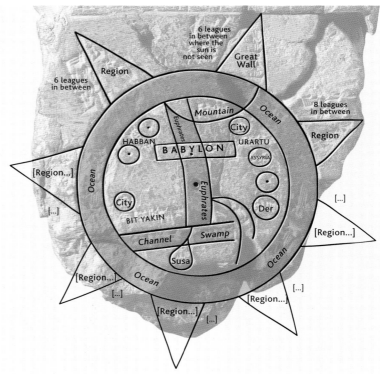

Few inscriptions from ancient Mesopotamia have ever achieved fame in the world outside cuneiform studies, but the Babylonian Map of the World is indisputably among them. This celebrated document is sometimes said to have been found at Sippar in southern Iraq, but the map itself and the associated writings were more probably copied from an earlier example from Babylon. By size and location Babylon here is the centre of a world both geographical and cosmic.

The map takes up the lower two-thirds of one side of the tablet. It is preceded by a descriptive mythological text. The other side contains a second text that applies more directly to the map itself. When held in normal reading position, the orientation of the diagram and the distribution of its components do not quite correlate with modern geography, but that is hardly surprising. The concern is with distant places, mythological events and creatures, and the world beyond the entirely familiar. The view represented in the clay is schematic, and might be likened to the bird's-eye view seen by Etana, the man who in Mesopotamian myth was carried up to heaven upon an eagle's back.[1]

The dominating feature of the map is the broad double ring: the central hole from some early 'pair of compasses' with which it was made is still visible. This ring is labelled *marratu*, 'salt-sea', and it is evident that the Babylonians shared with certain Greek cartographers the idea that an ocean flowed around the inhabited world. Within this boundary the important places and geographical features of the Mesopotamian heartland are represented by assorted (and mostly labelled) circles, oblongs or curves.

North to south (as shown) runs what is now known as the Euphrates river, straddled by a broad oblong that is labelled as Babylon. The spot in the middle of Babylon may even represent Etemenanki, the famous ziggurat restored by the neo-Babylonian kings. Due north is a bulging area labelled 'Mountain', from which the Euphrates may be seen to rise. The Tigris is not included. Below the river empties itself into areas marked as 'swamp' and 'channel' and from there into the sea. To east and west the map offers a sprinkling of circles. Three show a central dot but no name, two are identified merely as 'city', but two of the remainder are specifically labelled 'Der' and 'Susa'. 'Urartu' and 'Assyria' are located east of the

Euphrates, the former an unspecified area, the latter shown like a city within a circle. To the west are shown the Kassite tribal area 'Habban', and further south the area of the Bit Yakin, although both are properly located to the east of the Euphrates. A curved feature to the lower right west of the city of Der has a label that cannot now be read for certain.

A series of triangular projections juts out from the rim of the salt-sea. These are termed *nagû* in Babylonian, a word that may be translated 'region' or 'province'. At present five such triangles are preserved, in whole or in part, and it is not improbable that originally there were eight on the tablet. Four of the five carry short inscriptions exemplified by: 'Region; 6 (or 8) leagues in between'. The provinces seem to be equally spaced out round the perimeter, so perhaps this refers to the distance across the salt-sea to each. It has been suggested that their shape reflects that of an island, approached across the waters and seeming to rise out of the horizon.

One province alone has a longer text: 'Great Wall; 6 leagues in between, where the Sun is not seen'. The fragment that carries these particular words came to light in 1995 in the British Museum among a tray of small, unjoined tablet fragments. Wild celebrations met its identification; it fitted exactly into the hole in the map, and the reverberations even reached the television news in September of that year. The Great Wall that lies beyond perpetual darkness is not, however, the Chinese example, but probably that referred to in a literary composition about the world-conquering king Sargon I of Akkad (c. 2334–2279 BC).

Eleven tantalizing but fragmentary lines of text precede the map. Reference is made to the very creation of the world, as known from the epic *Enuma Eliš*, when the god Marduk defeated Ti'amat, the primordial Sea. The map tablet mentions 'ruined gods', known to be Ti'amat's creatures, and the bridge by which Marduk overstrode the waters – in which dwelt, among others, the viper and the *mušhuššu* dragon of Babylon. Other terrestrial animals created by

Marduk are listed, many of which, by Mesopotamian standards, were exotic: mountain goat, gazelle, zebu, panther, lion, wolf, red deer and hyena, monkey, she-monkey, ibex, ostrich, cat and chameleon. In addition, we learn that Uta-napišti (the Babylonian Noah), Sargon I himself and Nur-Dagan, king of Buršahanda (one of Sargon's celebrated enemies), also came to inhabit this freshly created land mass.

The inscription on the reverse side is more closely related to the map itself. It contains sections that describe the eight *nagûs* in turn, introduced as, for example, 'To the fourth region, where you travel seven leagues'. The whole passage is (as so often with the rarest texts) poorly preserved, but several times it gives unidentified measurements, such as 'are thick as a *parsiktum* measurement' or '840 cubits is its ...'. The text also refers to a winged bird that cannot complete a journey in safety, and to horned cattle that can run fast.

The carefully inscribed tablet was written by a scribe from the city of Borsippa. He was a descendant of a venerable scribe of that city called Ea-bel-ili.

FIG. 5

Walter Andrae, Watercolour showing excavations at Babylon

The excavation led by the German archaeologist Robert Koldewey on the central Babil mound on the early morning of 22 June 1902, as painted by the archaeologist Walter Andrae. 'I learnt something special from Koldewey; how to make the surface of our prosaic-looking mound appear three-dimensional to the observer, as though the sun were shining from the south-east'.[2]

AD 1902
Watercolour
H 20.0 cm, W 35.5 cm
Staatsbibliothek zu Berlin, SPK, Andrae Bequest 15/25
Andrae and Boehmer 1992: no. 90, pl. 60

to a belief that Hebrew was the most ancient language of all. The story of the Tower of Babel had a wide appeal and was often to be illustrated in European religious art.

The Bible also recounted how Nebuchadnezzar had ransacked the city of Jerusalem, killing many of its inhabitants and deporting others: 'by the waters of Babylon we sat down and wept, when we remembered thee, O Zion'. Nebuchadnezzar really had captured Jerusalem, imprisoning Jehoiachin, king of Judah. Later biblical legends dealt with the aftermath. These included the madness of Nebuchadnezzar (605–562 BC) and the magical graffito that appeared on the wall at Belshazzar's Feast and predicted the capture of Babylon that very night by the Persian king Cyrus. Moralistic tales recounted how, after refusing to obey royal commands which conflicted with their beliefs, Shadrach, Meshach and Abednego were saved by divine intervention from a fiery furnace, and Daniel from a lions' den. These stories helped perpetuate the name of Babylon as an embodiment of pagan power, arrogance, luxury and decadence. Biblical prophecies asserted that Babylon would be punished and become a desolate ruin.

The name of Babylon had also been familiar in the Greek world since at least the fifth century BC, one suggestion being that the Greeks added 'on' at the end of the name because of a similar-sounding city name which they already knew in Egypt. Babylon – including its magnificent walls, its palace and its tower dedicated to the god Belus, or rather the ziggurat dedicated to Bel or Marduk – featured in the writings of Herodotus, father of history. His account implies that he had visited the place personally, which would have been about 450 BC, but he may have used informants who had visited Babylon or originated there. Any stranger visiting Babylon could presumably have communicated easily in the widespread Aramaic language, but would hardly have been in a position to learn much about the city beyond what was obvious and what they were told. Ctesias, a Greek doctor who worked for the Persian king about 400 BC, and whose elaborate description

of Babylon survives in a compilation of histories made around 50 BC by Diodorus, is in some ways more informative than Herodotus but less reliable. For instance, according to Herodotus Babylon was built by several kings and by two queens, the semi-legendary Semiramis and Nitocris, both of whom, he recorded, worked mainly on projects connected with the Euphrates; according to Ctesias, however, Semiramis alone was responsible for almost everything. Better information was contained in the now fragmentary writings of a Babylonian priest, Berossus, who was writing in the early third century BC and clearly had access to copies of some of Nebuchadnezzar's royal inscriptions. Berossus gives the very name of this king and insists, rejecting Semiramis, that Nebuchadnezzar was responsible for the major buildings of Babylon. There are further snippets of information in other Greek and Latin writings, discussed below.

Herodotus says that the city-wall was about 89 km long and wide enough for a four-horse chariot to turn on. When later Greeks were compiling lists of the Seven Wonders of the World, some chose this wall as one of them.

Ctesias may have been the first Greek to describe the remarkable structure of the Hanging Garden or Gardens, where trees grew on raised terraces inside the royal palace, and this was generally accepted as one of the Wonders of the World. A gigantic stone obelisk attributed to Semiramis was also cited by Diodorus as a Wonder of the World. So Babylon had the exceptional privilege of possessing three monuments that featured in some lists of the Seven Wonders. Alexander the Great, after conquering Persia, contributed to the fame of Babylon by dying there in 323 BC; in AD 116 the Roman emperor Trajan, campaigning in the Orient, sacrificed to Alexander's spirit in the very room where he had reputedly died. In the early centuries AD the name of Babylon, when it occasionally appears in Greek and Latin literature, is increasingly that of a mysterious faraway oriental city. It was the setting chosen for the classical tale of the lovers Pyramus and Thisbe, who died by mistake like Romeo and Juliet (Fig. 6).

Later, in the seventh century AD, the Qur'an mentioned Babil in connection with the art of sorcery and two angels, Harut and Marut. One mound of ruins retained the name of Babil into the nineteenth century, and a story then told among people living in the neighbourhood, and also present in a book by Mas'udi, the tenth-century Arab writer, was that the two angels were imprisoned underneath this very mound, awaiting the Day of Judgement. Another local story was that the Almighty had destroyed Babylon, leaving only a solitary tamarisk tree; this tree was still alive in the nineteenth century, unusually far from water and growing on top of another mound near some ruins that bore the name of Kasr or Palace (Fig. 7). Meanwhile the records of serious Arab geographers helped to ensure that the knowledge of the location of the city was never lost, and the area was always known as the land of Babil.

Babylon, once it had lost its political status, retained practical significance as a seemingly inexhaustible source of high-grade baked bricks. The site differed in this respect from most of those mounds scattered all across the Middle East that represent the ruins of buildings made from unbaked sun-dried mud bricks, the traditional building material of the region. Mudbrick buildings have the advantage that they are well insulated in all seasons, but they need constant maintenance. Nebuchadnezzar knew how quickly they could deteriorate with neglect, and was determined that his own major buildings should last longer than those of his predecessors. He therefore chose to construct them of baked brick; his bricks are denser than any normally seen today, and their quality may never have been surpassed. The ironic result was that, after his buildings were abandoned, the walls did not merely collapse into commonplace mounds but were utilized as brick quarries, and parts of them have survived only because of the phenomenal scale on which Nebuchadnezzar built.

It has been said that much of Baghdad was constructed out of recycled Babylon bricks. They were extensively used in nearer towns in the region such as Hillah and Kufa, they were floated down the Euphrates to Basra, and in the nineteenth century they were the mainstay of the Hindiya dam constructed on the Euphrates, 14 miles north-west of Babylon.

The first European since ancient times to provide a description of the ruins of Babylon, albeit very brief, was Benjamin of Tudela, a rabbi from what is now northern Spain. He travelled extensively, visiting Babylon about 1170 AD; his account, in Hebrew, was published in 1543.[3] He states that the ruined streets extend for 30 miles, and he mentions the ruins of a palace of Nebuchadnezzar which was infested with snakes and scorpions, as well as a synagogue of Daniel. He refers to another palace of Nebuchadnezzar 'well known' as the location of the biblical Fiery Furnace, though it is not clear that he visited it. Later, however, after reaching Hillah on the other side of the Euphrates, he probably did visit a high ruin which he does not name but which he thought to be the Tower of Babel. Another rabbi, Jacob of Paris,[4] who describes itineraries across the region about 1240 AD, also mentions a tower of Nebuchadnezzar and a synagogue of Daniel at Babylon, on the way from Baghdad to Hillah. On the far side of Hillah he mentions a 'tower built by Nimrod'. Nimrod or Nimrud is a legendary figure who features in both Jewish and Arabic stories; he may be an avatar of the ancient Mesopotamian god Ninurta.

Benjamin's prime interest was in recording the various Jewish communities which he encountered, including that at Hillah, and the names applied by him and Jacob to ruins at Babylon must reflect traditions which they heard in the locality. We can make tentative identifications of the structures mentioned by him. Although the ruins did not really extend for 30 miles, his belief that they did is understandable because, as the scholar and collector Claudius Rich was later to remark,[5] 'The country is perfectly level, except where intersected by canals, which it is in a very surprising manner. These might very easily deceive the unpractised eye into the belief that they were vestiges of walls or buildings.' Benjamin and Jacob were undoubtedly correct in their identification of a palace of Nebuchadnezzar at Babylon. The one infested with snakes and scorpions could have been the mound commonly known as Babil, which is close to the road from Baghdad to Hillah; caves in the sides made it a notorious haunt of wild animals in the nineteenth century and they were still there in the 1960s. The synagogue of Daniel has either disappeared or been transformed into the shrine or tomb of some other person; it was presumably beside the Well of Daniel mentioned by Mas'udi as located near Babil, which both Jews and Christians visited during some festivals. Perhaps the synagogue was the oratory near Jumjuma, a village inside Babylon on the Hillah road; this oratory, a ruin by the nineteenth century, was said then to have been the tomb of a sultan.[6] Benjamin's Tower of Babel and Jacob's tower built by Nimrod are undoubtedly the same place, and correspond to the remains of a high and very imposing tower, the uppermost brickwork of which is split and partially vitrified; this had been the ziggurat of the god Nabu in the ancient city of Borsippa, on the west side of the Euphrates beyond Hillah. Rich records that the site was known to the Arabs as Birs Nemroud and to the Jews as Nebuchadnezzar's Prison.[7]

A handful of other European travellers passed through Iraq between the twelfth and fifteenth centuries. What was generally known or surmised about Babylon and the Tower of Babel may be summarized in the remarks of Sir John Mandeville (who never visited the site), written about 1355:[8] 'That is in the great desert of Arabia, upon the way as men go toward the kingdom of

FIG. 8
Georg Gerster, Aerial photograph of Babylon

The foundations of Nebuchadnezzar's Tower of Babel, the ziggurat Etemenanki, with its south-projecting staircase. Over the centuries Nebuchadnezzar's high-quality baked bricks were mined for recycling in new buildings. All that remains of Babylon's greatest monument today is a ghostly outline of ditches filled with murky water.

Taken in 1973
Georg Gerster/Panos

Western Face.

FIG. 9
Sir Robert Ker Porter, *A View of the West Side of Birs Nimrood, near Babylon*

The site of Birs Nimrud was a leading contender for the elusive Tower of Babel. It is situated some six miles south-west of Babylon, and had some Greek estimates been correct both it and the main metropolis could have been accommodated within the walls (see Fig. 91). In fact Birs Nimrud was a separate city altogether, ancient Borsippa.

AD 1818
Watercolour
From Ker Porter 1827: pl. 69

Chaldea. But it is full long since that any man durst nigh to the Tower; for it is all deserted and full of dragons and great serpents, and full of diverse venomous beasts all about.'

The 1498 discovery of a sea route round the Cape of Good Hope, linking Europe with Persia and India, led to the development of European commercial and colonial interests in the East, and to a continual interest in other faster or more direct routes.[9] One route went overland from the Mediterranean across Syria, south-eastward down the Euphrates to Falluja, across to Baghdad on the Tigris, and then on directly to Persia or to Basra, the Persian Gulf and the Indian Ocean. The route from Baghdad to Basra was either down the Tigris, or down the Euphrates by way of Hillah; the latter route passed within reach of Babylon. Consequently, from the sixteenth century onwards, a considerable number of Europeans – merchants, missionaries, scientists, diplomats, soldiers and adventurers – visited Iraq; and by the nineteenth century the route was an exciting alternative to the sea voyage for officers travelling to or from British India. Many of these men left descriptions of what they had seen.

The earliest of these new travellers from Europe brought with them a hotchpotch of legend and historical information relating to ancient Babylon, but no accurate maps since such things did not exist before the mid-eighteenth century, and their accounts of where they went are often puzzling and ambiguous. They nearly all had serious business to conduct; even if they had wanted to indulge in the exploration of ancient sites, it would usually have been impracticable for them to do so and liable to provoke local suspicions about motive. This was an insecure land with very mixed populations and shifting allegiances. Sovereignty was disputed between the Ottoman Turkish and the Persian empires. The Ottomans eventually prevailed and were to hold Iraq for most of the time until the First World War, but the countryside was often dangerous. Archaeological research would only begin to flourish in the course of the nineteenth century.

Although the early travellers were aware of Babylon, and some would have read Herodotus or other Greek classics as well as the Bible, they were not familiar with the Arabic and Hebrew itineraries and they did not know exactly where to find the fabulous city. The German physician and

The Fiery Furnace

In the Bible the three Hebrews Shadrach, Meschach and Abednego were thrown into a Fiery Furnace at Babylon for refusing to worship a golden statue set up by King Nebuchadnezzar. Early travellers to Babylon sought to identify the site of the Furnace itself. Rabbi Benjamin of Tudela, who visited in around AD 1170, reported a location 'well-known' as the site of the Fiery Furnace. This could perhaps have been the major palace mound at Babylon known to European visitors from the eighteenth century as Mujellibeh or Kasr, or sometimes even Babil.[10] This mound, which actually covers two adjacent palaces of Nebuchadnezzar in the centre of the city, was some distance from the road, which would explain why it was not mentioned by Jacob of Paris when he visited in about AD 1240. While Kasr means 'palace' or 'castle', there have been two views on the meaning of 'Mujellibeh'. An old proposal was that it meant 'house of the captives',[11] in which case this would be another candidate for Nebuchadnezzar's Prison as well as a possible location for his Fiery Furnace; we can deduce from an original Babylonian ration-list considered below (Fig. 130) that this area of the city is where the Judaean king Jehoiachin was in fact once held captive by Nebuchadnezzar. The meaning 'prison' is far fetched, however, and the natural meaning of Mujellibeh (as pronounced in the local dialect) – and the only meaning for the variant 'Maglub' that is also found – is 'overturned' or 'ruinous', which is a fair description of the site; Rich[12] uses the same name for the Babil mound.

A much better candidate for Benjamin's Fiery Furnace seems to be the mound of Ibrahim Khalil immediately beside the tower of Birs Nimrud, since this is where, according to Arab tradition,[13] Nimrud placed Abraham in a fiery furnace from which, like Shadrach, Meshach and Abednego, he miraculously emerged unscathed. One of the mounds in this vicinity consists of 'broken glazed bricks and vitrified earth',[14] possibly waste from kilns, which may have suggested the identification in the first place;[15] alternatively there is the vitrified brickwork of the ziggurat. Loftus[16] also mentions that, 'in several places where vitrified bricks appear in Babylonia', they are associated with this story about Nimrud and Abraham. On the other hand, if Ibrahim Khalil is Benjamin's Fiery Furnace, it is strange that he did not recognize it as adjoining what he took to be the Tower of Babel and describe the two together.

Yet another location for the Fiery Furnace is offered by Macdonald Kinneir:[17] in 1808 he was shown it near the so-called Tomb of Ezekiel, south-east of Hillah. This suggests a rival tradition or, perhaps more to the point, a thorough-going lack of interest, even among the local Jewish community, in the exact identification of such sites. The situation is confusing and anticipates the confusion of early nineteenth-century European travellers as they debated, with some spirit,[18] which mounds of ruins should be known by which names, something that really depended on who had happened to be their local informants and what previous travellers' books they had read. In 1894 Cowper remarked that, 'It seems curious, but is apparently the case, that the Arabs transpose and transfer the names from one mound to another in the most haphazard fashion';[19] it is still sometimes not obvious which mound a traveller is describing. The confusion was to be redoubled by European attempts to decide which of the mounds corresponded to monuments described in the Greek accounts of Babylon.

FIG. 10 *above*

Roman painting showing the three in the Fiery Furnace

This very early wall painting stands at the beginning of a long tradition of representing Babylon in art. In the Book of Daniel three Judaeans thrown into the Fiery Furnace by Nebuchadnezzar are protected by an angel and emerge unscathed.

3rd century AD, Fresco, catacombs of Priscilla, Rome

FIG. 11 *below*

'Les enfants dans la fournaise'

A medieval French Nebuchadnezzar inspects Shadrach, Meshach and Abednego in his own fiery furnace.

About AD 1109–11, Miniature painting in the *Bible of Etienne Harding* Bibliothèque Municipale, Dijon

FIG. 12

Remains of the ziggurat at 'Aqar Quf

Another candidate for identification as the Tower of Babel was the dramatic-looking ziggurat at the site of 'Aqar Quf (ancient Dur Kurigalzu), nearer to Baghdad than Babylon. This was built by a Kassite king, Kurigalzu, in about 1380 BC. The layers of reed matting between the courses of bricks that travellers had read about in Herodotus can still be seen in this modern photograph.

FIG. 13

Arch of Ctesiphon

The huge ruin of the famous sixth-century Sasanian palace popularly known as the Arch of Ctesiphon. This was frequently visited by travellers in Iraq, who found more to marvel at than they did at Babylon. This photograph is one of the first to be taken after the partial collapse of the arch in 1888.

AD 1892–4
Photograph from an album compiled in 1894
British Museum, BM 2007, 6025.1

botanist Leonhard Rauwolf, for instance, travelling in 1574, recorded that Falluja had been the ancient Babylon;[20] he had probably seen the ruins of the great medieval city of Anbar. In 1579 the Venetian jeweller Gasparo Balbi, and in 1583 John Eldred – one of a group of English merchants carrying letters from Queen Elizabeth to the emperor of China and the Mughal emperor[21] – also locate ancient Babylon at or near Falluja, extending along the road towards Baghdad.[22] Eldred describes Baghdad as the 'new city of Babylon'. This term, alluding to status rather than to topography, sometimes led people to suppose that ancient Babylon really did lie underneath Baghdad, although another candidate for the same status was the medieval city of Samarra. Eldred thought furthermore that the massive ruined ziggurat named 'Aqar Quf, which is surrounded by the mounds of ancient Dur Kurigalzu by the road between Falluja and Baghdad, constituted the stump of the Tower of Babel.

The French jeweller Jean-Baptiste Tavernier[23] who spent three weeks in Baghdad in 1652, agrees that the city was commonly (*d'ordinaire, vulgairement*) called Babylon; he knew that the real Babylon was elsewhere. He also knew of a walled city south of Baghdad on the Tigris that was said to be Babylon. Tavernier remarks that 'Aqar Quf could not possibly be the Tower of Babel, and that it is not worth visiting anyway. This last comment, reflecting the fact that ancient mounds do not have the visual charm of Greco-Roman ruins, goes far to explain why Babylon itself and many other sites in Babylonia failed to attract much interest before the nineteenth century. Even Jean Otter,[24] a capable Frenchman who was familiar with the Arab geographers and knew that the authentic Babylon was a little north of Hillah, took little interest when he passed close to the ruins in 1743; he remarks, presumably having inspected the nearby palm-groves from a distance, that all one can see there is a coppice (*un bois taillis*). In 1758 the Englishman Edward Ives,[25] usually an observant traveller, who published Doidge's illustrations both of 'Aqar Quf and of the great Arch of Ctesiphon, used the same route as Otter, but all he says of Babylon is that 'we walked up a little eminence [presumably Babil], where we saw a vast quantity of broken bricks and some cement'.

Every so often during the seventeenth and eighteenth centuries, other Europeans passed by the ruins. Some still supposed that 'Aqar Quf was the Tower of Babel, as this must be the provenance of a present made to the British Museum by Gustavus Brandes, a fellow of the Royal Society, in 1768. This was an unburnt mud brick, together with a specimen of the reeds that were laid as matting between every four or five layers of brickwork, which one Mr Magee had brought back from the 'Supposed Tower of Babilon ... about 4 Hours Distance from the City of Bagdat'. The brick was about 14 inches square and 5.5 inches thick, but before long, unfortunately, it was 'diminished very much, for it would not bear being handled, it crumbled into dust ... The reeds ... we were not able to find them anywhere in the Museum'.[26] A recent comprehensive study[27] has confirmed that few travellers published reminiscences of value for the study of Babylon itself, but there were exceptions.

One European had already taken serious note of the real Babylon as early as November 1616. This was Pietro della Valle, a rich young Italian who had undertaken an extended tour of the Orient because, as he says, he wanted distraction from a broken heart and was bored with Roman high society.

He was therefore an adventurer with leisure to explore. He decided while in Baghdad to take the risk of visiting Babylon, and consequently wrote the first careful description of one of the ruins. His party camped by the first mound he saw, namely Babil at the northern end of the city. He inspected the mound closely, noting that it was roughly square, with a perimeter of some 1,134 paces, and that its summit was much higher than the highest gable of the royal palace at Naples. There were several cavernous openings in the mound, but Pietro suspected they had not been parts of the original building. He made some slight excavations and observed that the construction incorporated both baked and sun-dried mudbricks, laid and secured with the help of bitumen, lime and reed matting. In 2000 this excavation was described by Antonio Invernizzi[28] as 'the first recorded scientific excavation in the East' and as 'scientific in a modern sense, for it was motivated by a pure desire for knowledge, a desire to ascertain the nature, the shape and the structure of the ruin, and not simply by the desire to collect precious objects'. Pietro collected

FIG. 14
Pietro della Valle

The intrepid traveller and scholar who visited many archaeological sites in Mesopotamia and Persia, writing a detailed description of what he saw at Babylon. An anonymous artist in his retinue also produced a drawing which was the first to show a tell (mound) site, namely Tell Babil, which was correctly identified as part of the city of Babylon but incorrectly as the Tower itself.

British Library
Frontispiece to *The Travels of Pietro della Valle into East India and Arabia Deserta*. Translated by G. Havers. London, 1665

samples of building materials to take back to Europe as curiosities. He further arranged for the mound to be drawn by the artist who accompanied him, and identified it as being both the biblical Tower of Babel and the tower of the god Belus described by Herodotus. While his hypothesis was wrong, it initiated a debate about this ruin that was to continue for nearly three hundred years. He ignored the other principal mounds at Babylon, which were off the road; but he later travelled on to Iran, studying the ancient Persian capital of Persepolis; and after further adventures in India he once again visited Iraq while returning to Italy. On this second occasion he passed by the ziggurat of the ancient city of Ur, and collected more bricks. Pietro della Valle was the first European to write intelligently on the cuneiform script, not yet deciphered at that time, in which ancient Near Eastern records were written.

In 1657 another Italian, Father Vincenzo Maria di S. Caterina di Sienna, travelled up the Euphrates to Hillah and then across to Baghdad. 'It is a very general opinion,' he writes:

> that this place [Hillah] was the ancient Babylon, which is proved by the site, being on the banks of the Euphrates, by the fertility of the adjacent lands, and by the ruins of magnificent buildings, which abound for many miles around; but, above all, by the remains of the Tower of Babel, which to this day is called Nimrod's Tower. We were curious to see these buildings, but finding that no one would accompany us for fear of robbers, we were compelled to give it up.[29]

In this account Father Vincenzo is effectively repeating information already known to Benjamin of Tudela, while giving an excellent reason why Birs Nimrud was not better known.

A significant visitor in the 1740s, soon after Otter, was the French missionary Emmanuel de St Albert, whose involvement with the Christian community in Baghdad earned him the ancient title 'Bishop of Babylon'. Emmanuel, like Pietro, had the advantage of residing for a time at Baghdad, and therefore had good opportunities to hear what the local people had to say about their own country and then to explore it. He drew attention to the fact, implicit but not specifically stated in Benjamin's account, that important remains existed on both sides of the Euphrates. One site, a hill north of Hillah on the east side of the Euphrates, was 'between two and three miles in circumference', and clearly corresponds to Mujellibeh and other mounds nearby; the other site was Birs Nimrud.[30] At both places Father Emmanuel collected square bricks, 'on which was writing in certain unknown characters'; the writing had been impressed, and the bricks from both sites bore the same impression. Such bricks, wrote the great French cartographer Jean-Baptiste d'Anville, 'would supply the literati, who are desirous of penetrating into the remotest Antiquity, with entirely new matter for meditation and study'.[31] Emmanuel remarks presciently that scholars may now have difficulty deciding which of the two sites was the better Babylon.

An important development at this time was in the quality of mapping. This was made possible by travellers who recorded their movements with exactitude, and by the persistence of d'Anville, who relied on evidence rather than estimates to create his maps. He had access to Father Emmanuel's unpublished report, and his discourse on the location of Babylon was published in 1755; there was another by de St Croix in 1789. Within Iraq of course the approximate location had always been known, but it now became increasingly recognized in Europe too. The full extent of the city however, and whether it really included Birs Nimrud, was to remain controversial for another century.

Carsten Niebuhr,[32] the one survivor of a Danish scientific expedition that transformed European knowledge of Arabia, considered the same problem in 1765. Approaching Hillah from the south, and seeing first the spectacular remains of the tower at Birs Nimrud, Niebuhr supposed that this probably corresponded to the tower of Belus described by Herodotus, and that Borsippa was therefore within the walls of Babylon. Niebuhr saw some 'small inscriptions on baked clay' near the shrine of Ibrahim Khalil. He also studied the foundations of brick walls at Kasr, the palace of Nebuchadnezzar in the centre of Babylon itself; he observed some unusual trees nearby and suggested that the building constituted the remains of the Hanging Gardens. This idea expanded the discussion over where exactly within Babylon the various monuments recorded in biblical and Greco-Roman sources might be located. Niebuhr also made an observation that in retrospect seems obvious but evidently needed saying at the time: that the Babylonians should not be dismissed as uncultured or illiterate simply because they had not left any beautiful stone buildings.

Another French priest, Joseph de Beauchamp, resident in Baghdad during 1780–5, adopted a novel and most informative approach to studying the ruins of Babylon: he interviewed someone who had been excavating there for years:[33]

> Here are found those large and thick bricks imprinted with unknown characters, specimens of which I have presented to the Abbé Barthelemy ... I was informed by the master mason employed to dig for bricks that the places from which he procured them were large thick walls and sometimes chambers. He has frequently found earthen vessels, engraved marbles, and about eight years ago a statue as large as life, which he threw amongst the rubbish. On one wall of a chamber he found the figure of a cow, and of the sun and moon, formed of glazed bricks. Sometimes idols of clay are found representing human figures. I found one brick on which was a lion, and on others a half-moon in relief ...
>
> The master mason led me along a valley which he dug out a long time ago to get at the bricks of a wall that from the marks he showed me I guess to have been sixty feet thick. It ran perpendicular to the bed of the river, and was probably the wall of the city. I found in it a subterranean canal, which, instead of being arched over, is covered with pieces of sandstone six or seven feet long by three wide ...
>
> I employed two men for three hours in clearing a stone which they supposed to be an idol. The part which I got a view of appeared to be nothing but a shapeless mass; it was evident, however, that it was not a simple block, as it bore the marks of the chisel, and there were pretty deep holes in it; but I could not find any inscription on it. The stone is of a black grain; and, from the large fragments of it found in many places, it appears that there were some monuments of stone built here. On the eastern side ... as I was told by the master mason, there were walls of glazed bricks which he supposed to have been a temple.

The items described in this passage are typical of the discoveries that were to be made during the full-scale German excavations commencing in 1899. Notable among them are the architectural decorations in the shape of glazed bricks, such as those which make up Nebuchadnezzar's grand Processional Way and Ishtar Gate. These structures were indeed located on the eastern side of the Kasr mound, as suggested by Beauchamp's quotation from his master mason. The massive object of black stone which Beauchamp partly uncovered but could not recognize is almost certainly the Lion of Babylon (Fig. 15) that was to be re-excavated at Mujellibeh in 1811 by Claudius Rich.[34] This massive but unfinished basalt sculpture shows a lion standing like Tippoo's tiger over a fallen man; it had probably been brought to Babylon by Nebuchadnezzar about 600 BC as loot after his conquest of Syria, and was displayed with other trophies in his new palace.

André Michaux, the botanist and compatriot of Beauchamp, who visited Baghdad about 1783–5, made a highly significant discovery of a different kind. This was a large black stone subsequently known as the Caillou Michaux, actually a Babylonian land record (*kudurru*) of about 1100 BC. The stone was partly carved with figures and symbols and partly covered with many lines of

FIG. 15
The Lion of Babylon

The Lion of Babylon, witness to the rise and fall of empires, maintained its commanding position against the skyline in 1964, and indeed still survives today. In 1829 Robert Mignan contemplated transporting it to England:[35]

From its vicinity to the river, (within five hundred yards,) little toil and expense would enable the antiquary to remove it from the mutilation of barbarians; and boats are procurable at Hillah, which would convey it to Bussorah. I trust I shall be believed when I state, that the want of funds was the only reason that prevented my transporting this valuable relic of antiquity to India; where no great expense would attend its embarcation for England.

George Keppel discovered in 1824 that the lion's mouth had been broken away; there is a story that a European visitor with a misguided sense of humour had thrust his fist into the hollow mouth and withdrawn it full of gold, after which someone had tried with gunpowder to extract more gold.[36] Removal of the lion was also considered by A.H. Layard in 1851, but he thought that it was 'either so barbarously executed as to show very little progress in art, or left unfinished by the sculptor. It would hardly be worth removal.' More recent scholarship agrees that the sculpture is indeed unfinished. In 1888 J.P. Peters commented on a hole partly drilled through the lion in search of treasure.

Photograph 1 January 1964

FIG. 16 *opposite*
The *Caillou Michaux*

The so-called Caillou Michaux, a Babylonian stone *kudurru*, or land-grant monument, discovered in 1783–4 by the botanist André Michaux. It was among the first Babylonian documents to come to Europe and to be published.

11th century BC, reign of Marduk-nadin-ahhe
Probably from Ctesiphon
Black limestone
H 45 cm
Bibliothèque Nationale de France, Cabinet des médailles, inv. Chabouillet 702
Michaux 1800; Steinmetzer 1922; Seidel 1968: 47–8, pl. 28; André and Ziegler 1982: 362

fine cuneiform writing. It was 'found at a day's journey below Baghdad, among the ruins of a palace known by the name of the garden of Semiramis, near the Tigris'. This is a surprising provenance since the name of Semiramis, though attached to Babylon in Antiquity and still associated with many monumental ruins in the Middle East, does not now seem to be used in southern Iraq. The Greek geographer Strabo refers to the so-called Wall of Semiramis, however, which crossed the modern course of the Tigris downstream from Baghdad, and it seems likely that the reference is to Ctesiphon. The great Arch of Ctesiphon (Fig. 13) is known as Taq Kisra, the throne of Kisra, but the city surrounding it was called the Garden of Kisra according to Mignan, who was there in 1827.[37] Kisra was Chosroes, a Sasanian king to whom great works are indiscriminately ascribed, and he may have swapped his identity with Semiramis. The Caillou Michaux demonstrated that the Babylonian cuneiform script was not only stamped on utilitarian bricks, such as those collected by Father Emmanuel, but that it was also employed to write long and elaborate texts. The Caillou Michaux was acquired for the French state in 1800, and fine engravings of it were published soon afterwards by the polymath Aubin-Louis Millin.[38]

Critically, throughout this period the gradual accumulation of information derived from visitors to Babylon and its environs was coincident with the European age of Enlightenment, when the spirit of scientific enquiry encouraged all kinds of investigation. As a writer in the *Critical Review* remarked in June 1780:[39]

That insatiable curiosity and love of the marvellous and astonishing, which is implanted in our natures, is never so agreeably flattered as by discoveries of unknown tracts, and the relation of strange and perilous adventures; voyages and travels, therefore, especially if written by men of credit and character, are generally read with more avidity than books of any other kind.

Babylon was by 1800 a natural subject for further research, potentially a classic Enlightenment project. There was at the time, however, no established mechanism to encourage, let alone fund, the disinterested pursuit of knowledge in the Orient. This depended on individual enterprise, or on the support of rich patrons or institutions such as the Society of Dilettanti in London, or on the patronage of rulers such as Louis XV of France and Frederick V of Denmark who were responsible for the travels of Otter and Niebuhr. The supreme example of a state-funded scientific expedition was the array of experts who accompanied Napoleon's military expedition to Egypt in 1798 and later published their records. There was no comparable support for archaeological research on ancient Babylon, but the directors of the Honourable East India Company, which ruled British India, still maintained the cultural interests promoted by their first Governor-General, Warren Hastings. They were also responsible for British interests in Iraq and in 1797, 'being always desirous to lend their assistance to those who may be employed in the elucidation of Oriental Antiquities' and being informed that at Babylon there were bricks inscribed in 'characters totally different from any now made use of in the East', gave orders that their Resident at Basra should send some of them to Bombay for dispatch to London.[40] This he did, and the bricks were soon followed by another far more impressive object, the East India House Inscription (Fig. 17), a large stone finely carved with far more lines of cuneiform than the Caillou Michaux. This stone was a record of some of Nebuchadnezzar's building works at Babylon and Borsippa; it had probably been deposited as a memorial in the foundations of the Kasr and been excavated by someone mining for bricks. An engraving of it was soon published.[41]

The publication of the Caillou Michaux and the East India House Inscription was prompted by a short but widely read book which had just appeared in London and was soon translated into German. In this *Dissertation on the Newly Discovered Babylonian Inscriptions* (1801), which discussed the bricks sent by the East India Company and a few seals, Joseph Hager pulled together the available evidence about Babylon and Babylonian writing and placed it in its historical context. Although some of his hypotheses about the influence of Babylon on Egypt and India have not stood the test of time, his main points were sound. For instance, he argued that the stamps on the bricks from Babylon were commonplace and repetitive, like those on Roman bricks, and formed whole sentences or words. He recognized that the script was not alphabetic, and that it had originally been written downwards rather than from left to right. Moreover, when he compared the Babylonian cuneiform inscriptions with those recorded from Persepolis in Iran, his first three conclusions were:[42]

1st, That the nail-headed (cuneiform) characters, found in Persia, are real characters and not ornaments, or flowers, as Dr Hyde and Professor Witte have supposed, nor magic and talismanic, as others have mentioned.

2nd, That they were used not in Persia only, as Tychsen and others believed, but also in Babylon and Chaldea.

🅔 FIG. 17 *opposite*
The East India House Inscription

The East India House Inscription memorializes
Nebuchadnezzar's building operations in stone.
After quoting his royal titles and describing his
personal piety, it describes the decorating of the
chapels of Marduk, Zarpanitu and Nabû in Esagil;
the reconstruction of the processional boat of
Marduk; the rebuilding of the *Akitu* house; the
restoration of the Babylon temples; and work
on the inner walls and on the Processional Way
of Marduk and the Ishtar Gate as well as on the
Southern Palace.

The stone is a masterpiece of archaizing
Babylonian epigraphy. Nebuchadnezzar's
craftsmen imitated perfectly the lapidary
characters of the much earlier age of King
Hammurapi to confer the authority of Antiquity.
Despite its great size the stone imitates the form
of many clay tablets, with a slightly rounded
reverse. An inscription of this type was no doubt
consulted by the Greek historian Berossus in
compiling his *Babyloniaca*. Another example
has only recently been published. [44]

Reign of Nebuchadnezzar (605–562 BC)
Found at Babylon before 1803. Presented to the East India
House Museum by Sir Harford Jones Bridges, and donated
to the British Museum in 1938
Stone
H 56.51 cm, W 50.16 cm, Th. 9.52 cm
British Museum, BM 129397
Fisher and Ryland 1803; Rawlinson and Norris 1861: 53–8
(original), 59–64 ('Hieratic'); Langdon 1912, Berger 1973:
Stein-Tafel X; Wallenfels 2008

3rd, That they were not derived from Egypt, as La Croze suspected; or of Bactrian origin as Hefren imagined, but derived from Babylon, which in point of culture was anterior to Persia; and, consequently these characters ought in future to be called rather Babylonian, than Persepolitan.

The Bible and the Greek records had always maintained that Babylon once held a central and fundamental place in the ancient Near East, but European scholars had been slow to accept this. By showing that the cuneiform script of Babylon was older than that of Persia, Hager opened the way to the recognition that Babylon might represent a literate civilization of very great age. He also pointed to the possibilities of reading the script 'by means of a great quantity of such characters, to employ the art of combination, and thus to decypher their meaning, (which we shall be better able to do, when more copious materials shall be procured from the East by the liberality of the Honourable East India Company)'.[43] In the event fifty years were to pass before Babylonian cuneiform was deciphered, but Hager had demonstrated the importance of Babylon itself and the great potential of further research there.

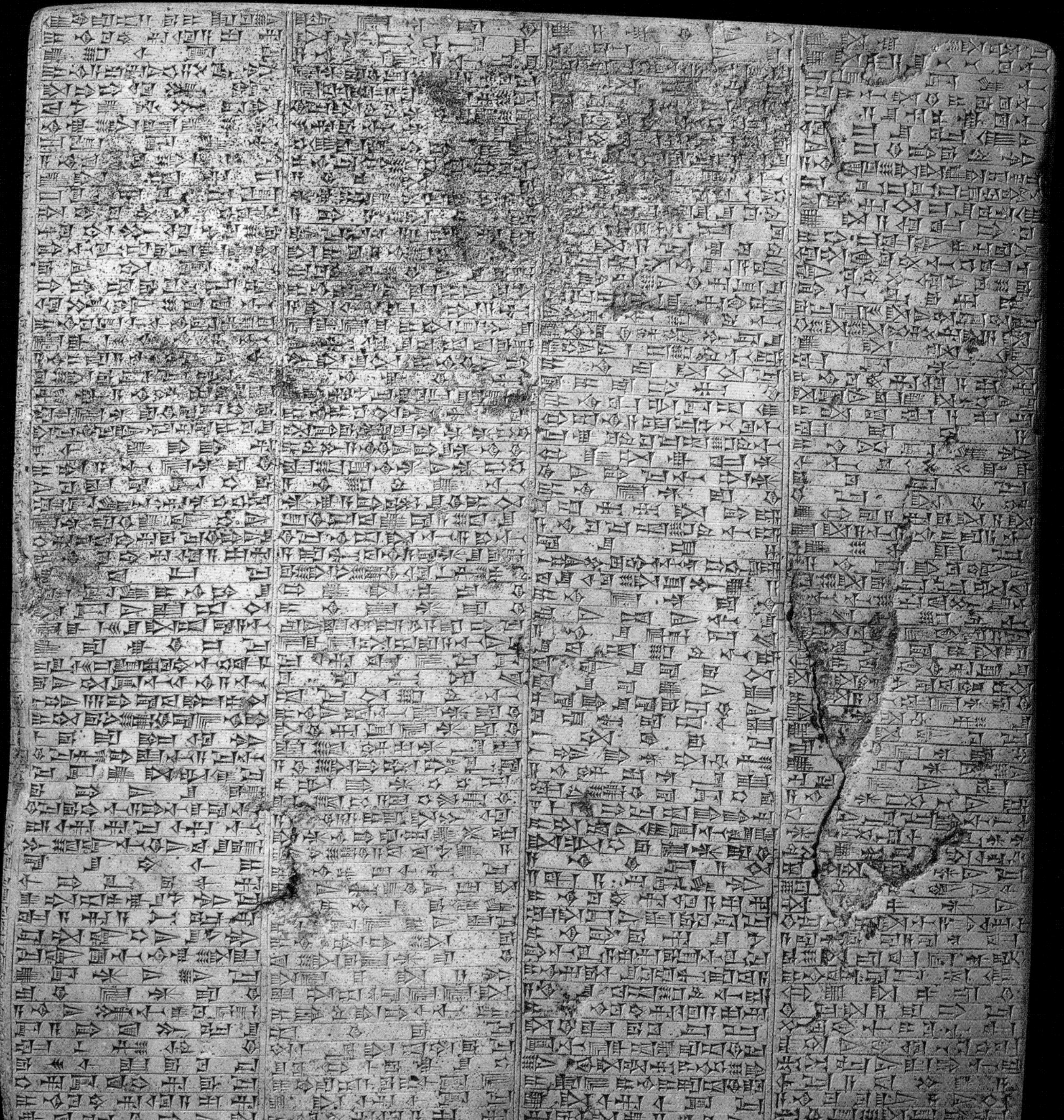

Notes: Babylon

1. See most recently Kinnier Wilson 2007.
2. Andrae 1961: 78–9, translated after Andrae and Boehmer 1992: 171.
3. Asher 1840: 106–7.
4. Adler 1930: 128.
5. Rich 1839: 29.
6. Rich 1839: 61.
7. Rich 1839: 73.
8. Layard 1895: 50–1.
9. Saleh 1966: 40–6
10 Buckingham 1827: 427.
11. Ainsworth 1888 II: 15.
12. Rich 1839: 68.
13. Rich 1839: 77.
14. Selby 1859: plan.
15. Ker Porter 1821–2 II: 328, pl. 9.
16. Loftus 1857: 31–2.
17. Macdonald Kinneir 1813: 282.
18. Ainsworth 1888 II: 16–18.
19. Cowper 1894: 317.
20. Rich 1839: 317–18.
21. Carruthers 1929: xix.
22. Rich 1839: 55, 320–1.
23. Tavernier 1678: 230, 238–40.
24. Otter 1748 II: 211.
25. Ives 1773: 269.
26. Van Rymsdyck and van Rymsdyck 1778: 34–5, table XIII.
27. Ooghe 2007.
28. Invernizzi 2000: 645.
29. Rich 1839: xxiv–xxv.
30. Rich 1839: xxxvi–xxxvii.
31. Hager 1801: xiv.
32. Niebuhr 1774–8 II: 287–91.
33. Rich 1839: 301–3.
34. Rich 1839: 36.
35. Mignan 1829: 186–7.
36. Koldewey 1914: 160
37. Mignan 1829: 69.
38. Millin 1802 I: pls viii–ix.
39. Anonymous 1780.
40. Hager 1801: xvi.
41. Anonymous 1803.
42. Hager 1801: 60–1.
43. Hager 1801: 56.
44. Wallenfels 2008.

The City
of Babylon

The City

In the nineteenth and twentieth centuries Babylon began to emerge from the dust. Increasingly detailed accounts, textual breakthroughs and excavations culminated in 1899 with the beginning of the large-scale excavations of the German Oriental Society (Deutsche Orient-Gesellschaft). In the following decades work was accomplished at the site that would have astonished the valiant workers of the preceding century, and in the expert hands of the German team the regal architecture of Nebuchadnezzar's capital was restored to life. The first-millennium BC city that emerged was itself at the end of a long historical tradition. Babylon had been a capital some twelve hundred years before, most significantly under Hammurapi (1792–1750 BC), the greatest of the kings of the Amorite dynasty, who established Babylon's pre-eminent status in southern Iraq and achieved immortality for himself through a monument now known – albeit inaccurately – as the world's first Code of Laws (see page 68). At Babylon itself little information from this, the Old Babylonian period, has come to light. This is because the corresponding archaeological levels are below the water table, and it is owing to work at other sites with their archaeological finds and many inscriptions that we are today relatively well informed about the Babylonia – and thus indirectly Babylon – of the second millennium BC. This book is concerned with a very short, though crucial, episode in Babylon's long history, the eventful years from 605 to 539 BC. The following sections deal accordingly with the rediscovery of this, Nebuchadnezzar's Babylon, and with the reality of the city itself.

FIG. 18
Thomas Phillips, Portrait of C.J. Rich (1787–1821)

Besides attempting to record the topography of Babylon, Claudius James Rich was an inveterate and cultured collector.[45] He accumulated more than 850 manuscripts in various oriental languages, many of great rarity and artistic or historical significance, together with an exceptional collection of coins, and he had an agent scouring the countryside for items of interest. These included antiquities, a modest market for which was beginning to develop at Hillah. Rich was well aware of the value of antiquities for the reconstruction of history, and was also probably the first visitor to Iraq to comment on the usefulness of knowing exactly where objects had been found.[46]

AD 1825
Oil on canvas
British Museum, painting 22

Nineteenth-century exploration and interpretation

Julian E. Reade

The history of research at Babylon in the nineteenth century embodied several different approaches, one of which is exemplified in the work of Claudius James Rich when British Resident in Baghdad. He visited the site in 1811 and 1817 on his own behalf, because it interested him. While glad to discover attractive antiquities, he acted primarily as a scholar impartially collecting field data in the hope of solving historical problems such as the topography of the ancient city. Henry Layard, the enterprising explorer who excavated briefly at Babylon on behalf of the British Museum in 1850–1, had a similar attitude although he was not himself sanguine about the prospects of work there. He is reported to have said, on returning from the site, 'There will be nothing to be hoped for from the site of Babylon except with a parliamentary vote for £25,000, and if ever this sum should be voted, I would solicit the favour of not being charged with its application.'[47]

Fulgence Fresnel, director of the state-sponsored French *Expédition scientifique en Mésopotamie* which worked at Babylon during 1852–4,[48] was also a careful scholar, although the final publication of the meagre results by his colleague, the Assyriologist Jules Oppert,[49] is thick with abstruse and misguided speculation. Some individual visitors to Babylon were also interested in elucidating the past; among them were John Macdonald Kinneir and his friend Captain Frederick in 1808, Sir Robert Ker Porter in 1818, and Colonel Henry Rawlinson, the gritty British Resident at Baghdad during 1843–55. The efforts of these and other men formed the background for the thorough-going professional excavations of the German archaeologist Dr Robert Koldewey, who worked at Babylon on behalf of the Deutsche Orient-Gesellschaft during 1899–1917.

Rich had been appointed to his Baghdad post as a brilliant and energetic young man, in order to watch for and hopefully thwart any intrigues that might have warned of an overland French invasion of the British possessions in India. He therefore indirectly owed his post to Napoleon, whom he met socially several times while visiting Paris in 1815. He was equally open in his relations with European scholars of various nationalities, and saw himself as participating – from a position of special advantage – in a project for the universal advancement of knowledge. Babylon, indeed, because the site was so difficult to understand and did not seem at the time to contain any great treasures of ancient art, was never the focus of the kind of nationalist rivalry that more productive sites like Nineveh attracted.

Rich,[50] noting that Babylon had 'never been either thoroughly explored, or accurately described', took it upon himself to provide the description, which was duly published in English in 1813 in *Mines de l'Orient* or *Fundgruben des Orients*, a journal published at Vienna. Between 1815 and 1819 Rich's paper was reprinted in England no fewer than three times,[51] which implies a remarkable interest in the subject even if the actual number of copies printed is unknown. It was published again long after his death, together with other material on Babylon.[52]

A memorable contribution made by Rich was that he published a plan of the site, actually made by a Captain Lockett who accompanied him. This enabled the reader to comprehend the written observations, which would otherwise have been impossible.[53]

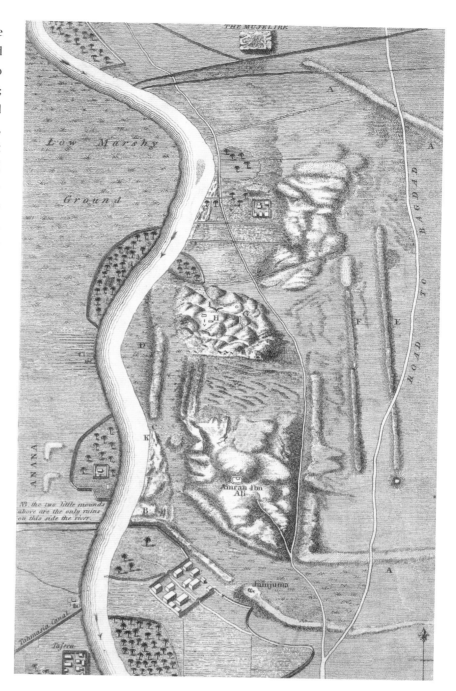

🄴 FIG. 19

Captain Lockett's map of the ruins at Babylon, as published by C.J. Rich

This, the outcome of Rich's personal survey of the site, was the first authoritative map of Babylon to be published. Rich's account sparked a lively controversy in Europe about the description of Babylon given by the ancient Greek historian Herodotus. For the first time ancient descriptions could be questioned on the basis of observations on the ground. The three principal mounds, north to south, are Tell Babil, the Mujellibeh or Kasr, and Amran ibn 'Ali.

Engraved by D. Read after C.J. Rich
Rich 1815: pl. 1

From the accounts of modern travellers, I had expected to have found on the site of Babylon more, and less, than I actually did. Less, because I could have formed no conception of the prodigious extent of the whole ruins, or of the size, solidity, and perfect state, of some of the parts of them; and more, because I thought I should have distinguished some traces, however imperfect, of many of the principal structures of Babylon. I imagined, I should have said: 'Here were the walls, and such must have been the extent of the area. There stood the palace, and this most assuredly was the tower of Belus.' – I was completely deceived: instead of a few insulated mounds, I found the whole face of the country covered with vestiges of building, in some places consisting of brick walls surprisingly fresh, in others, merely of a vast succession of mounds of rubbish of such indeterminate figures, variety, and extent, as to involve the person who should have formed any theory in inextricable confusion.

He would attempt to provide a 'plain, minute, and accurate statement of what I actually saw'.

Rich makes many acute observations on the building methods employed in the surviving structures at Babylon, but his main concerns are topographical. He describes how the Euphrates, although its course had changed slightly since Antiquity, ran roughly from north to south, close to the visible remains – almost all of which seemed at first sight to lie on the east bank.[54] Besides describing what he could see of the quay walls, as many scholars have done since, Rich identified three principal mounds or ruined structures on or near the east bank, and several others. The northernmost mound was the one known to modern scholars as Babil; for Rich and some other visitors of his time it was Mujellibeh (see page 23), a name found there again in 1872.[55] On top of Babil he excavated part of two passages that had been used for burials, effectively a catacomb; this was the mound that Pietro della Valle had thought to be the Tower of Babel and the tower of the god Belus described by Herodotus. Nearly 2 kilometres to the south was the more extensive mound best known as Kasr, notable for its solitary tamarisk and for the exposed stumps of fine brick walling in its northern half from which it gained its name of Kasr (palace); this was where Beauchamp's master mason had worked (see page 27), and where Rich himself exposed the Lion of Babylon, noting at the mouth 'a circular aperture, into which a man might introduce his fist'.[56] He observed Niebuhr's solitary tamarisk, and thought it might be a *lignum vitae*, not really a tree that had lived untended in such a climate. Rich[57] and probably most other nineteenth-century visitors thought that the mound was indeed a royal palace, as was eventually confirmed by the excavations of Koldewey,[58] who found there two palaces of Nebuchadnezzar and much else, notably the Ishtar Gate.

Nearly 1 kilometre further south was an even more extensive mound, parts of which had also been robbed for bricks; Rich calls this mound Amran after a shrine on top of it, and it is also known as Jumjuma after the village at its southern foot. Some distance to the east of Kasr and Amran there were parallel earthworks resembling an inner enclosure wall running from north to south; all the substantial remains of ruined buildings except Babil were between this wall and the Euphrates. An outer enclosure wall stretched south-eastward from Babil and then made a right-angled turn and came back to the southern end of Amran; the area between it and the river was roughly triangular, and was about 4 kilometres long from north to south and slightly less from east to west at its widest point.

Rich searched hard for significant mounds on the west bank of the Euphrates.[59] He thought he had had little success in the immediate neighbourhood of the other remains, although he did observe and plan what later turned out to be one of the western corners of the city-wall on this side; both corners were later identified by Selby.[60] He was, however, hugely impressed by the group of ruins at Birs Nimrud about 13 kilometres south-west of the Kasr mound, which Niebuhr had seen only from a distance.[61] He concluded that the tower of Birs Nimrud, rather than Babil, was the tower of Belus.[62] Among other reasons for his conclusion, he noted that the shape and altitude of the main ruin at Birs Nimrud suggested that it had been a tower, whereas the top of Babil was irregular but relatively flat. He was also disturbed by the burials he had found in the upper levels, which he clearly thought would have been inappropriate on a religious edifice; the possibility of their being late additions does not seem to have occurred to him. He was unhappy that Birs Nimrud was so distant from the other main ruins of Babylon, but it was just within the limits allowed by the enormous length which the Greek writers assigned to the outer city-walls. In fact the structure was really the ziggurat of the god Nabû in another city, Borsippa; this was ascertained in 1854 by Henry Rawlinson,[63] who excavated there and discovered two of Nebuchadnezzar's foundation inscriptions.

In 1815 Major James Rennell, the distinguished geographer who had already written on Herodotus and Babylon, challenged Rich's identification of Birs Nimrud as the tower of Belus, and maintained that Pietro della Valle had been correct in his suggestion of Tell Babil as the location.[64] This provoked Rich into revisiting the site and writing a second paper, published in 1818, which reaffirmed his views.[65] Seton Lloyd, the great twentieth-century archaeologist, was to comment that Rich's second paper 'virtually exhausted the possibilities of inference without excavation'.[66] However, although there were still some field observations to be made, Rich's enterprise had initiated a long period of speculation, occasionally punctuated by dissenting voices such as that of the archaeologist William Loftus:[67]

> In my opinion – and I have examined the ruins on four several occasions – it is now utterly impossible to recognize one single point in them as the remains of any of those sumptuous palaces described by the early historians. Rich, whose account and measurements are models of careful examination, has misled himself and others by his enthusiasm in endeavouring to identify certain of the ruins with the descriptions of Herodotus. I grant that it is a most pleasing subject to speculate upon, but it is perfectly hopeless, at this distance of time, to trace out any plan of the ancient city as it existed in its greatness and glory.

Two guests at Rich's Baghdad residence, James Silk Buckingham in 1816 and Sir Robert Ker Porter in 1818, visited Babylon and published accounts which largely supported Rich and amplified his observations. George Keppel, who went to Babylon in 1824, excavated the Lion of Babylon again.[68] Buckingham and Ker Porter were followed in 1827 by Captain Robert Mignan, who described what he saw with great care.[69] Ker Porter located additional remains on the west side of the Euphrates, actually outside the city-wall.[70] He also created an improved and expanded version of Rich's plan;[71] Mignan[72] made another informative plan of a wider area, extending south as far as Birs Nimrud. Much later, about 1855, the East India Company, still 'desirous to lend their assistance to those who may be employed in the elucidation of Oriental Antiquities', was to agree that Captain Felix Jones, commander of the *Nitocris*, the Indian Navy vessel that maintained British communications between Baghdad and Basra, should make a proper plan of Babylon. He did so about 1855, in a map which included 'all the neighbouring country';[73] his notes were unfortunately lost, unless they survive somewhere among the company's unpublished records in Mumbai. The work then devolved to his successor William Selby,[74] whose less extensive plan still covers Babylon and its vicinity, and adds some details of what may have been a system of defensive lagoons surrounding the city; Selby's plan also includes nearby Borsippa (Birs Nimrud). These plans, while sometimes contradictory, are invaluable early records of an ever-changing alluvial landscape.

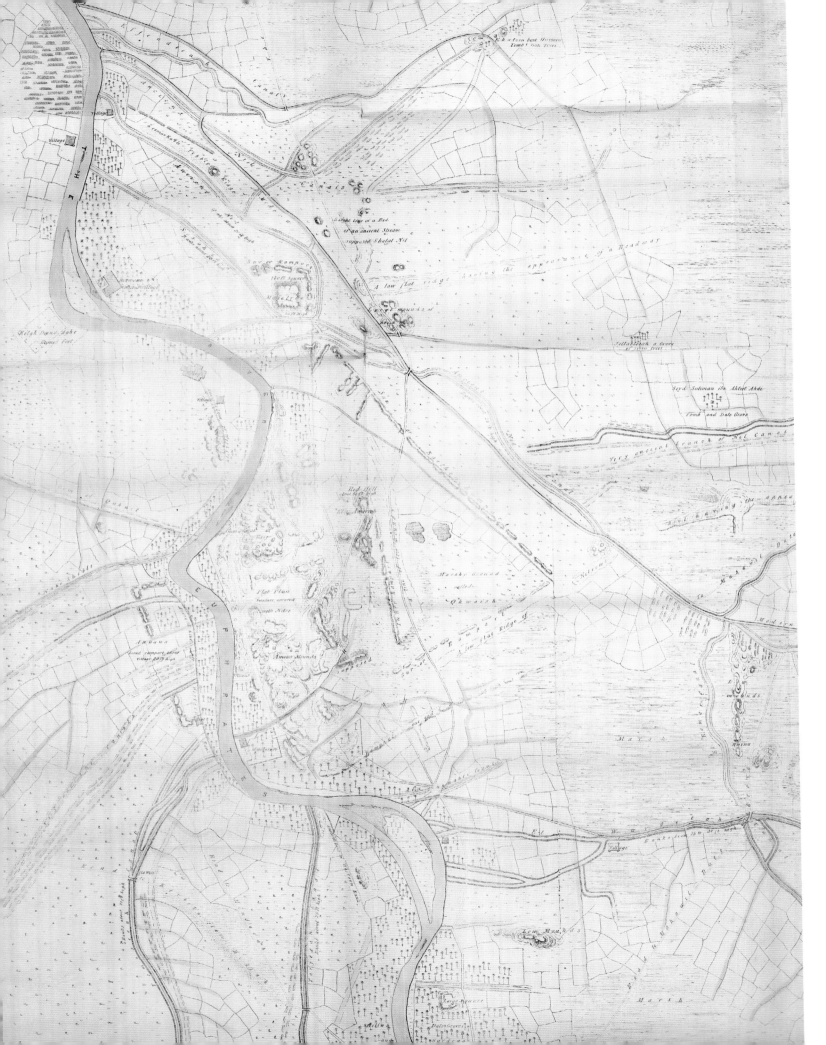

Nonetheless a common feature of nineteenth-century research at Babylon was that individuals who went there and wrote about the ruins were frequently unaware of conclusions that had already been reached by others. Whereas Rich's pioneering work was widely recognized, Ker Porter seems to have attracted little attention, while Buckingham and Mignan gained virtually none. Their books were too expensive, obscure or rare, and there are surely other travel books in various languages incorporating useful observations on Babylon which have still not attracted the attention they deserve. At the time, just as there were not yet any established mechanisms for funding research into the ancient Orient, so there were no clear procedures governing how best it should be published and publicized. A best-selling book was the best way, as Layard was to demonstrate with *Nineveh and its Remains* in 1849, but many people were making discoveries that were important in themselves but were not substantial enough to have entire books written about them and were unlikely to interest a publisher. The eventual solution would emerge in the form of regular journals, funded by subscription or otherwise, which were devoted to shorter papers on specific areas of knowledge. So the *Journal asiatique* started life in Paris in 1822, and the *Journal of the Royal Asiatic Society* in London in 1834, but both had a wide range of social, historical, literary and linguistic material to cover. Archaeology was hardly a mainstream subject.

Rich had been puzzled by the Babil mound, but Buckingham[75] contributed to its understanding by suggesting that 'the pile in question would therefore seem to be rather the elevated mound, on which a fortified palace, with all its offices, stood, than a tower or temple'. Ker Porter[76] had 'no doubt of its having been a groundwork, or magnificent raised platform, (like that of Persepolis, though there it was of the native rock;) to sustain habitable buildings of consequence'. Austen Henry Layard,[77] excavating at Babil briefly in 1850–1, recognized that a Nebuchadnezzar edifice had stood there, 'either on the level of the plain, or raised upon enormous piers and buttresses of brickwork'. He declined to speculate whether it had originally been a palace, the Hanging Gardens or a temple, but concluded that the tombs near the top were of the Greek period or later, and that the ruin had eventually been converted into a mudbrick fortress. Henry Rawlinson, however, who knew the area well, still insisted that Babil had been the tower of Belus; his views are undoubtedly those expressed in his brother's annotated translation of Herodotus:[78] 'it is the opinion of those best qualified to judge'. Layard's analysis was eventually to be confirmed by Koldewey,[79] who succeeded in recovering much of the original plan of Babil, calling it Nebuchadnezzar's Summer Palace. It was probably a palace attached to the city's military camp or arsenal; the fortress on top was Parthian, from the early centuries AD.

There were also more excavations at Babil which, being short term, never had any significant prospect of improving on Layard's results. Oppert[80] records a little inconclusive work there in 1852–3, but is mainly interested in demonstrating that Babil represented the 'Tomb of Belus', a building mentioned by some Greco-Roman writers and now generally thought, because ziggurats looked a bit like Egyptian pyramids, to be a romanticized name for the temple of Belus, the ziggurat of Bel. In 1864 Colonel Arnold Kemball, then British consul at Baghdad, dug at Babil for a month 'with the view of finally determining its character', but determined very little.[81] Rassam[82] dug there in 1879, proving to himself but to no one else that, because he had discovered a set of four fine wells and an underground water-channel, 'it was no doubt the site of the Hanging Gardens'. The Tower of Babel proved to be a similar preoccupation.

FIG. 20

Map of the ruins at Babylon by W.B. Selby

This detailed 1859 map was part of a much broader survey of Mesopotamia, and complements and develops Rich's earlier work – despite Selby's own reservations about the extent to which reliable interpretation of the ancient features at the site was possible.

Selby 1859: fold-out map

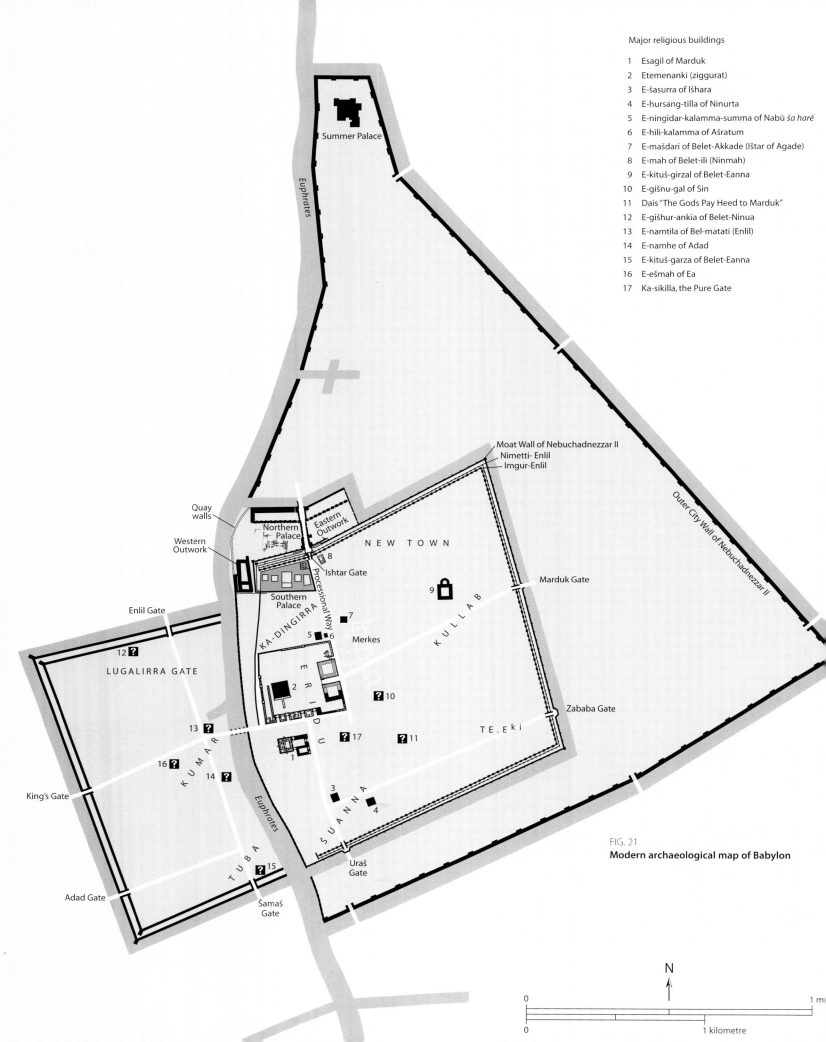

Major religious buildings

1   Esagil of Marduk
2   Etemenanki (ziggurat)
3   E-šasurra of Išhara
4   E-hursang-tilla of Ninurta
5   E-ningidar-kalamma-summa of Nabû *ša haré*
6   E-hili-kalamma of Ašratum
7   E-mašdari of Belet-Akkade (Ištar of Agade)
8   E-mah of Belet-ili (Ninmah)
9   E-kituš-girzal of Belet-Eanna
10 E-gišnu-gal of Sin
11 Dais "The Gods Pay Heed to Marduk"
12 E-gišhur-ankia of Belet-Ninua
13 E-namtila of Bel-matati (Enlil)
14 E-namhe of Adad
15 E-kituš-garza of Belet-Eanna
16 E-ešmah of Ea
17 Ka-sikilla, the Pure Gate

Summer Palace

Euphrates

Moat Wall of Nebuchadnezzar II
Nimetti- Enlil
Imgur-Enlil

Outer City Wall of Nebuchadnezzar II

Quay walls

Northern Palace

Eastern Outwork

NEW TOWN

Western Outwork

Ishtar Gate

Southern Palace

Marduk Gate

Enlil Gate

KULLAB

KA-DINGIRRA

Processional Way

Merkes

12

LUGALIRRA GATE

ERIDU

Zababa Gate

13

KUMAR

TE.Eki

16

14

King's Gate

3

Euphrates

SUANNA

Uraš Gate

TUBA

15

Adad Gate

Šamaš Gate

FIG. 21
Modern archaeological map of Babylon

N

0   1 m

0   1 kilometre

Robert Koldewey and the Babylon excavations

Michael Seymour

The detailed descriptions and informative plan produced by Claudius Rich in the early nineteenth century greatly enhanced European understanding of the site of Babylon. Following Rich a steady stream of travellers offered accounts containing additional details and differing opinions, but not further detailed exploration. From the 1840s excavations at the Assyrian capitals in northern Iraq transformed knowledge of ancient Mesopotamia, while at the same time decipherment of cuneiform scripts and languages progressed rapidly. For all this attention, however, Babylon itself still lay largely undisturbed. Though invaluable in recovering cuneiform texts from Babylon and Borsippa, Hormuzd Rassam's excavations[84] did not reveal much more of the city than was visible to Rich himself. It was not until the close of the nineteenth century that the newly formed Deutsche Orient-Gesellschaft (German Oriental Society) began large-scale excavations at the site.[85]

To some degree nineteenth-century excavators in southern Iraq were at a disadvantage to their counterparts further north. The characteristic mudbrick architecture of a region in which local stone sources were few and of poor quality made the identification of buildings difficult. In addition the efficient but dangerous combination of deep trenches and tunnelling employed by British and French excavators of Assyrian palaces to remove stone reliefs could not be used where there was no stone architecture to find or follow. Attempts to dig down to non-existent stone foundations only destroyed the mudbrick architecture itself,[86] and for a time a focus on recovering tablets rather than buildings seemed to be the most productive approach for archaeologists to take at sites in southern Iraq. When Robert Koldewey successfully excavated the city of Babylon, therefore, he not only uncovered one of the most important cities of the ancient world but also significantly advanced archaeological method in Mesopotamia.

FIG. 22
Robert Koldewey (1855–1925)

Photograph 1919 by L. Jessen
Staatliche Museen zu Berlin, Vorderasiatisches Museum

FIG. 23 *below*
Early days on the dig at Babylon

The tops of parts of the Ishtar Gate have been revealed. An elaborate railway system served to remove excavated materials to the dumps. The quantities were huge: the German excavations took eighteen years and exposed an enormous area.[83] Even so the excavations were only able to cover a tiny fraction of the ancient city.

Photograph 1902
Berlin, Deutsche Orient-Gesellschaft

Koldewey's previous work included participation in the short-lived Royal Prussian Museum of Berlin excavations at Surghul (ancient Nina) and al-Hiba (ancient Lagash) in 1887, where he gained experience of excavating large tell sites and of tracing mudbrick architecture. This background surely gave him confidence when assessing the potential for the excavations at Babylon, which he visited twice, in 1887 and 1897, prior to the start of excavations in 1899. He brought fragments of glazed brick back to Berlin, already suspecting that large decorative panels lay below the surface, and used these to help win support for the idea of major excavations at the site.[87]

> I saw a number of fragments of enamelled brick reliefs, of which I took several with me to Berlin. The peculiar beauty of these fragments and their importance for the history of art was duly recognised by His Excellency R. Schöne, who was then Director-General of the Royal Museums, and this strengthened our decision to excavate the capital of the world empire of Babylonia.

The timing could hardly have been better, since Koldewey was seeking sponsorship to excavate at Babylon at just the time when the idea of a national collection of Mesopotamian antiquities to rival those of England and France was solidifying into an organized body, the Deutsche Orient-Gesellschaft. German excavations had already been successful at Samothrace and Olympia; it was now hoped that new and spectacular discoveries could be made in Mesopotamia. The society enjoyed the support of the Kaiser himself and received donations from many wealthy industrialists.[88] It was founded with the explicit aim of conducting a large-scale Mesopotamian excavation to recover large quantities of monumental sculpture and cuneiform tablets for Germany. At the same time the new emphasis on scientific investigation meant that the high standards of recording associated with German excavations in Europe might now be transferred to Iraq.

Specific innovations attributed to the Deutsche Orient-Gesellschaft teams are the tracing of mudbrick buildings (hardly practised before Koldewey's work at Babylon and greatly refined by Iraqi specialists during the excavations at Babylon and Ashur)[89] and stratigraphic excavation (first practised at Ashur).[90] Perhaps even more importantly, in light of the destructive nature of archaeology, the recording of data was immensely more thorough than in any previous Mesopotamian excavations. Many of the German archaeologists (including Koldewey) had been trained as architects, and their contributions resulted in immaculate and highly detailed recording of the excavated architecture. Excellent drawings, plans and maps, coupled with minute description of both methods and findings, resulted in publications whose comprehensiveness was far ahead of its time. Particularly notable here is the work of Walter Andrae.[91] The Babylon publications are filled with his architectural plans and technical drawings, while in his spare time he engaged in a very different kind of recording: producing fine watercolours and pastels of the site, the landscape and daily life in the area around Hillah — including portraits and caricatures of everyone from high-ranking visitors to ordinary workers at the site.[92] Andrae went on to produce the reconstructions in Berlin that now form the centre of encounters with ancient Babylon for millions of visitors.

The characteristic standards of the German excavations had a profound impact on the Englishwoman Gertrude Bell, who visited the sites and corresponded with Koldewey and Andrae. Following the First World War, as Iraq's first Director of Antiquities, Bell set formal requirements for foreign excavators. These reflected the impression that Koldewey's work had made: the regulations included personnel required (notably an excavation photographer) as well as a division of finds with the newly formed Iraqi state. One might speculate that this latter policy also owed something to German excavations at Olympia, where Germany had not claimed a right to the

FIG. 24
Walter Andrae, Reconstruction drawing of the Ishtar Gate

Andrae, in common with many other German archaeologists, was a trained architect and an excellent draughtsman. The quality of recording at Babylon – through drawings, photographs, plans and notes – was exemplary, and far ahead of its time in many respects.

AD 1918
Drawing
Staatliche Museen zu Berlin, Vorderasiatisches Museum
Koldewey 1918: 32, pl. 20

excavated material and had even built a small museum at the site itself. Nonetheless, and perhaps reflecting her admiration for Koldewey, Bell allowed most of the huge quantity of finds from Babylon remaining in Iraq after the First World War to be shipped to Germany in exchange for donations of models and reconstructed reliefs to Iraq's new national collection.[93] (One of Gertrude Bell's most important and enduring legacies, the Iraq Museum, was founded in 1923 and opened in June 1926.) Once in Berlin the thousands of brick fragments excavated by Koldewey were put to spectacular use.

Walter Andrae was the first of Koldewey's assistants at Babylon, but was soon entrusted to direct his own major excavation at Ashur to the north. His contribution to Babylon can most keenly be felt in documentation and reconstruction. On the one hand the Babylon publications remain our most important sources for the temples and palaces of Nebuchadnezzar's city. On the other Berlin's Vorderasiatisches Museum itself, and most particularly the Babylon reconstructions around which it is built, are the work of Andrae, who became the museum's first director. Andrae organized and supervised perhaps the most complex and impressive architectural reconstruction in the history of archaeology: the rebuilding of Babylon's Ishtar Gate and Processional Way in Berlin. To achieve the reconstructions the hundreds of crates of glazed-brick fragments from Babylon were first desalinated and then pieced together to form the lions, dragons, bulls and floral features of which the monuments' decoration originally consisted. These figures were then supplemented with new bricks, baked in a specially designed kiln to achieve the correct colour and finish. The reconstructions include throne-room façades, the front part of the Ishtar Gate (visitors are often amazed to find that the monument they see is itself only part of a very much larger structure) and a major portion of the Processional Way.

The patient work of reconstruction was well rewarded, but there were also significant differences between the German excavations at Babylon and those of the English and French in northern Iraq half a century before. Whereas in these earlier cases the large stone reliefs reached the museums of Europe and went on display within a few years of their excavation, it was not until a decade after the excavations had finished – and more than a quarter of a century from their commencement – that the great reconstructions in Berlin were completed.[94] Moreover Babylon's excavator was barely more visible in Berlin than his finds. In Victorian England Austen Henry Layard had played a key public role, including his publication of the best-selling *Nineveh and its Remains*[95] in 1849. Indeed this period acted as a stepping-stone for Layard's continued career in public life as a politician. Koldewey, by contrast, hardly returned to Berlin at all. The most public face of the Deutsche Orient-Gesellschaft's work in Germany was therefore that of the Assyriologist Friedrich Delitzsch, whose views on Mesopotamian religion excited great controversy.[96]

Koldewey's reports from the site were published in the scholarly *Mitteilungen der Deutschen Orient-Gesellschaft* and *Wissenschaftliche Veröffentlichungen der Deutschen Orient-Gesellschaft*. Even his major book, *Das Wiedererstehende Babylon*, published in 1913,[97] took the form of a detailed, relatively dry archaeological report, although this did not discourage Agnes Johns from making a rapid English translation for publication the following year.[98] In a sense his publications are important for just this reason, marking the end of the scholar-explorer period and the beginning of more formal archaeological research in Iraq.

Further work at Babylon has since been carried out by Iraqi,[99] German[100] and Italian[101] scholars, and includes detailed research on the foundations of the ziggurat, but the achievement of uncovering and restoring to life the Babylon of Nebuchadnezzar is without doubt that of Robert Koldewey and Walter Andrae. The former would certainly have continued the excavations for many years had he not been compelled to leave by the advancing British Mesopotamia Expeditionary Force in 1917,[102] but what he had already achieved was staggering: enough to restore the heart of ancient Babylon and to present it to the world.

FIG. 25 *above*
Walter Andrae, Plan for Ishtar Gate reconstructions in Berlin

Walter Andrae (1875–1956) masterminded the spectacular reconstructions of the Ishtar Gate and Processional Way that now form the centrepiece of the Vorderasiatisches Museum in Berlin.

AD 1927
Watercolour
Handschriftenabteilung, Staatsbibliothek zu Berlin –
Preußischer Kulturbesitz

FIG. 26 *opposite*
The reconstructed Ishtar Gate

Staatliche Museen zu Berlin, Vorderasiatisches Museum

Koldewey's Babylon

Joachim Marzahn

⒠ FIG. 27

Inscribed brick of Nebuchadnezzar

Many thousands of the king's bricks bore a message with his name and titles. Nebuchadnezzar's ambitious building programme required huge numbers of bricks, and this led to a revival of the use of brick stamps. A cuneiform inscription was cut in reverse on the stamp so as to produce a readable text when applied to the still moist clay of the brick. Here, one of the workmen, Zabina, has spelled his name in Aramaic alphabetic letters before the clay dried: *zbn*.

Reign of Nebuchadnezzar (605–562 BC)
From Babylon, collected by C.J. Rich
Baked clay
H 32.5 cm, W 32.5 cm, Th. 8.0 cm
British Museum, BM 90136
Mitchell 1988: 77, no. 40

The wonder that Babylon has always inspired reflects the long-standing urban culture of Mesopotamia that reaches back to the third millennium BC and beyond. To this day the city epitomizes to all cultures the idea of a great and complex metropolis. Ironically, little enough of its former splendour has been preserved on the ground.

The building material *par excellence* in ancient Mesopotamia was alluvial clay, great quantities of which were freely available everywhere. The clay had always to be tempered with straw before moulding the bricks in a wooden frame and then drying them in the sun. Walls were made from these bricks using a mortar of exactly the same sort of clay, and the resulting structure was plastered with clay as well. This building principle applied to all major architectural structures in Babylonia, irrespective of size and function, with the drawback that constant care and renovation were required to prevent buildings from relatively rapid decay. This matter is referred to in countless inscriptions by royal patrons who proudly list the renovation of decrepit buildings and monuments of an earlier age among their achievements: 'I had rebuilt, and provided for, the shrines of Babylon and Borsippa. I completely restored Etemenanki, the ziggurat of Babylon, and E-urimin-anki, the ziggurat of Borsippa, with bitumen and baked brick, and completed the work.'[103]

A standard Neo-Babylonian clay brick was square in shape, measuring approximately 33 by 33 cm, with a thickness of 8 cm to enhance stability. Half-bricks were employed at corners. Large buildings of great height required massive strength, so walls could be 3–4 metres thick, if not more, to resist the pressure. Rooms built in this way therefore appear in excavated ground plans as small and elongated, although they were not so in reality.

To increase stability reed mats were placed at certain intervals, serving to distribute weight and to prevent vertical splitting. Bitumen, likewise readily available, was used as waterproofing material and applied to roofs, drains and sanitation facilities. It also served to guard against rising damp, which was crucial in view of the high water table at Babylon especially. Flat roofs without waterproofing were susceptible to rain and weather damage since they too were constructed with clay on reed mats over beams.

These very practical considerations explain why archaeologists are fortunate to find impressive remains today of ancient Mesopotamian architecture. Most of it has perished, while the destructive forces of armies, nature and weather have often been compounded by the recycling of ancient bricks as building material, again especially at Babylon. The excavators of the city found that several of their hosts' houses incorporated bricks of Nebuchadnezzar, clearly identified as such by stamped cuneiform inscriptions.

It is natural to wonder how the architecture in the public spaces of Babylon looked. Brick facings were everywhere, while the impressive size of many of the urban structures, even when of a private nature, was remarkable. Characteristically Babylonian buildings were structured around large central courts, as in later Iraqi architecture. Ground plans of palaces and temples are mainly distinguishable from those of

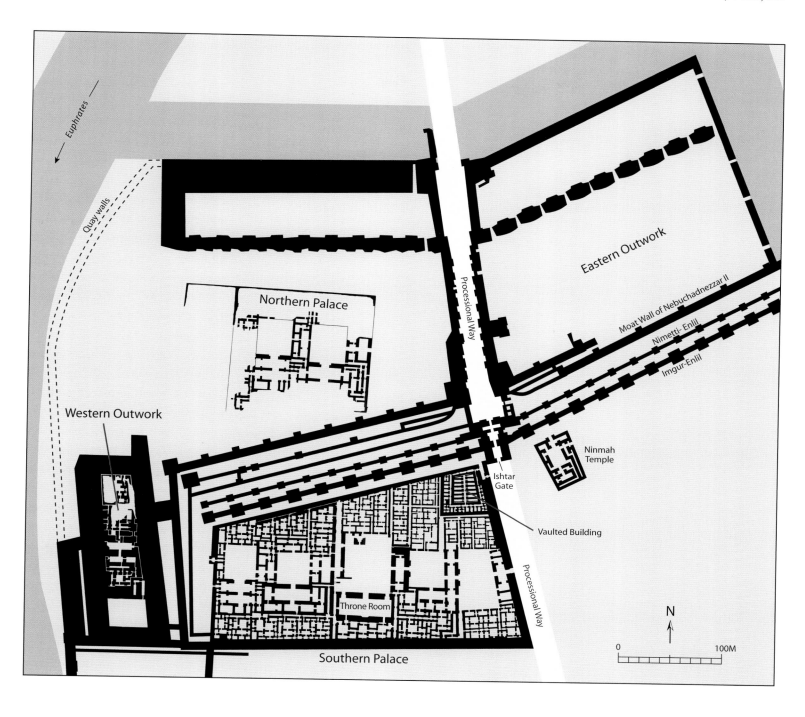

Euphrates

Quay walls

Northern Palace

Western Outwork

Eastern Outwork

Processional Way

Moat Wall of Nebuchadnezzar II

Nimetti- Enlil

Imgur-Enlil

Ninmah
Temple

Ishtar
Gate

Vaulted Building

Throne Room

Processional Way

Southern Palace

N

0   100M

FIG. 28
Nebuchadnezzar's Southern Palace

This map shows at once the great size of Nebuchadnezzar's palace and the sites of the Vaulted Building and the Western Outwork, both of which have been put forward as possible locations for the Hanging Gardens. As well as the great courts the palace contained hundreds of smaller rooms. Nebuchadnezzar's throne room is visible in the centre, while the Ishtar Gate may be seen at the north-east corner of the palace.

domestic dwellings by their immense size and the thickness of their walls. For example the Southern Palace of Nebuchadnezzar in the inner city measured 325 by 220 metres, a huge building even by today's standards. The whole structure of the temple enclosure around the ziggurat was even larger.

The impression that these buildings must have looked bare, given the yellow-brownish clay from which they were structured, is misleading. Babylonian architecture made use of different techniques to build up wall features. The walls were structured using grooves and niches, and sometimes they incorporated slightly projecting pillars. Urban dwellings were not always

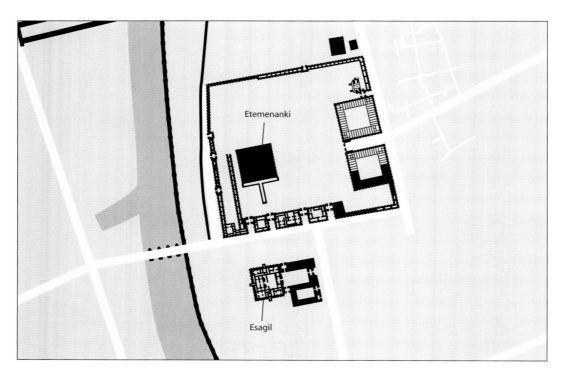

constructed along straight lines. Quite often the direction of the wall was broken up in a saw-like manner 'which gave the streets of Babylon a very characteristic appearance, quite distinct from those outside Babylonia'.[104]

Important buildings incorporated projecting towers that rose above the height of the roof. In addition entrances quite often had pronounced gateways with inclining stepped sides. The tops of the walls were set off with crenellations. It is easy to imagine the effect of changing shadows and moving sunlight, and their shade served to cool the walls.

FIG. 29
Esagil and Etemenanki

Esagil was the most important of all Babylon's temples. By the time of Nebuchadnezzar it was already ancient, having been established even before the reign of the great Old Babylonian king Hammurapi in the eighteenth century BC. The temple was the seat of Marduk, who gradually achieved status as the primary god of Babylonia. The old Sumerian name of the temple, Esagil, means 'House Whose Top is High'. The building complex contains shrines for Marduk and his consort, Zarpanitu, and is constructed around three courtyards with elaborate doorways. Immediately to the north lies the ziggurat Etemenanki, whose similarly old name means 'House of the Foundation Platform of Heaven and Earth'.

FIG. 30 *opposite*
Unglazed brick relief showing a bull and dragon

The lowest sections of the Ishtar Gate were constructed in unglazed bricks that featured the sacred animals in relief. The glazed panels were produced later. All unglazed portions were out of sight by the time of Nebuchadnezzar's final building stage, as the ground level of the Processional Way was constantly rising.

Reign of Nebuchadnezzar (605–562 BC)
From Babylon
Baked clay
Staatliche Museen zu Berlin, Vorderasiatisches Museum, VA Bab 1976

There were no windows in the modern sense since it was essential to keep out heat and dust; a door facing the courtyard was normally sufficient to let light into the rooms. The floors inside buildings were simple compacted clay, with or without a lime slip. The paved courtyards were usually of plastered brick. These generalizations apply throughout architecture because in Babylonia stone was far too rare and costly to be used as a building material. Where necessary, clay bricks could be hardened considerably: in palaces and temples one does encounter fired bricks laid in asphalt or lime slip/mortar. Stone slabs were, however, used for thresholds and the door-posts on which door beams turned.

Walls were usually plastered with clay and might be covered with a lime slip, whose white colour would have enhanced the walls' appearance. The bases or doorways might be painted in different colours. Some remnants of mural paintings do survive at Babylon, but they are too small to reveal the original design.

This general picture of Babylonian architecture, including fortifications and gates, reflects the results of the German excavations, bearing in mind that they are restricted to Neo-Babylonian levels. Nonetheless in those areas where earlier occupation levels could be reached the picture looks similar. Babylon had an established tradition concerning layout of the administrative centres, streets and living quarters, and this underwent little change over time.

Even from afar the walls and towers of Babylon, crowned by the temple-tower of Marduk, would have been a clearly visible and famous landmark. For a first-time visitor the mass of crowded buildings domestic and public, with narrow passages and sudden open spaces, must have been bewildering. We have to assume that some areas of the inner city were not built up since excavation could find no trace of architecture there, but the view was always dominated by the overarching foci of divine and state power.

Nebuchadnezzar's wonderful blue and yellow bricks were an outstanding feature. Although neither glazing technology nor brickwork relief was new, the combination was startling in its originality and indeed artistic effect. Neo-Babylonian decoration technology far superseded earlier

FIG. 31
Glazed brick relief showing a *mušhuššu* dragon

The beast, called *mušhuššu* in Babylonian, is a composite, with a snake's head, eagle's talons and a lion's torso and striding legs. Such dragons were sacred to the god Marduk, and were esteemed by the Neo-Babylonian kings in particular for their power to drive off enemies and evil spirits:

I cast seven bronze savage mušhuššu, who spatter enemy and foe with deadly venom.

Inscription of King Neriglissar (560–556 BC)

Reign of Nebuchadnezzar (605–562 BC)
From Babylon
Baked and glazed clay
H 116 cm, W 167 cm
Staatliche Museen zu Berlin, Vorderasiatisches Museum, VA Bab 4431
Borger 1975: no. 168; Westenholz 1996: 207, pl. 9; Seipel and Wieczorek 1999 vol. 1: 152, 154

craftsmanship, and successive periods at Babylon showed relief bricks without glazing, glazed flat bricks, and ultimately relief bricks with colourful glazing. These were used to decorate the most public monuments with reliefs depicting animal, rosette and palmette designs in shining colours. This sophisticated decoration was limited to a few structures that represented the power of the gods and the king. Among these the Processional Way and Ishtar Gate complex was the most important, because it linked a non-sacred structure, part of the city fortifications, with a high sanctuary. This road, coming from the north, was used during the New Year festival procession by the gods together with king and court. They came from the festival house outside the city in a ceremony meant to secure rule over the empire for a new year. By extending the palace buildings beyond their previous boundaries, north of the gate there emerged a street enclosed by walls, to be decorated with brick reliefs. At the end of this passage was the gate named 'Ishtar is the one who defeats her enemies', covered with glazed bricks on all its outer sides.

The walls along the Processional Way were clad for about 180 metres with pictures of lions and other ornamentation on their lower sections, and these were enhanced by a coloured stone floor that went further into the city. The amazing Ishtar Gate, composed of an ante-gate in the

FIG. 32
Glazed brick relief showing a bull from the Ishtar Gate

Reign of Nebuchadnezzar (605–562 BC)
From Babylon
Baked and glazed clay
Staatliche Museen zu Berlin, Vorderasiatisches Museum

outer wall and the main gate in the larger inner wall of the city, with a 48-metre-long passage, was decorated with no fewer than 575 depictions of animals (according to calculations by the excavators). These pictures, of bulls and dragons representing the holy animals of the weather god Adad and the imperial god Marduk, were placed in alternating rows. These were fit surroundings for the New Year procession heading towards Esagil, the Marduk sanctuary named 'House Whose Top is High' in the centre of the city.

Another building with similar decoration was part of the inner city palace where the throne room of the king was situated in the central court. Its façade, 56 metres in length, had three entrances, the middle one leading towards the throne dais. It showed a huge mural of glazed relief bricks with depictions of walking lions framed by decoration, and on the upper level were palmette motifs and floral elements.

Parts of both structures, street and city gate – as well as the façade of the throne room – have been reconstructed from thousands of small fragments and filled in with modern replacement bricks where needed, and may be seen today as one of the highlights of the Vorderasiatisches Museum in Berlin.

FIG. 33
The Processional Way

This photograph shows part of the modern installation in the Vorderasiatisches Museum, Berlin. The reconstruction is built up from thousands of original fragments supplemented by bricks that were specially manufactured for the purpose.

Reign of Nebuchadnezzar (605–562 BC)
From Babylon
Staatliche Museen zu Berlin, Vorderasiatisches Museum

These structures were surely not the only ones where glazing was used, but so far we cannot prove that there were further buildings. Only close to the main gate to the inner city palace of Nebuchadnezzar have small fragments of glazed bricks been found, and these were too few to allow reconstruction. One can assume that this palace was a prime site for splendid decoration since any visitor to the ruler of the four quarters of the world had to be impressed. This palace was never open to everyone, but certain areas were frequented by staff, servants, guests, diplomatic envoys and other persons who came to petition the king and his administration.

No one who saw Babylon's glazed-brick reliefs gleaming in the spring sunshine for the New Year festival would ever have forgotten the strange beauty and power of these monuments. It is fitting that their few surface traces – small, enigmatic fragments collected by Robert Koldewey during his early visits to the site – should have inspired the excavation and rediscovery of the great city in modern times.

ⓔ FIG. 34
Glazed brick relief showing a lion

Reign of Nebuchadnezzar (605–562 BC)
From Babylon
Baked and glazed clay
H 124 cm, W 231 cm
Staatliche Museen zu Berlin, Vorderasiatisches Museum,
VA Bab 4376
Borger 1975: no. 169; Seipel and Wieczorek 1999 vol. 1:
152, 155.

FIG. 35
Glazed brick panel from the throne room

A particular series of panels was found in
Nebuchadnezzar's throne room. They show
palmettes and floral motifs as well as the favoured
regal lions.

Reign of Nebuchadnezzar (605–562 BC)
From Babylon
Baked and glazed clay
Staatliche Museen zu Berlin, Vorderasiatisches Museum

A tour of Nebuchadnezzar's Babylon

Andrew George

E FIG. 36
Head of a dragon

The dragon that appears to such good effect in Nebuchadnezzar's brick relief panels was sometimes also reproduced in the round. Here the central recess probably held a jewelled inlay, as did the eyes. The forked protruding tongue that is now almost completely missing was made of iron.

6th century BC
Babylon(?); acquired in about 1890
Bronze and iron
H 15 cm, L 10 cm
Paris, Musée du Louvre, département des Antiquités orientales, AO 4106
Heuzey 1906, pl. 4; Lambert 1984

Babylon reached its greatest glory as a city during the reign of Nebuchadnezzar II (605–562 BC). It was then the capital of an empire that stretched from the Persian Gulf to Gaza, and from the mountains of Greater Armenia to the desert wastes of northern Arabia. Nebuchadnezzar conducted an elaborate programme of rebuilding and renovation in the city, paying particular attention to its monumental buildings and public spaces: temples, palaces, walls and streets. The Babylon that was excavated by Robert Koldewey between 1899 and 1917 was largely his creation.

Babylon was a great religious centre, known as the Sacred City. At its heart were fourteen different sanctuaries, and another twenty-nine were distributed through the rest of the city. That was quite apart from the hundreds of street-side chapels and shrines. This tour of Nebuchadnezzar's Babylon reflects that reality. It adopts the route followed every year by the procession of the god Nabû, who entered the city in the south, visited several of the principal religious buildings and went past many of the important sights, and left the city in the north. The visit of Nabû was part of the New Year festival, a series of rituals that signified the triumph of Marduk, the god of Babylon and king of the gods, over the Sea. Nabû's role was as Marduk's helper, for he was Marduk's son.

The procession arrived by barge from Borsippa, Nabû's cult-centre 12 miles south-west of Babylon, on the 5th day of the month Nisannu, docking on the east bank of the Euphrates just downstream of the city at Red Gate quay. The next day it passed through the city-wall at the Uraš Gate. The wall was in fact two walls: a lower outer rampart and a taller inner wall, called respectively Nimetti-Enlil and Imgur-Enlil, the 'Bulwark of Enlil' and 'Enlil Showed Favour'. When the procession arrived inside the gate it went a few blocks north along a great ceremonial way called Nabû-dayyan-nishishu (Nabû is the Judge of his People), but then turned right, down a back street to the temple of Ninurta. This was E-hursang-tilla (House where the Mountain is Annihilated), which was rebuilt by Nebuchadnezzar's father, Nabopolassar. It was the location for a ritual in which Nabû smashed the heads off two figurines, a symbolic rite that demonstrated his prowess as a warrior equipped to slaughter his father's enemies.

The procession then left E-hursang-tilla, rejoined the ceremonial way and headed north to the centre of town, past the temple of the goddess Išhara. It was about 460 metres to the great gate that led into the precinct of Marduk's temple. Either side of this gate, called Ka-sikilla, the 'Pure Gate', were the statues of the twin divine judges Madanu and Nergal who forbade entry to any evil-doer. The Holy Gate was where Babylonians in legal disputes swore on Marduk's divine weapon, and where the god of Babylon dispensed 'justice at the gate'. Nabû's procession passed through it, into the Sublime Court. Nearby were Esagil, the great sanctuary of Marduk, and the temples of many other deities – including the sanctuaries of Marduk's father, the god Ea, and his paramour, the Mistress of Babylon, Zarpanitu. Nearly all the land between the Holy Gate and the River Euphrates was crammed with religious buildings. This part of the city was the centre of the Babylonian cosmos and was called Eridu, the name of a very ancient city that signified the primeval cult-centre.

For the Babylonians Marduk's temple was the holiest place on earth. Its name, Esagil, means 'House whose Top is High'. No one knows who founded

Esagil, but it was already in existence by 1850 BC. It was desecrated in 689 BC when Sennacherib of Assyria sacked Babylon and took Marduk's statue back to Ashur, and it had to be completely rebuilt as a result. Sennacherib's son Esarhaddon died before the work was finished, and Marduk's statue did not return home until the reign of *his* son, Ashurbanipal. The temple stood until late in the Parthian period, *c.* AD 100, and was probably the last of the great Babylonian temples to succumb to neglect and time.

Esagil was huge: 86 by 79 metres, with gateways 9 metres high and walls 4 metres thick. Nebuchadnezzar lavished attention on the cult-rooms: there were gold, silver and gemstones everywhere, and great doors and beams of Lebanese cedar. Throughout the temple were images of strange monsters – serpents and dragons, lion-demons and scorpion-men, bison and mermen; statues of dragons and goat-fish and sphinxes stood guard at its entrances. The plaster walls of a Babylonian temple were usually decorated in black and white using washes of gypsum and bitumen, but Nebuchadnezzar achieved the same effect in Esagil by using inlaid panels of lapis lazuli and alabaster.

Marduk was not the only deity who resided in Esagil; his wife Zarpanitu occupied a suite of rooms called E-hal-anki, 'House of the Mystery of Heaven and Earth', and another part of the temple was given over to Nabû, who stayed in his parents' house, as it were, when he was in Babylon. As well as that, all the gods of the pantheon had a shrine in the building and the Babylonians often called it the 'palace of the gods'.

Attached to Esagil was Ubshu-ukkinna, an enclosed courtyard where the gods assembled at the New Year to pay homage to Marduk and Nabû. The two gods were enthroned on a gold-plated platform called the Dais of Destinies and charged with bringing order to the cosmos. When they came back from the Akitu temple, where their battle with the Sea was symbolized in ritual, they sat on the Dais of Destinies again to decide the fate of the cosmos for the coming year.

At dawn on 8th Nisannu Nabû's statue resumed its procession, leaving its chambers in Esagil, traversing the temple precinct and turning left out of the Pure Gate. Immediately outside was a shrine called Iqullu-ilu-ana-Marduk (The Gods Pay Heed to Marduk), the first of many stations on the road to the Akitu temple. The procession moved north along the ceremonial road called Ay-ibur-šabu (May the Arrogant not Prevail), the scene of many a military triumph since Nabopolassar threw off the yoke of Assyria in 612 BC. The road's surface had been remade by Nebuchadnezzar with baked bricks set in bitumen, and paved with breccia slabs.

On the left Nabû's party, now in convoy with a much larger procession led by the king and Marduk, soon reached the wall of the ziggurat precinct, which accompanied the road for 400 metres. Behind this wall, in an enclosure that stretched all the way to the River Euphrates, was the ziggurat E-temen-anki, the 'Foundation Platform of Heaven and Earth'. The ziggurat was a giant tower made up of multiple storeys like a stepped pyramid, but with a flat top. The number of storeys has been a matter of dispute (Herodotus reported eight), but was beyond doubt seven. Nebuchadnezzar faced the last storey with glazed bricks that shone dark blue, as if tinged by contact with the sky. On its south side a triple staircase gave access to the top of the first stage. The passage from there to the top was probably via interior staircases.

The tower took nearly a hundred years to rebuild after Sennacherib's engineers wrecked it. Esarhaddon had its foundations laid, but Ashurbanipal did not finish it, even though he ruled for

ⒺFIG. 37
Terracotta dragon plaque

This mould-produced plaque is likely to have been manufactured for the domestic market. The *mušhuššu* dragon would serve to protect a household from enemies.

About 800–550 BC
Purchased from E. Géjou, 1911
H 9.1 cm, W 10.0 cm
British Museum, BM 103381
Oates 1986: 170

forty years. Construction was interrupted after his brother Šamaš-šuma-ukin rebelled in 652 BC, triggering a bloody civil war from which Ashurbanipal eventually emerged victorious. Work resumed when Nabopolassar drove the Assyrians out and became king in Babylon, but the structure was not finally completed until the reign of Nebuchadnezzar II, in about 590 BC. The long period of construction probably informed the biblical legend of the Tower of Babel. The Persian king Xerxes disabled the ziggurat after the Babylonian revolt of 484 BC, and took part of its foundation deposit back to Susa in triumph. The ruins were dismantled by Alexander the Great and his successors in preparation for a reconstruction, but that never took place.

Archaeological survey of the site where the tower stood established that its base covered an area 91 by 91 metres. According to a Late Babylonian mathematical exercise called the Esagil Tablet, the tower was as high as it was wide – but this may be a statement of an ideal that was never realized. In its overall dimensions and division into seven stages the tower replicated the boat in which Uta-napišti survived the Babylonian Flood, for both were microcosms of the universe. The Esagil Tablet reports that each stage was slightly smaller, so that the last measured 48 by 45 cubits. This top storey was 30 cubits tall and was not solid like the other six, but took the form of a temple suspended between heaven and earth. Marduk dwelt there, on a great throne in the holy-of-holies, along with Nabû and a few other gods in separate chapels. There were two beds, one in the bedchamber, and a second in the courtyard. Herodotus picked up a rumour that a ritual of sacred marriage took place there, when a woman lay on the bed and waited for Marduk to come to her, but there is no corroboration from Babylonian sources. The rituals of this high temple were a mystery which none would reveal.

After leaving the ziggurat enclosure behind, the procession passed the little temple of the goddess Ashratu. Just behind it was the more important temple of Nabû as divine crown prince. Reconstructed by Nebuchadnezzar, this temple was the location for a ritual in which the king's son was installed as crown prince and given the regalia of office. Its name was E-ningidar-kalam-ma-summa, 'House which Bestows the Sceptre of the Land'. Off to the right was a smart neighbourhood, where the temple of the Mistress of Akkad lay two blocks east of the procession road. The temple E-mašdari was built by Nabopolassar or Ashurbanipal.

The procession passed over the eastern canal that took water for irrigation from the Euphrates to the fields east of the city – Libil-hengalla it was called, 'May it Bear Plenty'. The bridge, also renewed by Nebuchadnezzar, was made of cedar and fir beams coated in bronze and laid three deep to create the deck.

Ahead on the left loomed the gigantic walls of the old palace built by Nabopolassar and refurbished by his son, who had to raise its floors to protect it from rising damp at a time when the water table was rising. It was not big enough, or perhaps still not dry enough, to meet Nebuchadnezzar's needs, and he extended it by adding a further palace on its north side, across the city-wall. But the old palace provided good enough lodging for those foreign kings who were deported to Babylon when their territories became provinces of the empire. Among them was Jehoiachin, formerly king of Judah – which Nebuchadnezzar had subdued in his seventh year, 597 BC, and again eleven years later. Documents recording his oil-rations were found in the palace storerooms and reveal that Jehoiachin and his retinue became permanent guests of the king.

The procession reached the city-wall at the Ishtar Gate. On the right of the road was E-mah, 'Sublime House', the temple of the Mother goddess rebuilt by Ashurbanipal and repaired by Nebuchadnezzar. In front of the gate was a shrine called Ishur-izziz-Marduk, which means 'Marduk Turned and Stood'. This was another station on the road to the Akitu temple. Here lamentation-priests chanted a Sumerian litany begging Marduk not to be angry on his journey. The king got down from his carriage and himself slit the throats of two sacrificial lambs. After their blood had drained away he presented their heads to Marduk and emptied two bottles of wine on to the roadway to wash away the stain.

The Ishtar Gate was also called Ishtar-sakipat-tebiša, 'Ishtar Repels her Attackers', a name that invoked the help of the goddess of war in the city's defence. It earned the epithet 'Entrance of Kingship' because it was where the kings of gods and men together re-entered Babylon in triumph after the symbolic rituals of the Akitu temple. The gate was raised so that it stood at the crown of a low elevation, with the road sloping off in both directions. Its massive structure, 25 metres from the roadway to the top of its four towers, was faced with blue-glazed bricks. Rows of bulls and dragons alternated on its surfaces, picked out in relief by specially moulded bricks glazed in yellow and ochre.

From the top of the gate an observer could see the whole city spread out below them. Back

FIGS 38, 39
The Ishtar Gate reconstruction

The arrival of much material needed for the reconstructions in Berlin was delayed by the First World War, while the essential desalination and reassembly project in the museum meant that it was not until 1930 that the public at large could see the Ishtar Gate and Processional Way for the first time.

Reign of Nebuchadnezzar (605–562 BC)
From Babylon
Baked and glazed clay
Staatliche Museen zu Berlin, Vorderasiatisches Museum

down the procession road, across the open space of the ziggurat's precinct, one could see the east façade of Esagil. Dominating the view was the ziggurat Etemenanki itself, which rose up from behind Nabopolassar's palace in the middle distance, all but its lowest stage fully visible over the palace battlements.

Behind the ziggurat the Euphrates flowed right to left, brown as a clay pot, and disappeared to the south in a haze of sunlight. Midway down its course was the bridge that had been built to replace the ferry and connect the two halves of the city with a permanent structure. Across the bridge were the western quarters. Amid the dense warrens of residential housing, palm plantations and vacant lots, the distinctive structures of temples showed up, easily recognizable from their size and sunlit façades striped with shadow. Among the thirteen temples of west Babylon were some very old foundations, including temples of Enlil, Adad and Šamaš that went back to the era of King Hammurapi, twelve hundred years before Nebuchadnezzar.

The western quarters were enclosed by a defensive oblong, on three sides by the city-wall, and on the fourth by the quay wall on the river's west bank. There were four gates in the city-wall, and four more in the circuit of the wall that enclosed the eastern quarters. Their names are preserved in sequence: the gates of Enlil, the king, Adad and Šamaš in the west; and of Uraš, Zababa, Marduk and Ishtar in the east. Looking south-east from the Ishtar Gate, a line of date palms revealed the course of the canal Libil-hengalla from the bridge on the procession road to the temple of the goddess Belet-Eanna, and beyond to the city-wall. Another major landmark in the east was the temple of the Moon god, another very ancient foundation restored by Nebuchadnezzar.

Urban sprawl spilled out of the gates of Zababa and Marduk along the roads to Kish and Kutha. Beyond that Nebuchadnezzar's new outer wall loped across the field of vision, making a dog-leg around the eastern city from the Euphrates just downstream of the Uraš Gate, north-east towards Kish, and then north-west to the Euphrates 2 kilometres north of the Ishtar Gate. At the north end of this wall, well away from the city, Nebuchadnezzar built another palace for use in summer when the city air was stifling and its smells at their worst. Its ruins, called Babil, kept alive the name of Babylon until the modern era.

Outside the Ishtar Gate, across the other side of the procession road, was the palace extension built by Nebuchadnezzar to enlarge the urban residence he inherited from his father. The Greek authors reported that Nebuchadnezzar built a terraced garden there (the Hanging Gardens). There is no Babylonian account of it because no outsider ever glimpsed it, even from the city-walls. It would not do to have soldiers leering at the ladies of the harem.

Because of the palace extension the area immediately outside the Ishtar Gate was heavily fortified, but the great walls either side of the Processional Way matched the Ishtar Gate for beauty. Friezes of white lions marched along the walls of blue-glazed brickwork as if issuing forth from the city to prey on the countryside. The road led down to the river, where endless palm plantations lined the bank. Further upstream, though, between the landing stage and the Summer Palace, was a garden planted with many other kinds of trees. In it could be seen, half obscured by poplars and tamarisk, a small temple. This was the Akitu temple, where Marduk and Nabû defeated the Sea and her forces of chaos.

Neither inscriptions nor excavation yield anything like a complete overview of the city as it appeared in its heyday. But between them, texts and archaeology can give us a glimpse.

FIG. 40

Herbert Anger, *View of the Ishtar Gate and Processional Way*

This view over the city of Babylon, which incorporated the latest archaeological information and was based on a drawing by Eckhard Unger, soon became well known in its own right. In the foreground a procession passes through the Ishtar Gate. Koldewey's suggested location for the Hanging Gardens in the Vaulted Building adjacent to the Southern Palace – a proposal which has since been superseded – is here discreetly endorsed.

Colour print after watercolour, AD 1927
Unger 1931: frontispiece

FIG. 41 *bottom left*

***Tintir = Babylon*, the ancient listing of Babylon's features**

A compilation listing the city's religious buildings and sacred features, which no doubt fulfilled an important role in school teaching. This fragment of a larger manuscript originally contained the whole of the five individual tablets that make up the ancient compilation known as *Tintir = Babylon*.

6th century BC, hand of Nabu-kin-apli
From Babylon
Clay
H 14 cm, W 13 cm
Staatliche Museen zu Berlin, Vorderasiatisches Museum, VAT 13101
Unger 1930: pl. 82; Unger 1931: pl. 43, 45, 46a and 49; George 1992: ms z, pl. 1

FIG. 42 *bottom right*

***Tintir = Babylon*, Tablet I in Babylonian and Greek**

In this example from a first-century BC school environment, the first twelve lines of Tablet I are given in Babylonian cuneiform on one side and in Greek alphabetic transcription, shown here, on the other.

About 1st century BC
From Babylon; purchased from Messrs Spartali & Co. 1879
Clay
H 12.2 cm, W 8.6 cm, Th. 2.7 cm
British Museum, BM 34798
George 1992: ms c, pl. 6; Geller 1992: 82–3, no. 16; Westenholz 2007: 273, no. 16

Ancient descriptions: the Babylonian topographical texts

Andrew George

The Babylonians would not have recognized 'topographical texts' as a genre of their written record, but the term is used today to refer to texts that help modern scholars to reconstruct the topography of the cities of ancient Mesopotamia. Most such texts are concerned with Babylon, for this city was the political, religious and cultural centre of Babylonia during most of the first millennium BC. They fall into two groups: (a) texts that list epithets of the city, its religious buildings and sacred features; and (b) texts that present dimensions of one or other of the city's monumental structures.

Foremost among the first group is a text called by the ancients *Tintir = Babylon*. This composition has been reconstructed from more than sixty Neo-Assyrian and Late Babylonian cuneiform manuscripts – that is clay tablets and fragments of the first millennium BC. The manuscripts of *Tintir* date to the period 700 to 61 BC, but the text was probably composed hundreds of years earlier. It was a common copy-book of Babylonian apprentice scribes during their education, and inculcated in them both practical knowledge of the capital and the ideology of Babylon and its patron god, Marduk. It begins with the fifty-one Sumerian names of Babylon, of which Tintir is the first. The point of this initial list is to celebrate Babylon as the centre of the world, not by praising it in a connected text but by attributing to it venerable Sumerian epithets and explaining them in Babylonian. The pedagogical value of studying this list is self-evident. Many of the epithets were formerly the property of older cities – especially Nippur, the old Sumerian religious centre of Babylonia. Their adoption by Babylon is a clear demonstration of the new theology and ideology that arose from Babylon's rise to power in the second millennium. Column i of Fig. 41 holds part of this list, as does the obverse of Fig. 42. The reverse of the latter preserves a Greek transcription of the list, a crib demonstrating that student scribes were still learning *Tintir* in the first century BC, when Greek had become a language of the Babylonian elite.

Tintir = Babylon continues by listing the Sumerian ceremonial names and divine occupants of shrines in Esagil, the temple of Marduk. The entire pantheon was housed in this building and many gods had at least one shrine. The second column of Fig. 41 holds a fragment of this list, which was at least 110 lines long. The next preserved section of the text is a list of Sumerian names of the forty-three temples of Babylon, beginning with Esagil and Etemenanki, Marduk's ziggurat. This list is organized by city-quarter. Because we know where the quarters were, the recovery of the list has allowed the identification of several excavated temples by name. The text then turns to shrines of Marduk, 55 in number. These bore Babylonian names, not Sumerian. They were not inside the great temples but scattered in and around the city in public places. Some of them have also been excavated.

The text *Tintir = Babylon* concludes with the gates, walls, waterways and streets of Babylon. These also bore ceremonial names in Babylonian, for they were invested with religious significance. As points of exit and entry and routes of the processions of Marduk and the great gods, these features of the city were the backdrop to the great festivals of the Babylonian religious calendar, and by association they were almost themselves divine. A fragment of this section survives on the reverse of Fig. 41 (right-hand column). The end of the text is truly topographical: a list of the ten city-quarters of Babylon, each identified by name and one or more prominent landmarks. This has been a key passage for identifying the different parts of the city on the ground, along with the gates and temples associated with them. The end of this section is preserved on the reverse of Fig. 41 (left-hand column).

The second group of topographical texts is based more on measurements. Two structures received special attention. The first was the wall of Babylon. Not only did the wall defend the city, but it was also a symbolic barrier between the ordered world of the city and the chaotic realm of nature. It had a counterpart in the night sky, where it was identified as the great square of Pegasus. Perhaps for this reason its measurements were the subject of scholarly study. The Late Babylonian fragment in Fig. 44 is part of a clay map of Babylon showing the south-west section of wall, with a city-quarter and a waterway inside the Gate of the Sun god; on the other side is a metrological commentary on the wall that gives their approximate dimensions. Another metrological tablet in the British Museum concerned with Babylon's wall is Fig. 43. Where they can be compared with extant remains, the measurements presented in this text are extremely accurate and no doubt derived from practical experience rather than academic speculation. The text probably stems from a detailed survey of the state of the wall when Nebuchadnezzar II succeeded his father, Nabopolassar, as king of Babylon in 605 BC.

Another set of texts focuses on the cult centre of Marduk, which comprised Esagil, his sanctuary at ground level, and Etemenanki – his ziggurat. The Neo-Assyrian tablet Fig. 46 gives the dimensions of the main building of Esagil in two cross-sections. Matching its data to the remains of the temple is fraught with

FIG. 43
A topographical exercise

This tablet contains short extracts from several different school exercises. Alongside lines from the topographical text *Tintir = Babylon*, this trainee scribe practised snippets of bilingual magic and lists of objects made from wood, reed or terracotta.

6th–5th century BC
From Babylonia
Clay
H 10.6 cm, W 6.0 cm
British Museum, BM 54626
George 1992: ms 1ee, pl. 10

E FIGS 44, 45

Plan showing Tuba, an area in south-west Babylon

This highly unusual tablet preserves part of a well-executed map of one section of Babylon. The modern line drawing below gives its location within the city at large. The other side of the tablet contains a teacher's didactic commentary on the measurements of the inner city-wall of Babylon, called Imgur-Enlil.

Probably reign of Nebuchadnezzar (605–562 BC)
From Babylon; purchased from Messrs Spartali & Co. 1879
Clay
H 7.9 cm, W 10.7 cm
British Museum, BM 35385
Pinches 1882: 152; George 1992: no. 16, pl. 28, fig. 5

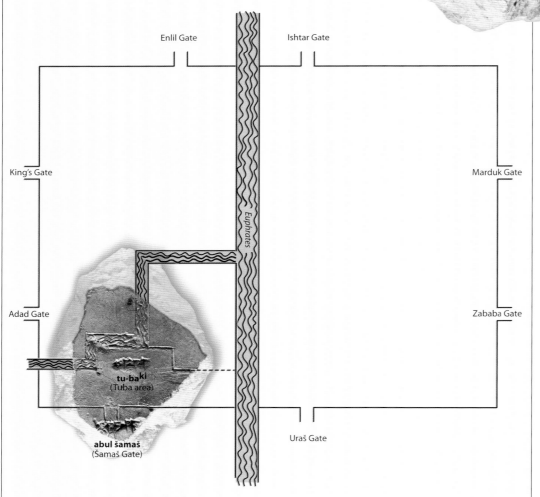

Enlil Gate

Ishtar Gate

King's Gate

Marduk Gate

Euphrates

Adad Gate

Zababa Gate

tu-ba^{ki}
(Tuba area)

abul šamaš
(Šamaš Gate)

Uraš Gate

FIG. 46 *opposite*
Measurements of Esagil and Ezida

Designed to be hung up like an amulet, this Assyrian document gives dimensions for parts of Babylon's most important temples: Esagil of Marduk and Ezida of Nabû. The former include the Chariot House and Court of Bel-Marduk, as well as chapels of Ea, Beltiya and Anu-and-Ishtar. The text may relate to rebuilding by Esarhaddon after the destruction wrought in Babylon by his father Sennacherib in 689 BC.

7th century BC
From Ashur
Clay
H 14 cm, W 6.3 cm, Th. 1.5 cm
Staatliche Museen zu Berlin, Vorderasiatisches Museum, VAT 9961+10035
George 1992: no. 14, pl. 26–7

difficulty because the temple's ground plan was not fully recovered, and because the text and the ground plan clearly bear witness to different rebuildings.

The ziggurat Etemenanki was the structure that gave rise to the biblical myth of the Tower of Babel. Ziggurats were stepped towers surmounted by small temples. A schematic diagram, thought by some to represent a ziggurat in profile, appears on the Late Babylonian tablet Fig. 47. In the first millennium BC ziggurats were usually attached to a large temple at ground level, but at Babylon Etemenanki was 250 metres distant from Marduk's great cult-centre, Esagil. The most famous metrological text that holds data about Etemenanki is the so-called Esagil Tablet. The text is best known from a Late Babylonian tablet written at Uruk in 229 BC and now in the Louvre, illustrated in Fig. 109.

The text of the Esagil Tablet begins by giving the dimensions of two courtyards in the precinct of Esagil and then turns its attention to the measurements of the ziggurat. It gives first the base area of the tower and then the measurements of the sanctuary at the ziggurat's top, including the length and breadth of Marduk's bed.

The text concludes with the tower's exterior dimensions, stage by stage. The motivation for the text is not description from reality but mathematical, for some of the data are set out as mathematical problems and others are repeated in units drawn from different metrological systems. One gets the sense that teachers used the ziggurat as a giant model for instructing students in geometry and metrological conversion. Thus it is unwise to use the Esagil Tablet as a blueprint for reconstructing the tower. It presents only an idealized, schematic structure.

In addition to texts of obvious topographical importance, there are other documents that can help in reconstructing the plan of Babylon and the layout and fittings of its sacred buildings. Babylonian and Assyrian kings were inveterate builders, for the maintenance of the gods' earthly abodes was an essential duty in their mediation between heaven and earth. The custom was for the builders of monumental structures to leave inscriptions embedded in the brickwork, recording the name of the god for whom the work was done and the identity of the builder. Often these inscriptions contained much more

ⓔ FIG. 47
A Babylonian ziggurat in side view

This school tablet shows what was probably originally a seven-storey ziggurat in elevation. Measurements of length and height for each stage are noted in cuneiform. The lowest level is only 21 metres to a side, which suggests either that the building was a small ziggurat or that this is a scale exercise modelled on Etemenanki in Babylon. Part of the building is labelled: 'View of the face of the House of Anšar'; other passages suggest that Anšar here is a name of Marduk.

Hand of Nabu-šuma-iškun, descendant of Ahi'utu (7th century BC)
Probably from Babylon
Clay
H 6.35 cm, W 5.08 cm
Excavated by Hormuzd Rassam, 1880
British Museum, BM 38217
Wiseman 1972

information, such as historical accounts of campaigns and information about the circumstances that led to the construction work. Some Babylonian building inscriptions quote topographical details, including lines of the temple list from *Tintir = Babylon*. Others give details of furnishings. Several relevant inscriptions were left by the last great Assyrian king, Ashurbanipal (669–631 BC). He spent much time and effort beautifying Babylon and the cult-centre of Marduk. In one inscription he describes a bed of Marduk and his consort, the goddess Zarpanitu, that he placed in their bedchamber in Esagil (Fig. 48). This was not the bed in the ziggurat temple, but its counterpart at ground level – where a ritual of divine marriage was carried out annually. Details such as these allow us slowly to flesh out the extant ruins and the two-dimensional plans of archaeologists. Not only can we recover something of the topography of Babylon and its sacred buildings, but also we can use other cultic sources to populate the streets and temples with gods, kings and the onlooking crowds. Thereby we gain a fascinating glimpse of gaudy ritual, and a sweet whiff of incense.

FIG. 48
Objects from Assyria for the Marduk temple in Babylon

This document records King Ashurbanipal's much-publicized return to Babylon of the ornate bed of Marduk and Zarpanitu and the throne of Marduk. His grandfather Sennacherib had taken these items from Babylon when he sacked the city in 689 BC, and Ashurbanipal's action was part of the Assyrian effort to make good the physical and spiritual damage done at that time. Ashurbanipal wrote his own name on the throne in place of that of Sennacherib, who had dedicated the booty to Ashur and Ninlil in the city of Ashur.

7th century BC. Kuyunjik (Nineveh), excavated by Sir Austen Henry Layard
Clay
H 16.5 cm, W 14.6 cm, Th. 2.2 cm
British Museum, K.2411
Streck 1916: 292–303; Millard 1964: 20–3

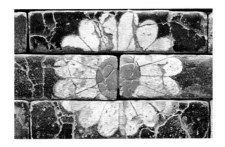

The Dynasty

Neo-Babylonian kings at Babylon

Jonathan Taylor

In 612 BC the armies of Babylon and Media rampaged through the streets of Nineveh, the last of the great capital cities of Assyria. During the seventh century BC the Assyrian Empire had reached its zenith, controlling a territory that extended from Iran to Egypt, including the city of Babylon. By the 620s BC the Assyrian grip over Babylonia had weakened substantially. Out of the strife arose a rebel general named Nabopolassar who seized the throne at Babylon and founded a new dynasty.[105] Nabopolassar ruled from 626 to 605 BC, consolidating his empire and building his capital at Babylon. To the east the Medes, erstwhile vassals of Assyria, had risen to dominate Iran and cooperate with the Babylonians. After the dramatic fall of Nineveh, the victorious allies divided Assyria's empire between them,[106] unaware that within a century both their realms would in turn be subsumed into the even greater empire of Cyrus II of Persia.

A small group of Assyrian survivors fled westwards to the city of Harran. Fearing the advance of the Babylonians, Egypt stepped in to assist the Assyrians, but without success. The decisive blow was struck at the bloody Battle of Carchemish in 605 BC, when Nabopolassar's eldest son, Nebuchadnezzar, crushed the last remnant of this force. The victorious Babylonians pursued the surviving Egyptians, with the effect that 'not a single man escaped to his own country',[107] but invasion of Egypt was averted by news of Nabopolassar's death. The crown prince hurried back to Babylon to claim his inheritance unimpeded.

Nebuchadnezzar, king of justice

The new king, Nebuchadnezzar II (605–562 BC), was quick to build on his father's achievements. His inscriptions present him as an archetypal Babylonian monarch: wise, pious, just and strong. Even his name was auspicious; it echoed that of the king who had famously rescued Marduk's statue from Elam and established that god as head of the pantheon.[108] In a remarkable document known to scholars as 'Nebuchadnezzar, king of Justice', we learn that Babylon had been beset by abuses and injustice: 'the strong used to plunder the weak' and 'regent and prince would not take the part of the cripple or widow before the judge'. But now Nebuchadnezzar 'was not negligent

E FIG. 50
'Nebuchadnezzar, king of justice'

This literary composition extols Nebuchadnezzar as man and ruler, just, benevolent and strong:

Then a second time because of criminal and unjust acts he came back for judgment. The king commanded (?) the troops; they cut off his [the criminal's] head and sent it throughout the land. They cut off a stone head, made it into the likeness of that man's head, and had inscribed on that man's head: 'A man whose case has been judged, the tablet of whose verdict has been written, and whose tablet has been sealed, but afterwards he returns for judgment – in like manner his head shall be cut off' and fixed it onto the outer gate of that law court for all to see. [109]

Reign of Nebuchadnezzar (605–562 BC)
Babylon
Clay
W 14.0 cm, H 10.0 cm
British Museum, BM 45690
Lambert 1965

in the matter of true and righteous judgment, he did not rest night or day, but with counsel and deliberation he persisted in writing down judgments and decisions arranged to be pleasing to the great lord, Marduk, and for the betterment of all the peoples and the settling of the land of Akkad'.[110]

It was a royal duty to maintain and restore temples and to strengthen the city's defences. Nebuchadnezzar set about these tasks with great relish. The ancient imperial city was already vast, but under the new king it was to attain unprecedented grandeur. He worked on Babylon's immense network of walls, protecting the city from flooding and from invasion by foreign armies. He also saw to the spiritual protection of his empire, restoring the main temple precinct dedicated to Marduk as well as a host of other temples in cities across the land.

The great king deserved a palace to match. Whereas previous kings had built palaces wherever they pleased and only came to Babylon for the New Year festival, Nebuchadnezzar situated his palace in Babylon, making it a focal point for the new empire. Supplementing his father's already gigantic residence, he built two new palaces, the first on the northern edge of the inner city, the second to the north of the city beside the River Euphrates. This, the so-called 'summer' palace (it had ventilation shafts of a type still used today for cooling houses in the Middle East), he described as 'a building to be admired by the people, a linking point of the land, a gleaming sanctuary, my royal abode'.[111] In the corners of his buildings Nebuchadnezzar buried clay cylinders telling of his pious deeds.

The Neo-Babylonian kings of Babylon

Ancient cuneiform king-lists give us the names of Babylonian rulers, and, helpfully, some even include the dates of their reigns.

Ancient Mesopotamian names were meaningful. Nabu-kudurri-uṣur, known to us as Nebuchadnezzar, means 'O Nabu, protect my child!' The names that are familiar today derive from the Bible or classical sources, and have thus tended to undergo slight changes. Below are the names of the six Neo-Babylonian kings as they are most familiarly known, with their Babylonian originals:

Nabopolassar, 626–605 BC (ancient name Nabu-apla-uṣur)
Nebuchadnezzar II, 605–562 BC (ancient name Nabu-kudurri-uṣur)
Amel-Marduk, 562–560 BC
Neriglissar, 560–556 BC (ancient name Nergal-šar-uṣur)
Labaši-Marduk, 556 BC
Nabonidus, 556–539 BC (ancient name Nabu-na'id)

Amel-Marduk is more familiar to readers of the Bible as Evil-Merodach, while 'Labynetus' – mentioned in some Greek sources – is a name probably derived from Nabonidus. The Neo-Babylonian dynasty came to an ignominious end with the Persian conquest in 539 BC.

The Old Babylonian *Code of Hammurapi*

When Hammurapi (1792–1750 BC) came to the throne in Babylon his kingdom was only one of several in southern Iraq. By the end of his reign he had secured Babylon's position as capital and established a wide sphere of influence. Yet it was not for diplomatic guile or military prowess that Hammurapi came to be remembered, but as a law-giver.

Hammurapi's laws are best known through this massive black stone, originally one of many set up around the kingdom towards the end of his reign. A florid prologue expounds on the king's divinely supported status as shepherd of the people, while the epilogue threatens dire curses against anyone who might seek to pervert his justice. In between are inscribed some three hundred legal pronouncements, the 'just decisions which Hammurapi, the able king, has established and thereby directed the land along the course of righteous behaviour and proper conduct'.

Hammurapi's laws, a paradigm of right and wrong behaviour, became a classic text, studied by countless generations of scribes. Copies occur in the royal library of Assyria as well as from the time of the Neo-Babylonian kings. The description of Nebuchadnezzar's benevolent actions in the tablet known as 'Nebuchadnezzar, king of justice' (Fig. 50) placed him in a tradition of responsible rulers that already stretched back more than a thousand years to Hammurapi and his predecessors.

FIG. 51
Reign of Hammurapi (1792–1750 BC)
Susa, excavated by Jacques de Morgan, 1901–2
Basalt
H 225 cm, W 70 cm, Th. 47 cm
Paris, Musée du Louvre, département des Antiquités orientales, Sb 8
Scheil 1902; Bergmann 1953; Finet 1973; Roth 1995: 71–142; André-Salvini 2003

The Greeks would later marvel at the architectural splendours of the city. Even as late as the thirteenth century AD, the Arab geographer Yaqut records that Bukhtnassar (Nebuchadnezzar), a king who ruled over the entire earth, diverted the water of the Euphrates 'fearing that the city wall would be torn down', and had as his palace the *Sarh* (a word referring to an impressive construction).[112]

Nebuchadnezzar's extensive building programme consumed enormous resources and required a large workforce, including many skilled craftsmen. Fortunately, he had a ready supply of workers, thanks in part to his successful foreign policy. Soon after his coronation he marched back west to confront the Egyptians once again, and spent the next ten years asserting his control over the small states of the Levant.[113] These subject states had long proved difficult to rule; caught between major powers, they constantly shifted allegiance, striving and conniving to loosen the grip of their imperial masters. Heavy clashes with Egypt in 601 BC left Babylon weakened. The kingdom of Judah saw an opportunity and withheld tribute payments. Having regathered his strength in 600 BC, however, Nebuchadnezzar moved against the Arabs in 599 BC[114] and then Judah in 598 BC, besieging and soon capturing its capital, Jerusalem.

Soon after this Babylonian historical documents largely fall silent. In 595/4 BC the king faced rebellion at home but was able to put it down within a month, capturing and executing the guilty party, and disposing of his estate.[115] A tantalizing reference is made in a cuneiform tablet[116] to further conflict with Egypt in 567 BC, against the pharaoh Amasis. Other than this we rely mostly on classical and biblical sources. Josephus[117] tells us that Nebuchadnezzar laid a 13-year siege to Tyre, while Ezekiel 26–28 provides a lengthy description of Tyre's sins and its destruction at the hands of Nebuchadnezzar. Some sources are beset with confusion. Megasthenes in his

Ⓔ FIG. 52

Barrel cylinder of Nebuchadnezzar

It was standard practice among Babylon's kings to deposit clay cylinders in the foundations of buildings. These were intended as messages to posterity as well as to any future king who might come upon them in their own building or rebuilding operations. Often written in exemplary script on fine clay, such cylinders speak of royal achievements as well as piety, and can be precious historical sources.

In this inscription the king typically declares his personal devotion and describes his extensive building programme, but not his military activities.

Reign of Nebuchadnezzar (605–562 BC)
From Babylon
Clay
W 24.0 cm, D 10.0 cm
Paris, Musée du Louvre, département des Antiquités orientales, AO 1506
Langdon 1912: 111–21 (no. 14); Berger 1973: 289–90

FIG. 53

Foreigners in Babylonia

We can be sure that society in the capital city at Nebuchadnezzar's time was very cosmopolitan. Foreigners arrived as traders and merchants, mercenaries and prisoners. Occasionally their names surface in cuneiform texts. Here, for example, individuals with clearly Egyptian names are mentioned among other foreigners, as being entitled to receive rations.

Probably 6th century BC
Probably from Sippar, excavated by Hormuzd Rassam, 1882
Clay
H 4.4 cm, W 3.2 cm
British Museum, BM 57337
Wiseman 1966

History of India even claimed that Nebuchadnezzar surpassed Heracles, and had successfully invaded north Africa and Spain.[118]

The Bible details Nebuchadnezzar's best-known deed: in 587 BC Judah again rebelled. The Babylonian king sacked Jerusalem and again deported part of the population. This relatively trivial episode in Nebuchadnezzar's reign (from a Babylonian perspective) would come to dominate his legacy, condemning him to infamy in the Old Testament.

A period of instability

After a long and illustrious reign Nebuchadnezzar II died in 562 BC, to be followed by a series of kings with very short reigns. The first of these was his son, Amel-Marduk. There is some evidence – both from contemporary texts and from later sources – to suggest that he may have acted as regent during the final stage of Nebuchadnezzar's reign, but little else is known about him. Berossus' description of him as one 'whose government was arbitrary and licentious'[119] seems to find confirmation in a fragment of Babylonian text that bemoans the inappropriate behaviour of this king.[120] Amel-Marduk may be the same person as Nabû-šuma-ukin, a son of Nebuchadnezzar who composed a literary account of how court slander had him falsely imprisoned by his father, and how Marduk saved him. On his accession he is said to have ordered the release of Jehoiachin, imprisoned ex-ruler of Judah (Jeremiah 52:31–32).

Amel-Marduk's brief reign was brought to an end in 560 BC when he was murdered by his brother-in-law, Neriglissar. Earlier documents from Nebuchadnezzar's reign show Neriglissar as a businessman with extensive land holdings. He is mentioned as governor of Bît-Sin-magir in a list of Nebuchadnezzar's court officials,[121] and is one of the high-ranking Babylonian officers recorded by Jeremiah at the siege of Jerusalem in 586 BC. Neriglissar fought successful campaigns in the north-west but died in 556 BC, to be followed on the throne by his son, Labaši-Marduk. The young king only survived three months before being murdered in turn. According to Berossus friends plotted against him on account of his wickedness.

The rise and fall of Nabonidus

The coup that toppled Labaši-Marduk was led by a mysterious figure with the name of Nabonidus. His origins are cloudy. Perhaps he was Herodotus' 'Labynetus', who had been peace-maker between the Medes and Lydians when the battle at the River Halys was halted by an eclipse on 28 May 585 BC. His father was probably a noble; Nabonidus' inscriptions refer to him as a learned counsellor. More is known about his mother, Adda-guppi, a devotee of the Moon god, Sin, from distant Harran. When she died in 547 BC, aged over 100 years, her passing was marked with a remarkable account of her life, known as her 'Autobiography'.[122] In it we discover that 'Sin had become angry with his city and his temple and went up to heaven' (this refers to the earlier destruction of the temple in Harran, apparently by the Medes, when the last remaining Assyrians were ousted in 610 BC). Adda-guppi had shown devotion to the Moon god since the days of the last Assyrian kings that continued through the reigns of Nebuchadnezzar, Amel-Marduk and Neriglissar. Eventually Sin heard her prayers. In recognition of Adda-guppi's piety the Moon god called her son to kingship – this is how Nabonidus justifies his claim to the throne. In his own inscriptions Nabonidus plays the reluctant king: 'I, who, not knowing, had no thought of kingship for myself'. The 'Autobiography' also claims that Adda-guppi and her son served Kings Nebuchadnezzar, Amel-Marduk and Neriglissar faithfully, while others neglected them.[123]

In Adda-guppi's account Sin appears to the queen mother in a dream, setting out his vision for the future: 'With you, I will place the return of the gods and the habitation of Harran in the hands of Nabonidus, your son. He will build Ehulhul and he will complete its work. He will make Harran more perfect than it was before and he will restore it. He will grasp the hand of Sin, Ningal, Nusku and Sadarnuna and cause them to enter Ehulhul.'

The restoration of Ehulhul, Sin's temple in Harran, was to consume much of Nabonidus' energy. From various accounts it is clear that with him Sin occupies a more prominent role than might have been expected for a king of Babylon. Marduk was the state god and head of the pantheon and it is he who is usually 'king of the gods' and who calls his appointee to kingship. Nabonidus' religious convictions caused him notoriety and trouble as a radical and a heretic.[124] Certainly he did not conform to the norms of Babylonian kingship. Nowhere is this manifested more clearly than in his prolonged absence from Babylon, and his setting up a rival capital in the recently conquered Arabian town of Teima. His motives for this dramatic move are not clear; possibly it involved lucrative trade routes, perhaps too there was more freedom to initiate religious reforms, or sickness was involved. Nabonidus saw it thus:[125]

> The sons of Babylon, Borsippa, Nippur, Ur, Uruk, Larsa, priests and people of the centres of Akkad sinned against his great divinity [i.e. Sin], whenever they strove they sinned, ignorant of the anger of Nanna, king of the gods. They forgot their duty. Whenever they talked it was treachery and not loyalty. They devoured each other like dogs. They brought about disease and famine amongst themselves, diminished the population. As for me, I took myself away from Babylon …

Whatever the motive, the consequences of this departure were serious. For the Marduk priesthood the very cosmic order was threatened, although the Babylonian chronicler records these events concisely and matter-of-factly: 'The king did not come to Babylon in the month Nisan. Nabû did not come to Babylon. Bel did not come out. The akitu-festival did not take place.'[126]

During Nabonidus' protracted absence from the capital his son, Belshazzar, was appointed regent over Babylon. The inscriptions dating to his regency show that he himself supported the cult of Marduk in other quarters, but trouble was brewing. To the east King Cyrus of Persia had turned against his uncle, Astyages of Media, and assumed leadership over a vast territory. Perhaps in reaction to this new threat Nabonidus returned to Babylon after ten years at Teima to resume his traditional royal duties. His post-Teima period inscriptions, however, attest to his efforts to have Sin replace Marduk as head of the pantheon, and there can be little doubt that his heretical behaviour paved the way for Cyrus to take the city in 539 BC. After some skirmishing the Persian army is reported to have entered the most heavily fortified city in the world without a fight. King Nabonidus was captured and possibly exiled;[127] Belshazzar disappears from view.[128]

 Thus ended the last native dynasty of Babylon. Despite the apocalyptic strain adopted by the Old Testament prophets, there was no 'fall' as such. Babylon was to become the largest of the Persian capitals and, briefly, the capital of Alexander's ever growing world empire before its gradual fading from the political scene in later centuries.

Ⓔ FIG. 54 *following pages*
Glazed brick relief showing a lion

Reign of Nebuchadnezzar (605–562 BC)
From Babylon
Baked and glazed clay
H 105 cm, W 227 cm
Paris, Musée du Louvre, département des Antiquités orientales, AO 21118
Fitz 1991

Life and Letters

Tablets at Babylon and the British Museum

Julian E. Reade

FIG. 55

The first published drawing of a Babylonian cuneiform tablet

Cuneiform writing was not yet deciphered when Carl Bellino (1791–1820), the gifted German secretary to Claudius Rich at Baghdad, made the drawing from which this engraving was prepared for publication. His achievement is all the greater in that the copy is extremely accurate and faithful to the original. Like Rich, Bellino died young, but he would have undoubtedly become a great scholar in his own right, as the then new field of Assyriology gathered momentum. We now know that Rich's tablet – an early specimen for the British Museum collection – was an undated Neo-Babylonian record of dates from fields located by the New Canal opposite the Šamaš Gate at Babylon. The tablet is now numbered BM 30040.

Engraving by S. Hall after original drawing by Carl Bellino
Rich 1818: pl. 9 no. 5

One of the cuneiform tablets collected by Claudius James Rich seems to be the first such object ever to be illustrated in a publication, and his specimens were among the first to enter the collections of the British Museum. Tablets at that point were sufficiently unusual to get the nickname of 'love-letters',[129] but there have been tens of thousands since. This tablet formed part of what has come to be known as the Kasr Archive, legal documents belonging to a governor of Babylon about 400 BC.[130] At the time, naturally, the script was still undeciphered, but Joseph Hager's hopes for the decipherment had begun to be realized in the work of the philologist Georg Grotefend of Frankfurt. By 1802 Grotefend had read the names of three Persian kings on inscriptions from Persepolis. This 'learned and ingenious person' had also turned his attention to the inscriptions from Babylon, most obviously the bricks, and 'those who consider the importance of the undertaking will rejoice to learn that Dr Grotefend is prosecuting his inquiries with unremitting ardour'.[131] Rich encouraged a correspondence between Carl Bellino, his own German secretary,[132] and Grotefend. Bellino had an exceptional ability at copying the cuneiform script; this would not be remarkable for a modern scholar knowing the signs, but Mignan,[133] referring to the densely inscribed terracotta cylinders which were placed as memorials in the foundations of Babylonian buildings, aptly remarked that they 'are covered with the small running-hand alone, executed with such delicacy and nicety, that to copy them is a task almost impracticable'. Bellino made what is generally accepted as an outstandingly clear copy of one of them, this actually from Nineveh, but Rich's collection did eventually include two from Babylon so that Grotefend probably had access to as many inscriptions as were then available. Among them were two of Rich's most important acquisitions, a stone land record resembling the Caillou Michaux and a carved stela showing the last king of Babylon, Nabonidus (Fig. 152). It must have seemed that a breakthrough in the decipherment was imminent, if only enough inscriptions could be found.

Other visitors looked for antiquities too. In 1818 Ker Porter[134] came away with one of the terracotta cylinders, presumably from the foundations of Nebuchadnezzar's palace. In 1824 Keppel[135] studied the inscriptions on the bricks, comparing the different stamps on those found in the ruins with those that paved the veranda of the house in which he was staying in Hillah; he presented one brick to the Calcutta Asiatic Society. He also found some cylinder seals and discussed the iconography of three which he presented to the British Museum. Mignan[136] found a cylinder too:

> with the greatest difficulty ... in one of the innumerable unexplored winding passages, at the eastern end of that remarkable ruin the Kasr, or great castellated palace. It was deposited within a small square recess, near a fine perfect wall, the kiln-burnt materials of which were all laid in bitumen, and the ground was strewed with fragments

of alabaster sarcophagi, and enamelled brick, still retaining a brilliant lustre. Many fractured masses of granite of inconceivable magnitude (some chiselled in a pyramidal form,) prevented my penetrating far into this intricate labyrinth; the way to which is by a souterrain, and must be entered in creeping posture.

Mignan records and illustrates several other finds, including exceptionally large inscribed bricks. The Babylon bricks were normally at most 14 inches (35.5 cm) square, but he found a platform made of bricks that were 19.75 inches (50 cm) square and 3.5 inches (9.0 cm) thick.[137] He removed two of these, presenting one of them to Sir John Malcolm, governor of Bombay.

Excavations at Babylon in this period were following the precedent set in 1616 by Pietro della Valle. Unless for some reason objections were raised, there was no restraint on the excavation and export of antiquities until the first Ottoman law governing such activities was promulgated in 1874. Pietro had dug primarily out of scientific curiosity, and so to some extent did Rich, Keppel and Mignan. Rich kept his collection, which he had largely acquired by purchase, and his widow eventually sold it to the British Museum in 1825. The then vast sum of £7,500 that she received, after some haggling, was almost entirely on account of his wonderful collection of manuscripts and coins, not for his Babylonian antiquities. The British Museum also acquired Ker Porter's collection. Keppel[138] recommended that other travellers who were passing through Iraq 'ought to provide themselves with instruments for digging, which would both facilitate their researches, and in all probability amply repay their curiosity'. There are two motives here, scientific and acquisitive; in the event Keppel, son of the Earl of Albemarle, behaved as a public-spirited gentleman and gave at least some of his acquisitions to scientific institutions, the Calcutta Asiatic Society and the British Museum. Mignan[139] employed up to thirty men on one of his excavations at Babylon; while he had been pleased to excavate some coins and seals at Ctesiphon, he seems to have been content at Babylon with varieties of inscribed bricks which he could compare with one another. The objects which he[140] thought worth illustrating for his book consisted of a broken glazed brick of the Persian period showing a rosette, his inscribed cylinder (although no real attempt was made to copy its inscription), eight small corroded bronze figures ('valuable and interesting, as being the earliest specimens of the metallurgic science'), and the inscriptions on two bricks (reproduced upside down). He was attempting to show the kinds of things that were to be found at Babylon, and their scientific interest. He presumably kept most of these things, but in giving a brick to the governor of Bombay he was hopefully placing it in the public domain where anyone might inspect it. This at least is what happened to some Assyrian sculptures presented to the governor about 1850, which are now in Mumbai's Shivaji Museum.

The practice of casual digging for antiquities at Babylon seems to have lapsed over the next few years. Several visitors to the site published reminiscences, but their books and those of others throughout the nineteenth century mainly repeat the observations and speculations of the past, sometimes larded with eloquent passages from the Bible about the dreadful fate that had overtaken the blasphemous city. It must have become evident that work there was unlikely to produce either scientific results or attractive antiquities, and visitors who wanted antiquities could buy them more conveniently in Baghdad, where they were brought from many different sites.

Nonetheless while Babylon was returning to deserved obscurity in the eyes of Europeans in Baghdad, it was attracting renewed interest in Europe. The decipherment of Babylonian cuneiform had proved far more difficult than can possibly have been expected in 1800. Grotefend failed to make any significant advance on his original breakthrough; anyway this only covered the Persian version of the script, which was entirely different from the Babylonian and far simpler. The

FIGS 56, 57
Henry Rawlinson and Edward Hincks

Rival decipherers side by side, as they seldom were
in real life.

56
**Sir Henry Creswicke Rawlinson
(1810–1895)**

AD 1860
Mezzotint by Samuel Cousins, after an 1850 painting by
Henry Wyndham Phillips (the location of which is now
unknown)
H 50.4 cm, W 38.2 cm
British Museum, 1872, 0309.463

57
Reverend Edward Hincks (1792–1866)

Date unknown
Artist unknown
Oil on canvas
H 106 cm, W 82 cm
Trinity College, Dublin

key lay in a vast inscription written by the Persian king Darius on a precipitous rock at Bisitun in Iran; it was written in three scripts, one used for the Old Persian language itself, one used for the Elamite language spoken in southern Iran, and one used for Babylonian. The inscription was extremely difficult and perilous to reach, let alone to copy, but Henry Rawlinson succeeded in doing so in 1836, and again in 1847 when he needed more details. Several scholars had contributed to the final decipherment of the Persian script in 1846; the most notable of them was an Irish clergyman, Edward Hincks. Rawlinson, who must have reckoned that his feats of mountaineering entitled him to a good share of the credit, claimed he had reached the same results independently. During the 1840s many inscriptions in the Assyrian script, which was closely related to Babylonian, also became available from excavations in northern Iraq. These enabled Hincks, with Rawlinson trailing in his footsteps and making some contributions too, to decipher Babylonian in turn; all the basic work had been done by 1850.[141] Rawlinson was unwilling to be thwarted twice in his hopes of fame and then, having a far more convincing presence than his rival and publishing in far more accessible journals, skilfully diverted credit for the decipherment to himself. From 1855 on he presided triumphantly over the slow publication of the innumerable cuneiform inscriptions that had been brought back from Assyria to the British Museum.

Meanwhile Babylon was his baby. Rawlinson had moved into politics, where he had firm views on such matters as the Russian threat to India, but as a politician he could never experience the same control over his surroundings and unquestioning respect as he had enjoyed when British Resident in Baghdad. There was no serious question, however, over his status as the high master of cuneiform studies, father of Assyriology as he was later entitled (the discipline itself is so-called because at the time there were far more Assyrian than Babylonian inscriptions) and he could still command. He promoted cuneiform studies with determination and conviction, all the more so as the sheer range of subject-matter in the Assyrian inscriptions became more apparent, and as it gradually emerged that Babylon had been only the last of a succession of major cities in southern Iraq. The history of the land stretched into a past so remote that its inhabitants, in their earliest writings, had even been using an unknown language, the one we now call Sumerian. In April 1867, commenting at the Royal Asiatic Society on Bewsher's paper about Habl al-Sahr, Rawlinson declared emphatically that 'The country to which Lt. Bewsher's paper referred, was the cradle of civilization. In it were first cultivated ... the natural sciences and that study of art which afterwards spread through the world.'[142]

This was a more satisfactory arena in which to display his abilities than in the interpretation of contradictory Greek historians. Rawlinson's reference to the study of art is disingenuous since he himself had limited time for it; he had several times irritated Layard by denigrating the artistic value of Assyrian sculptures. Knowing the contents of the Assyrian tablets as he did, however, he could reasonably hope that cuneiform studies would contribute to understanding the origins of the natural sciences.

He therefore greeted with proprietary interest the appearance on the Baghdad market between 1873 and 1878 of thousands of cuneiform tablets, many of which seemed to come from Babylon; there were 3,000 tablets stored in a single group of jars according to one account.[143] They included what has now been recognized as a unique series of astronomical diaries which set out the behaviour of the moon and planets year by year, together with records of ordinary and extraordinary contemporary events including the weather. There were many business archives and tablets of other kinds. Modern Assyriologists are still engaged in finding, cataloguing and publishing them, but already in 1903 the remarkable scholar H.V. Hilprecht[144] reflected that documents dating between the seventh and fifth centuries BC had:

> revealed to us an entirely new phase of Babylonian civilization. We became acquainted with the every-day life of the different classes of the population, and we became witnesses of their mutual and manifold transactions. We obtained an insight into the details of their households, their kinds of property and its administration, their incomes and their taxes, their modes of trading and their various occupations, their methods in irrigating and cultivating fields and in raising stocks, their customs in marrying and adopting children, the position of their slaves, and many other interesting features of the life of the people. Above all, these tablets showed us the highly developed legal institutions of a great nation, thus furnishing an important new source for the history of comparative jurisprudence. There is scarcely a case provided against by the minute regulations of the Roman law which has not its parallel or prototype in ancient Chaldea.

Rawlinson wanted the British Museum to maintain its pre-eminence, and his own, in the field of Assyriological study by procuring more tablets by excavation at source rather than by competitive purchase; the government accepted this view, and money was provided. Opportunely in 1878 Henry Layard, now Sir Henry, became ambassador in Constantinople. He was probably the first British ambassador to speak Turkish comfortably and really know how to behave in polite Ottoman society; he also represented a government whose fleet was, at least as he and the Turks hoped, waiting in the Aegean ready to repel an imminent Russian threat to Ottoman provinces in the Balkans and possibly to Constantinople itself. With these advantages Layard was able to persuade the sultan to waive the stringent conditions of the 1874 antiquities law which required excavators to surrender everything they found to the Sublime Porte. The permit which Layard obtained and which, as he says, 'caused him much more difficulty than getting possession of Cyprus'[145] was valid for two years and renewable for another two.

The work of excavation was entrusted to Hormuzd Rassam, whose approach contrasted drastically with that of Rich. Rassam had been born in Mosul in northern Iraq, working there originally as Layard's right-hand man during the latter's highly successful excavations. He then had a distinguished career, mostly in southern Arabia, as administrator and trouble-shooter in the service of the Indian government, after which he retired to England. He reluctantly agreed to be called out of retirement in 1877 in order to organize further excavations at various sites in Iraq on behalf

FIG. 58
Hormuzd Rassam (1826–1910)

Rassam was born in Iraq, worked with A.H. Layard on his excavations, and later became agent and excavator for the British Museum in his own right. Later photographs of Rassam show him in Western dress, after he moved to England.

About AD 1854
Photograph after collodion negative by Philip Henry Delamotte
Swansea Museum, SWASM:SM1987.845.79

of the British Museum. The work at Babylon itself lasted through 1879–82, but Rassam was often back home, resigning or attempting to do so, because he had never agreed to do much more than initiate excavations for someone else to take over. Fieldwork was largely left in the hands of local supervisors answerable, in some degree, to successive British consul generals in Baghdad who had other duties to occupy their time.[146]

Rassam had been instructed to find as many cuneiform inscriptions as possible. He did record some architecture at sites in the Babylon region, while at Babylon itself, 'had it not been for my scruple not to waste public money on such an object, which is of no material value to the British Museum, I should certainly have gone about differently to discover some clue to the positions of the important parts of the old city'.[147] He and the supervisors followed instructions, however, acting primarily as hunters after antiquities, and obtained a phenomenal collection. As a consequence Rassam's work has been unfairly regarded as little better than that of the other most successful nineteenth-century excavators of Babylon. These were the villagers and dealers who had always used Babylon as a source of income, digging for bricks to sell, and who had presumably first stumbled about 1872 on whatever large cache of tablets it was that precipitated the flood of discoveries through the 1870s. Tablets were more valuable than bricks and they started to be found at many sites; Babylon may have been the most productive, but Ibrahim Khalil next to Birs Nimrud was also a major source. Rassam[148] explains how dealers sometimes paid for tablets by number, which encouraged villagers to break their larger finds into two or more pieces, while the prices charged to foreigners in Baghdad were liable to be a hundred times as much as those paid to the villagers who had found them. He himself employed the same villagers, and arranged that they should be entitled to keep and sell any plain bricks they found while he was to have anything required for the British Museum. While there were some thefts from Rassam's excavations, he was clearly good at dealing with the people he employed and there seems to have been relatively little trouble.

During 1879–82 Rassam's men worked in five main areas in Babylon, with great success in two of them. Rassam thought that the Kasr mound, part of which was the area most heavily mined for bricks, was too badly disturbed to merit much attention, although he 'always found inscribed tablets mixed up with the rubbish'. He did, however, excavate part of the Ninmah temple on the northern edge of Kasr; we have a plan of some rooms[149] which can be identified because they were later re-excavated by Koldewey. When in Baghdad in 1878 Rassam had reported that tablets were then coming from Kasr, and this must have been correct in at least one instance, because among the inscribed material which he bought for the British Museum at the time was a foundation cylinder for the Ninmah temple.[150] There even exists a letter from the dealer who had the cylinder in Baghdad, describing how it was said to have been found, in a place with an iron door. Rassam was aware, however, as he remarks elsewhere, that dealers were not reliable sources of information. Rassam also excavated at Babil, where he found some arrangements for the supply of water; and at the Homera mounds, where he found nothing on which to report.

Rassam divides the Amran mound into two: Amran on the north and Jumjuma on the south. The northern part is where Koldewey eventually located the temple of Bel or Marduk, and this is presumably where Rassam's men found a fine stone stela of the Assyrian king Ashurbanipal, 668–631 BC, that was dedicated in a shrine of the god Ea (Fig. 59), and two more black stones of the Caillou Michaux type, one from the reign of an early twelfth-century king of Babylon, Melishipak,[151] and another naming a member of the temple staff.[152] A very important document

FIG. 59
Ashurbanipal rebuilds Babylon

The great king of Assyria is shown in traditional form, carrying a brick basket on his own head. Like his father, Esarhaddon, Ashurbanipal sponsored a major programme of restoration at Babylon to make up for the sacrilegious destruction of the holy city by his grandfather Sennacherib.

Reign of Ashurbanipal (669–631 BC)
From Babylon, found in the ruins of Esagil
Pinkish marble
H 35.9 cm, W 22.2 cm, Th. 6.4 cm
British Museum, BM 90864

reputedly found at or near Amran, possibly in the riverside wall, was the so-called Cyrus Cylinder, discussed below (Fig. 161). This famous cylinder was broken during excavation, and one pilfered fragment eventually found its way to Yale University in the United States.

Apart from small objects of miscellaneous kinds which were always emerging, there were hundreds of cuneiform tablets or fragments found at Amran, and apparently even more at the southern corner of the city near Jumjuma, where Rassam's men dug through mudbrick walls alongside the inner face of a city-wall. They were unable to plan the walls, but Rassam records that legal contracts were found here, which suggests it was an area of private housing. This is virtually all that can be said about the archaeological provenance of Rassam's Babylon tablets, and although he himself tried to ensure that tablets from different sites were packed and labelled separately, much of this information was lost before they came to be entered in the acquisition registers of the British Museum, so that it is often difficult or impossible to tell at a glance whether a particular tablet was found at Babylon or at one of his other sites such as Birs Nimrud. The different original archives have to be reconstructed from the evidence of the texts themselves, and the Museum in fact received so much more than it had bargained for from Rassam's excavations – including innumerable fragments that it would never have considered purchasing – that much of this work is still in progress. As a consequence, unless it was simply that age had mellowed him, Rawlinson by 1888 was far less proprietorial. At that time Peters[153] consulted him on which site he should choose to excavate, the explicit aim being the acquisition of a good collection of objects for the University Museum of Philadelphia. Rawlinson suggested that they should try Babylon; Peters understandably thought it was too large and confusing.

There is one very distinctive small tablet group which Rassam found at a site he called Eligrainee, situated a few miles north of Babylon itself. They are a thousand years older. They were written in the Old Babylonian period, best known for the code of laws inscribed at the time for a king, Hammurapi of the First Dynasty of Babylon, who had actually built the first Babylonian Empire; his existence was not yet suspected. Koldewey was to find houses of similar age deep beneath the floors of houses in Nebuchadnezzar's city.

Excavation was easier than conservation. Rassam noted in 1880:[154]

Unfortunately all the inscriptions found are on unbaked clay, which gets very damaged as soon as they are exposed to the air. We have lately found a very large tablet of this description, about 10 inches (25 cm) long, (the largest that has yet been found, I believe, in Babylon or Nineveh) containing two columns of fine inscription which has already been very much damaged; and my fear is that if it is sent to England in its present state, not a sign of the inscription would remain on it by the time it reaches the British Museum.

Rassam recognized that he himself was no Bellino, adept at accurate copies of an unfamiliar script, and his employers would provide neither an Assyriologist nor even a camera. Rassam therefore continues:

There is an Arab among our workmen here who had been in the habit of finding these kinds of unbaked clay tablets and who had tried, with success, to preserve them by baking them in hot ashes. I am going to get him to try one or two pieces before me, and if I find his process prove successful I will have the large tablet baked in the same way before I send it home.

The principle that the most sensible way to conserve cuneiform tablets was to bake them in the field as soon as practicable after excavation was thus invented by one of the villagers at Babylon. It has its critics but was widely accepted in the twentieth century, and the process was refined in the British Museum.

Beginning in 1899 Robert Koldewey led the Deutsche Orient-Gesellschaft excavations that were to uncover the monumental remains of Nebuchadnezzar's city. Although driven by an interest in architecture, the German excavations also led to the scientific recovery of numerous cuneiform archives, most of which are now held by the Vorderasiatisches Museum in Berlin. Koldewey's work at Babylon was halted in 1917 when, after three years of hard fighting, a victorious British army was advancing on Baghdad from the south. As with the tablets recovered by Rassam, work on the translation and publication of the huge corpus of texts excavated by Koldewey continues today. The historic rations tablet shown in Fig. 130 is just one example.

Uncovering life at Babylon

Irving Finkel

How is one to imagine life in the Babylon of King Nebuchadnezzar II? It was a vast, complex and bustling urban world; a city of renown since the time of law-giver Hammurapi more than a thousand years earlier; and already ancient when Nebuchadnezzar began to put his stamp on a new capital for a new age.

The official architecture, religious or secular, gave out an unmistakeable message of prestige and looked-for immortality. Nebuchadnezzar, who had personally witnessed the demise of all-powerful Assyria and was all too aware of the transitory nature of empire, operated on a truly grandiose level, as we have seen. Meanwhile within the great walls of the city and for much of the surrounding terrain, a great and contrasting population lived out its days. The nature of this urban conglomerate can perhaps be partly imagined on the basis of the modern Middle Eastern world, but it can often be more precisely gauged from contemporary Babylonian documents. A profusion of cuneiform inscriptions on clay echo the words and daily deeds of the state and the people.

Most of the institutions – religious, military and economic – were not new to the time. Sophisticated commerce without an underlying currency system, for example, had flourished since the turn of the third millennium, and in fact the great majority of surviving texts are economic in nature. Terms for loan, interest, mortgage and a dozen others were stock in trade to merchants and by the period treated in this book Babylon must have accommodated a wide spectrum of dealers, traders and speculators. We know most, as it happens, about the largest banking families, powerful dynasties that bought and sold property in such cities as Nippur and Babylon itself, imported and exported expensive goods, and secured profitable marriages – like

FIG. 60 *below*

Model of the ziggurat and surrounding area of Babylon

AD 1938
Designed by Walter Andrae, built by Günter Martiny
Staatliche Museen zu Berlin, Vorderasiatisches Museum, VAG 1070

FIG. 61
The Creation of the World

Babylonian documents record everything from everyday administration to religious belief and – as in the case of this tablet – ideas about the order of the universe. The creation of the world received its fullest account in the Babylonian Creation Epic, or *Enuma Eliš*. Its narrative is concerned with the struggle against chaos and the creation of mankind from divine blood and clay to serve the gods for all time. The epic witnesses the elevation of the god Marduk to the head of the pantheon. This process involved the creation and centralization of Babylon as the focal point of Mesopotamian culture:

When Marduk heard this,
His features glowed brightly, like the day:
'Then make Babylon the task that you requested,
Let its brickwork be formed, build high the shrine.'
The Anunna-gods set to with hoes,
One (full) year they made its bricks.
When the second year came,
They raised the head of Esagila, the counterpart to Apsu,
They built the upper ziggurat of Apsu,
For Anu-Enlil-Ea they founded his … and dwelling.
He took his seat in sublimity before them,
Its pinnacles were facing toward the base of Esharra
(the ziggurat)
After they had done the work of Esagila,
All the Anunna-gods devised their own shrines.
The three hundred Igigi-gods of heaven and the six
hundred of Apsu all convened.
The Lord, on the Exalted Dais, which they built as his
dwelling,
Seated the gods his father for a banquet,
'This is Babylon, your place of dwelling.
Take your pleasure there, seat yourselves in its delights!'

6th century BC (?)
Babylonia
Clay
H 11.5 cm, W 8.8 cm, Th. 3.2 cm
British Museum, BM 93016
Foster 2005: 470–1

others before and after – to guarantee the survival of their holdings. We can thus follow the life of the courts that arbitrated disputes from a wealth of administrative and legal documents that survive, with the judges' findings carefully written out on clay tablets to be hoarded by the protagonists against future claims.

Cuneiform texts survive in abundance. Their preoccupations, of course, are primarily the central institutions of the state: the king, the army and the temple. Each of these factions had its own priorities and, with the help of writing, projected its own image and needs. Writing beyond these 'public' spheres was, however, far more restricted in distribution, with the lasting consequence that the great proportion of the population, urban and rustic, lived their lives independent of it. On the rare occasion that a document was required in such a family, to provide it there were professionals schooled to produce documents that were legally unambiguous, signed and sealed to the satisfaction of all parties. The result of this reality is that we have but scant evidence for the lives – and especially the thoughts – of the great abundance of the population, who like all mankind have found themselves at the mercy of war, illness, famine and other misfortunes, usually with no direct record left. Personal or private writing hardly occurs on any level; there was an unspoken consensus, very probably, of the uses to which cuneiform writing on clay could fittingly be put.

Cuneiform sources as a whole, formulaic and straitjacketed though they might sometimes seem, do grant us glimpses of what one might call the humanity beneath: irony and sarcasm in letters, the desire for sons in medicine, neurosis and persecution complex in magic, humour in literature and piety in religion combine to create an accessible image of a world where the individual was never valued for their own sake, where human life was cheap and life expectancy not great, but which – despite the undoubted strangeness of many of its institutions – is no longer so inaccessible to us.

> Speak to Sin-shemi; thus says Lu-Hani: I am praying for you in the temples of Bau and Ningirsu. The omens are clear, so I wrote to you. Intercede for me, save me! Give me one shekel of silver that I can eat and not be carried off. I am doing good on your behalf. Send five fish. I swear that there are none here for Bau.
> A LETTER FROM BABYLON[155]

Writing at Babylon

Writing, as far as archaeology can tell us, appeared for the first time within the world of the ancient Near East and very probably in Iraq itself. The first experiments in recording language in graphic form certainly took place well before 3000 BC, and it was not long before the original pictographic symbols drawn on tablets of clay had evolved into the fully developed, classical cuneiform script that has preserved for us today the Sumerian and Akkadian languages of Iraq and other languages too.

Cuneiform, a complex and multi-value system, consisted of graphic signs that were themselves made up of individual wedge shapes deployed in a great variety of combinations. Each component was impressed into clay using a prepared, straight-cut stylus – hence the Latinate name 'cuneiform', meaning wedge-shaped. The developed use of the script came to function with surprising flexibility and adaptability. Words could be written with a single sign, but increasingly were spelt in syllables whereby a given word was broken down into 'sound bites' and an appropriate syllabic sign supplied for each.

The apprentice scribe faced the problem that there was always more than one sign available to write a given syllable, while at the same time each of those syllable signs often had additional phonetic (sound) values. Cuneiform signs were thus always multi-functional. This system made its demands on the reader, but helpful aids could be added, such as phonetic complements (to help in the correct choice of reading) or determinatives (to indicate meaning – to show, for example, that the following word was a god, or made of wood or the name of a river).

Cuneiform script was used to write on clay tablets for well over three thousand years; the latest dated cuneiform tablet comes from the second century AD. Cuneiform was never easy to master, and few convincing attempts to simplify it or streamline the system are detectable during its venerable history. No one advocated literacy for all; the whole process of maintaining the tradition and training new scribes was characterized by a sense of non-innovative responsibility, coupled with something of the clique or guild. There is every likelihood that the arrival of alphabetic writing after 1000 BC was not greeted with enthusiasm by the professional writing class, and that the 'old-fashioned system' was carefully guarded and promulgated in the face of this new and more easily-mastered system of writing that was, theoretically at least, available for all.

Professional, trained scribes were thus always few in number, and in ancient Mesopotamia we are paradoxically presented with a highly literate ancient culture in which literacy itself was always only available to, and transmitted by, a very small minority of individuals. Nevertheless cuneiform came in time to function as an adaptable vehicle for Sumerian (the oldest language we can identify for certain) and the various dialects of Semitic Akkadian (including Babylonian) within Iraq, as well as a handful of quite unrelated languages in the surrounding landscape, such as Elamite in Iran, Hittite in Turkey and Hurrian in Syria.

The durability of sun-dried clay has meant that vast quantities of inscriptions, usually more or less ephemeral in content, have survived in the ground to await the archaeologist's spade. The decipherment of cuneiform in the middle of the nineteenth century opened up a whole world of history, ideas and human activity. Such was its richness and extent that this huge inheritance is still being tackled by scholars today.

Writing and learning were deeply conservative. The kings and scholars of the Neo-Babylonian dynasty inherited a wealth of traditional lore that reached back in some cases over thousands of years. Sumerian, a language with neither ancient nor modern relatives, long survived its extinction as a spoken tongue because so much religious and other important literature was couched in it. Semitic Akkadian, in its dialects of Assyrian (north) and Babylonian (south), proved much easier for the decipherers, and ironically the history of the Akkadian language today is better documented than that of many Semitic tongues that are still in use.

Study of Sumerian and Akkadian together dominated the school curriculum in the second and first millennia alike, and some knowledge of Sumerian, and understanding of texts written in it, persisted among scholars until the final demise of cuneiform altogether, probably in the second century AD. Dictionaries, lists of signs, words collected by subject-matter or meaning appeared almost with the script itself, providing an inflexible backbone for teaching and learning, and likewise proving crucial for our contemporary understanding of cuneiform texts.

Cuneiform teaching was strictly supervised, and the uses to which the script could be put were traditional and rigid. Literature is almost invariably anonymous and personal writing of any kind is very rare. As remarked above, the half-million or so surviving tablets in world collections principally reflect the world of the state – the king, the army, religion, and the economy – law, property and inheritance, and how these factors affected the cities and what we might call the upper classes.

A great wealth of cuneiform inscriptions survives from Babylon from the seventh century BC through to the first century AD, a span that reaches from the time of the Neo-Babylonian kings on through the Achaemenid and Seleucid and into the Parthian periods. The bulk of these, some twenty thousand pieces, are now housed in the British Museum, with important parallel collections in, principally, the Vorderasiatisches Museum in Berlin, as well as related archives that have been discovered at other southern Iraqi sites, chiefly Uruk. As with cuneiform sources in

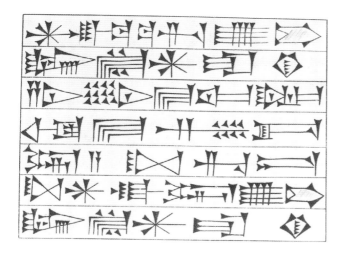

FIG. 62
Drawing of a Nebuchadnezzar brick

A deft nineteenth-century copy of the inscription from a single brick used in one of Nebuchadnezzar's great building operations at Babylon. The copy was made by Carl Bellino, long before any word of the script could be read.

The cuneiform text itself, in elegant, old-fashioned writing, signals the king's most crucial cultic responsibility: the upkeep of the temples Esagil of Marduk, and Ezida of Nabû, Marduk's son. The inscription reads:

Nebuchadnezzar (Nabu-kudurri-uṣur), king of Babylon,
Provisioner of Esagil and Ezida,
Eldest son of Nabopolassar (Nabu-apla-uṣur),
King of Babylon

Engraving after a drawing by Carl Bellino; Rich 1818, pl.10, no. 6

FIG. 63
Glazed brick panel with royal inscription

The identical Nebuchadnezzar inscription occurs in its most lavish incarnation on this glazed brick panel from the Ishtar Gate complex.

Reign of Nebuchadnezzar (605–562 BC)
From Babylon
Clay with coloured glaze
Staatliche Museen zu Berlin, Vorderasiatisches Museum

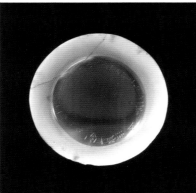

ⓔ FIG. 64 *above*

A compendium of esoteric sign lore

These ancient-looking clay fragments are all that is left of a secret compendium from a scholarly academy at Babylon. The scribe has included the most ancient, third-millennium BC 'pictographic' symbols (from which the cuneiform signs originally derived) for each 'modern' sign. In addition each sign is allotted a secret number, written in minute script. Such secret numbers could be used to encode texts such as astrological omens where readership was restricted, and we know that there was more than one number system available.

Reflected here is genuine understanding of the earlier history of Mesopotamian writing, and early tablets were no doubt keenly sought after for analysis by scholars. King Ashurbanipal of Assyria (669–631 BC) had kept similar texts in the Nineveh library, claiming that he could read 'texts from before the Flood', while an Assyrian fragment from the alternative capital Nimrud shows that new historical inscriptions could be written out in these earliest signs.

After 600 BC
From Babylon
Clay
(left) H 5.9 cm, W 6.0 cm; (right) H 9.4 cm, W 4.7 cm
British Museum, BM 46603 and 46609
Pearce 1996

ⓔ FIG. 65

An inscribed royal 'eye-stone'

An eye-stone, dedicated, according to its elegant inscription, by Nebuchadnezzar himself. Specially cut agates of this type had been favoured for royal dedications by earlier Kassite kings, and the old practice was clearly once more in fashion under the Neo-Babylonian kings at Babylon. How such stones were put to use is unknown.

Reign of Nebuchadnezzar (605–562 BC)
From Babylon
Cut agate
D 4.2 cm, Th. 1.5 cm
Paris, Musée du Louvre, département des Antiquités orientales, AO 7706
Delaporte 1923: 93, A.827

general, the overwhelming majority concerns the economy and administration of Babylon, but there are major holdings of literature of all kinds – from hymns, prayers and the Epic of Gilgamesh, to lexicography, mathematics and astronomy, as well as astrology, magic and medicine. These resources often originate in some form of archive, be they those of the powerful banking families like the Babylonian Egibi or the learned scholarly academies in which history, the future, and the patterns of events were carefully documented and considered. Work on all these genres progresses apace, as does our understanding of many facets of the ancient Babylonian world.

E FIG. 66
The Aramaic alphabet in cuneiform.

This remarkable tablet of about 500 BC captures interaction between the age-old syllabic cuneiform writing used for the Akkadian (Babylonian) language and the new alphabetic Aramaic that ultimately displaced it. This school exercise uses cuneiform syllabic signs to write out the *sounds* of the individual Aramaic alphabet letters, such as would be learned by a child (see right).

This document is, so far, unique. It must originate in a teacher who imposed an innovative writing exercise on pupils who were bilingual in Akkadian and Aramaic. The letter order has survived and is that of the modern Hebrew alphabet.

About 500 BC
From Babylonia
H. 7.0 cm, W. 3.0 cm
Clay
British Museum, BM 25636
Finkel 1998; Geller 1997-2000: 144-6

a	*la*
be	*me*
ge	*nu*
da	*sa*
e	*a-a-nu*
u	*pe*
za	*tsu*
he	*qu*
te	*re*
ia	*shi*
ka	*ta*

Nebuchadnezzar II, like other kings of ancient Iraq, favoured the use of 'ancient-looking' signs for his royal inscriptions, and it is a curious fact that the short brick inscriptions and more prolix records that confronted the Babylon visitor everywhere could have been read with facility by King Hammurapi twelve hundred years earlier. The scribes who produced monuments like the East India House Inscription (Fig. 17) must have had access to reference ancient-sign lists that gave them a dependable model, since imitating archaic writing was much more complex than painting 'Ye Olde Tea Shoppe' on a wooden board today. Inscribing error-free bricks for the king's building programme must have been a wearisome and unending matter. As in earlier ages things could be speeded up by the use of reverse-cut cuneiform stamps on a kind of production line.

How long the Babylonian form of Akkadian lasted as a spoken and written tongue in ancient Iraq remains quite uncertain. As the first millennium BC unfolded Aramaic – a distinct member of the Semitic linguistic family – came gradually to supplant historic Akkadian on many levels, starting in the market place and ending as the *lingua franca* and language of official proclamation. This process is detectable to us now in various ways, such as certain Aramaic influences on Babylonian grammar and syntax, or Aramaic loan-words borrowed into Babylonian – like *zayyit* (olive), replacing the native word *sirdu* that had been the common term since the third millennium. In addition there are tablets in Babylonian with marginal summaries in Aramaic for convenience, bricks with Aramaic signatures by workmen, a school text that rehearses the sounds of the Aramaic letters in cuneiform and, in one unique case, an entire spell in the Aramaic language written out in cuneiform script (Fig. 68).

E FIG. 67 *left*

Aramaic letters in ink

This very late (151–150 BC) document in Babylonian concerns the sale of a plot of ground near the Great Gate of Šamaš in the city of Uruk in southern Iraq. Nanaj-iddin transfers the land (which belongs to his wife Antum-banat) in return for a payment of 10 shekels of silver to Antipatros. After a guarantee there is a list of witnesses and the date, the third day of some month in year 161 of the Seleucid era. A single summary line of Aramaic across the reverse allowed easy retrieval.

Ink summaries to cuneiform documents are known from the seventh century BC onwards. By the time this contract was written it is likely that the individuals concerned no longer conversed in Babylonian at all. More commonly such Aramaic labels were scratched in to the clay.

151–150 BC
From Uruk
Clay
H 8.6 cm, W 9.2 cm, Th. 2.9 cm
Paris, Musée du Louvre, département des Antiquités orientales, AO 7037
Contenau 1929: no. 246; Rutten 1935: 182 ; Vattioni 1970

E FIG. 68 *right*

Aramaic language in cuneiform script

This highly unusual inscription is a magical incantation in the Aramaic language but spelled out in cuneiform signs. Although so far unique, the tablet cannot have been without parallels. The hand is that of a highly experienced cuneiform scribe. The magic is concerned with defeating a human rival who has made trouble through malicious slander and gossip. There are hints that the spell might derive from an older Babylonian magic tradition known as *Egalkura* (Entering the palace), which fulfilled much the same function. The spell begins:

You took a binding from a wall
and I locked(?) you out from the door.
To place him(?) under my tongue,
I brought the prattler home …

About 350 BC
From Uruk
Clay
H 9.3 cm, W 7 cm, Th. 2.1 cm
Paris, Musée du Louvre, département des Antiquités orientales, AO 6489
Geller 1997–2000; Müller-Kessler 2002

E FIG. 69 *left*

Aramaic graffiti on a Babylonian brick

A glimpse that alphabetic Aramaic was understood by a far greater proportion of the population of Iraq than cuneiform had ever been is afforded by this Babylonian brick (see also Fig. 27 above). This brick is one of many in which workmen scrawled their names in Aramaic letters before the clay had dried hard in the sun. Here the Aramaic reads *zbn*', the personal name Zebina.

Reign of Nebuchadnezzar (605–562 BC)
See Fig. 27

The decline of the cuneiform script itself has been well summed up recently:[156]

> Cuneiform writing was still in use for utilitarian as well as scholarly purposes down to about 100 BC, at least at Uruk and Babylon. After that time, the use of tablet and stylus is only known from Babylon, increasingly restricted to astronomical records and horoscopes. The latest dated administrative records, the Rahimesu archive from Esangil, are dated around 90 BC, and two 'parchment scribes,' presumably using Aramaic or Greek writing, are mentioned in them. The latest medical texts are of Achaemenid date …; historiographic texts, ritual prescriptions, and omen compendia are known from Seleucid times …, with perhaps a few of early Arsacid date. Traditional literary and scholarly texts, even bilingual Sumerian-Akkadian hymns, continued to be copied and presumably used in the cult at Babylon well into the first century AD.

Many languages besides Aramaic must have been spoken and heard in the Babylonian metropolis. For example the Egyptians named in ration-lists (e.g. Fig. 53) no doubt spoke their own language among themselves. There must have been many speakers of Persian in the city, as well as other tongues, but no record of these has yet survived on the Iraqi clay on which we are so dependent.

For Greek, however, we do have certain evidence of a remarkable kind. Among the assorted collections that go back to the 1870s occur some sixteen fragmentary pieces that must have originated in a late school environment at Babylon. In these standard exercises cuneiform on one side of the clay tablet is matched by transcription into Greek script on the other. There has been debate about both the date and function of these documents. Most probably they belong between 50 BC and 50 AD. One suggestion is that the tablets reflect Babylonians learning Greek. Others have argued that the Greek *transcripts* were being used to teach correct Babylonian (and Sumerian) pronunciation, or that these are Greeks learning Babylonian to gain access to their traditional and much-famed wisdom.[157] In fact there is very little alternative evidence to show how prevalent knowledge or use of Greek might have been in Babylonia after the Neo-Babylonian and Persian periods, but at the very least these manuscripts embody interchange between Babylonian and Greek, and give a medium for the mutual flow of ideas such as are discussed below.

FIG. 70
School tablets in Babylonian and Greek

Only a small number of school texts of this kind survive. Each tablet contains on one side the traditional Babylonian school exercises in cuneiform, and on the other a Greek 'crib'. The texts chosen are usually passages from the traditional cuneiform dictionaries or bilingual incantations in Sumerian and Akkadian.

a) BM 33769, part of a hymn to Šamaš, the Sun god, also known from earlier copies in cuneiform.

b) BM 35458, a sign list that gives Sumerian signs, their pronunciation, and their sign names.

About 50 BC – AD 50
From Babylon
Clay
a) H 5.0 cm, W 5.7 cm
b) H 8.5 cm, W 6.2 cm
British Museum, BM 35458, 33769

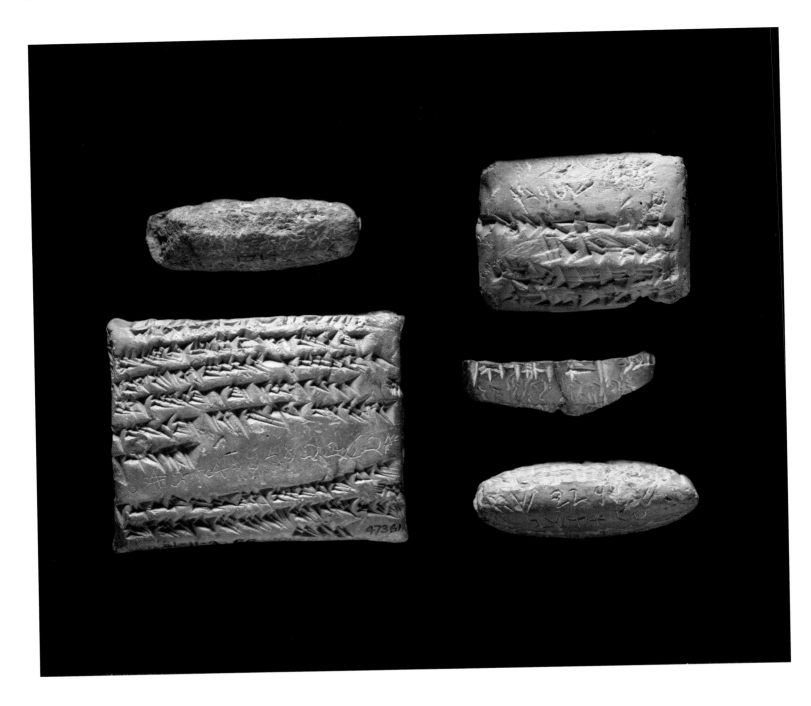

FIG. 71
Some odd characters

There are a small number of clay tablets on which mysterious short inscriptions are found alongside the cuneiform text. A few examples are shown here.
On Babylon tablet BM 47361 (bottom left) an 'Indian' alphabet is inscribed across the top edge and the reverse. The tablet concerns the sale of a slave, whose 'left hand was marked with the name of Ina-Esagil-lilbir, son of Bel-eteru.' The document is dated to the 11th day, 12th month and 23rd year of either Artaxerxes I or II (442 or 382 BC). All the names mentioned are Babylonian. The nature of the script, and why it is there, remains unexplained.

Clay
British Museum, BM 47361, BM 54221; BM 55787; BM 79708; F 233
For BM 47361 see Pinches 1883

Religion and belief

Reconstructing and understanding ancient religious life and belief remains one of the most complex tasks of modern scholarship, largely because summaries or syntheses of religious thinking were never written and because religious evolution and change are immensely difficult to document.

The Babylonian language, as far as we know, contains no word for 'religion' as such. This is no trivial point of philology: the corollary was that the whole range of experience that is distinguished and described as religion in the modern world was taken for granted in ancient Mesopotamia. The gods existed, and were sometimes even visible; they affected the lives of people – sometimes diligently, sometimes through oversight – and everyone who worried about such things knew, more or less, how things worked in the universe. Ritual, prayer, cultic practice, magic and divination all reflected an essential umbrella of many divinities, and each in their own fashion attempted to secure good, well-being, prosperity and safety.

Nebuchadnezzar undoubtedly took seriously his role as linchpin of the kingdom and empire – in which stability and success were contingent on his relationship with Marduk, the chief god of the Babylonian pantheon – and his fulfilment of cultic responsibility. The annual cycle was punctuated by such ritual and cultic demands, and the temples of the land followed this lead, with their own calendars, rites of service and ritual observation. For most of the population, however, these central activities were unknown and mysterious.

The gods – and they were many – had been ruling their universe since time immemorial. The Mesopotamian pantheon of the second millennium BC preserved a substantial older Sumerian presence, and Babylonian religious activities of the first millennium BC still incorporated Sumerian cult practice and therefore to some extent Sumerian thinking. Among both Sumerians and Babylonians the gods were seen to reflect the human world: a few were kings, some were important, many more far less so. Theologically minded scribes periodically sought to bring order out of chaos and, following an age-old susceptibility for word-lists, identified this god with that and allotted them places within the courts of the unassailable great gods, such as Šamaš the Sun god and Sin the Moon god. Over the centuries individual gods achieved outstanding status. An, the original head of them all, remained shadowy from the remotest times. Ashur and Ninurta each came to prominence under the Assyrians to the north, while among the Babylonians Marduk, his wife Zarpanitu and his son Nabû had practically dominated the pantheon since the dynasty of Hammurapi in the early second millennium BC.

The king had express responsibilities towards his gods. Traditionally a royal birth was divinely ordained and supervised, and a pious ruler always had the comfort of knowing that the forces of heaven were behind him. Military campaigns and building programmes alike profited from this awareness. In Nebuchadnezzar's time the great temple institutions with their long-established priesthood were a major force to be reckoned with, and their power and affluence must have proved irksome to more than one ambitious king who was not content to sit out his reign in idleness. The royal year was punctuated by cultic responsibility, culminating in the deeply significant New Year festival, when major participation by the ruler served to reinforce the balance of things in the kingdom and ensure that the coming year would proceed in accordance with what had been ordained.

E FIG. 72
Statue of a god

There must have been many statues of Babylon's hundreds of gods. Temples had their large cult-images and housed votive donations of sculpture, and the city's artisans must have produced endless figures of gods for street shrines and private houses. However, surviving sculptures of gods and goddesses are rare. This small figure with its divine horned headdress was buried in the doorway of the Southern Palace at Babylon. It would have functioned as a protective device to keep out evil forces. Comparison with other foundation figures from temples suggests that this statue represents a messenger god, perhaps Papsukkal.

Probably 6th century BC
From Babylon, Kasr
Clay
H 15.5 cm, W 7.5 cm, Th. 4.5 cm
Staatliche Museen zu Berlin, Vorderasiatisches Museum, VA Bab 3135
Klengel-Brandt and Cholidis 2006: no. 693

The extent to which the monumental temples and their cult statues were open to the greater public is unknown, and indeed private religion remains to a large extent elusive to us. Individuals had a personal god or goddess to whom they looked for protection. It is probable that families had enduring relationships with a particular god which would sometimes be reflected in personal names. The mass-produced figurines and plaques of clay that have been found in many excavations would be hawked by vendors outside the temples to provide focus or comfort in many domestic settings; but the truth remains that the mass of documents concerning the gods, their identities, needs and ritual was probably not the concern of private individuals, especially those who lived outside the cities.

The period broadly covered in this book (the late seventh and sixth centuries BC) saw many facets of life in flux, and religion was among them. One manifestation of this was a tendency among certain first-millennium theologians to look askance at their inherited pantheon, producing the theory that the most important gods, each with their area of responsibility or specialization, were but aspects of the one central god, Marduk. The idea can be traced earlier, in Assyria, where Enlil was treated to a similar theological 'upgrade', but it is likely that under Nebuchadnezzar many would have agreed with the position adopted in the following passage (from Fig. 73):

> Uraš is Marduk of planting
> Lugalakia is Marduk of ground water
> Ninurta is Marduk of the hoe
> Nergal is Marduk of war
> Zababa is Marduk of battle
> Enlil is Marduk of lordship and deliberation
> Nabu is Marduk of accounting
> Sin is Marduk as illuminator of the night
> Šamaš is Marduk of justice
> Adad is Marduk of rain
> Tišpak is Marduk of hosts
> Ishtaran is Marduk of …
> Šuqamunu is Marduk of the trough
> Mami is Marduk of potter's clay …

In a similar way, as we have seen, King Nabonidus later evinced an exclusive preference for the Moon god, Sin, evidently as a consequence of his upbringing, which led him to defy the Marduk clergy and go his own way entirely.

The extent to which this period of evolving monotheistic theology might have had its influence on Judaean thinkers who found themselves in Babylon at this time, and therefore might have affected the development of Judaism, is an important question that cannot yet be answered.

Divination

A crucial aspect of Mesopotamian daily life was fortune-telling, a hallmark intellectual activity with roots also in the remote third millennium BC that operated on many levels with considerable subtlety. The underlying assumptions reflected a cosmic theatre of cause and effect at work in the world that could be both understood and responded to, if not manipulated. In essence a particular occurrence that had once coincided with a certain event would (or could) have parallel consequences if repeated. It was essential, therefore, to document such associations, and truly

ⓔ FIG. 73
All the gods are one?

In first-millennium Babylon certain theologians speculated that the important gods of the traditional pantheon might be seen as aspects or manifestations of a single god. This small tablet lists fourteen independent and powerful gods, who are explained as specific aspects of the god Marduk. The repeated writing of Marduk's name can easily be distinguished in the right-hand column, while the sign that in each case precedes it, that for 'god', occurs with each of the names in the left-hand column of the individual gods who are listed there.

The same idea surfaces in a long sequence of hymnal passages known from Assyrian and Babylonian tablets alike, which elaborate through well-known epithets the way in which Marduk appropriates the divine attributes of his peers.

Adad

Marduk   of   rain

Reign of Nebuchadnezzar (605–562 BC)
From Babylon
Clay
H 4.0 cm, W 3.0 cm
British Museum, BM 47406
Pinches 1896: 1–3; King 1908: pl. 50; Lambert 1964; Parpola 1995: 399

ⓔ FIG. 74
Divination by horoscope

This third-century BC tablet from Babylon collects predictions based on the details of a child's birth. It can be seen that while some of the births have exalted consequences, others do not:

- A child is conceived (when) the sun in 5 x 4, the moon in 5 ..., Jupiter and Mars in 5 are favourable. That child will become king.

- A child is conceived when the moon flutters(?) 1 cubit in front of Regulus. Jupiter and Venus stand in his place, ...'s appear (?). The child conceived (at that time) will become king.

- Jupiter set, Venus acronychal rise, the child is conceived: that child will become the chief temple administrator.

- Mercury in the womb of his mother ... establishes, the child will be afflicted by leprosy.

3rd century BC
From Babylon
Clay
H 11.2 cm, W 8.9 cm, Th. 2.4 cm
British Museum, BM 32488
Unpublished

E FIG. 75
Stamp seal showing a priest and altar

A priest worships before an altar on which is seated a couchant *mušhuššu* dragon as well as divine standards, the spade of Marduk and the stylus of Nabû. Above the scene is a crescent, symbol of the Moon god. By the Neo-Babylonian period (the late seventh and sixth centuries BC) stamp seals of this type had largely taken over from cylinder seals.

6th century BC
Chalcedony
H 3.3 cm, W 2.6 cm, Th. 1.7 cm
From Babylonia
Paris, Musée du Louvre, département des Antiquités orientales, AO 4366
Delaporte 1920: 92, pl. 29

E FIG. 76
Stamp seal showing four cult scenes

Modern impressions from this most unusual four-sided seal show a moon standard; a priest before divine symbols of Marduk, Nabû and Sin; the forked lightning rod of Adad; and a cultic boat with divine star. In function this object is clearly to be distinguished from conventional seals. Perhaps the images were needed in a ritual, for example to be impressed on offering cakes.

6th century BC
From Babylon
Limestone, pierced through for suspension
L 2.3 cm, W 1.5 cm, Th. 1.2 cm
Staatliche Museen zu Berlin, Vorderasiatisches Museum, VA Bab 1651
Jakob-Rost 1997: no. 260

colossal effort was devoted to the collecting, copying, arranging and ultimately interpreting a great traditional body of omen literature. As with laws in a code, or medical recipes in therapy, omens began with the telling word *šumma* (if), and were referred to by cuneiform librarians as 'the *Ifs*'.

Traditional divination systems involved contrasting approaches, varying from examination of spontaneous and unprovoked phenomena such as chance happenings in the street, the behaviour of certain animals or birds, types of abnormal births, and planetary movements in the heavens. Variations from the norm or the expected were carefully indexed. The other approach involved deliberate operations that were known to provoke an answer, such as the examination of a slaughtered sheep's liver for abnormal markings or the dropping of oil into water for message-bearing patterns.

Historically speaking, predicting the future in ancient Mesopotamia was the province of central authority. Thus we know a great deal about divination under the final, powerful kings of Assyria and the extent to which they were guided by the authoritative practitioners who surrounded them. For the period of the Neo-Babylonian kings themselves there is less direct evidence; tablets with omens were copied in the traditional way, but it is only in the succeeding Achaemenid, Seleucid and even Arsacid periods that the sources reveal a clear picture. It is evident that in the interim a kind of democratization had been at work; the private application of divination, and especially astrology, suggests the dawning of some new sense of individual identity and worth. At the time of the Neo-Babylonian kings most state divination was based on astral events.

The first millennium also saw the flourishing of divination techniques that were either unknown or less common in earlier times, such as the interpre-

🄴 FIG. 77
An oracular fish

Cuneiform omens are almost invariably found written out on clay tablets, often collected in authoritative compendia. By contrast, here a single omen concerning an abnormality in a fish has been written over the two sides of a bronze model of a dogfish.

The right flank of the fish has two fins, but the left side only one. All physical abnormalities in the animal kingdom were deemed ominous. This object was probably first made in clay, inscribed, and cast in a mould. The passage reads:

If a fish lacks a left fin(?), a foreign army will be destroyed. The 12th year of Nebuchadnezzar, king of Babylon, son of Nabopolassar, king of Babylon.

Such an anomaly could always be fished up, or bought in the market, but once found could hardly be disregarded, and there was probably an understanding that such finds should be reported to the experts, so that the necessary steps to avert any bad implications could be carried out. While certain specimens could be kept in salt or honey, in this case an accurate record of a specific type, its oracular consequences and year of the find, 592 BC, are recorded in a permanent form for archiving and consideration by diviners. No specific military triumph can yet be linked with the date on this fish, but the rarity of the object suggests that some major event lay behind it.

Probably 592 BC
From Babylon
Bronze
L 8.2 cm, W 2.5 cm, Th. 2.0 cm
Staatliche Museen zu Berlin, Vorderasiatisches Museum, VA Bab 4374
Jacob-Rost 1962; Klengel-Brandt 1992: 188

E FIG. 78
Personal cylinder seal of the god Marduk

Hard-stone cylinder seals were an important symbol of personal identity in ancient Mesopotamia. Seals were carved with scenes and often included the bearer's name, as they were rolled on clay tablets in place of a written signature. It was also thought that the gods needed seals, hence this unusually large specimen.

In this seal Marduk and his sacred animal, the *mušhuššu* dragon, are clearly visible. The inscription records that the seal had been presented on behalf of his own life and that of his family by the earlier Babylonian king Marduk-zakir-shumi (854–819 BC). The original donation was accompanied by a necklace so that it could be worn by the Marduk statue in the temple.

Reign of Marduk-zakir-shumi (854–819 BC)
From Babylonia
Lapis lazuli
H 19.3 cm, Th. 3.7 cm
Staatliche Museen zu Berlin, Vorderasiatisches Museum, VA Bab 646
Koldewey 1900: 11ff; Wetzel, Schmidt and Mallwitz 1957: 36ff, no. 15; Frame 1995: 103ff

E FIG. 79
Personal cylinder seal of the god Adad

Adad, clutching lightning forks, wears an elaborate robe. The primary inscription reads: 'Property of the God Marduk. Seal of Adad of Esagil'. A second inscription records that the seal was returned to Babylon, following its removal by the Assyrian king Sennacherib at the beginning of the seventh century BC, by his son Esarhaddon.

9th century BC
From Babylonia
Lapis lazuli
H 12.5 cm, Th. 3.2 cm
Staatliche Museen zu Berlin, Vorderasiatisches Museum, VA Bab 647
Wetzel, Schmidt and Mallwitz 1957: no. 14, pl. 43a–d; Marzahn et al.1992 no. 67; Frame 1995: 165ff

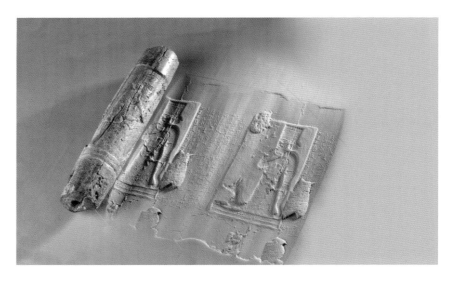

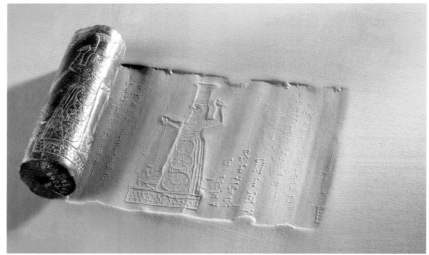

E FIG. 80 *opposite*
Babylon's New Year festival

This tablet was written down long after the period of the Neo-Babylonian kings, but its description of the annual New Year festival no doubt reflects what happened when Nebuchadnezzar himself 'took the hand of Bel'. His doing so ensured that Marduk would guarantee safety and prosperity for the country for the coming year. The accompanying festival lasted from the 1st to the 12th of Nisannu (our April). The gods went in procession out of Esagil, down the Processional Way to the Akitu House. Part of the journey was by boat.

The illustrated tablet is one of several known pieces that give details of this most important ritual activity. Here the fourth day saw the symbolic recitation of *Enuma Eliš*, the Creation Epic, in which Marduk's defeat of chaos led to the creation of the world and the institution of Esagil (see Fig. 61).

> *When this is done [and after] the second meal of the late afternoon, the urigallu priest of the temple Ekua recites Enuma Eliš (while lifting his hand?) to the god Bel. While he recites Enuma Eliš to the god Bel, the front of the tiara of the god Anu and the resting place of the god Enlil shall be covered.*

After 500 BC
Baked clay
H 19.0 cm, W 11.4 cm, Th. 3.4 cm
From Babylon
Paris, Musée du Louvre, département des Antiquités orientales, MNB 1848
Dhorme 1911; Thureau-Dangin 1921: 128–48, 153–4; Pritchard 1969a: 331–4; André and Ziegler 1982: 223, no. 165

ⓔ FIG. 81
Onyx sceptre

This object is evidently a sceptre, although its specific function is uncertain. It is formed of pieces of agate that were originally mounted on a central bronze pin; the modern reconstruction shown here is only provisional. It seems unlikely that so delicate an object was regularly used as royal regalia. It was perhaps reserved for a particular ritual or held by a divine statue.

After 500 BC
From Babylon
Onyx
L 38.4 cm, D 4.5 cm
Staatliche Museen zu Berlin, Vorderasiatisches Museum, VA Bab 1625
Wetzel, Schmidt and Mallwitz 1957: 36, no. 7; Meyer 1961: 7ff; Marzahn et al.1992: no. 68; Völling 1998: 197ff

tation of ominous dreams. Earlier kings slept overnight in temples to experience such a dream, and among the upper classes encyclopaedias explained the significance of specific dreams, such as suddenly finding oneself naked in a public street. In the mid-first millennium there was a shift that meant private individuals could use the dream system to answer their own questions, with the help of a professional dream interpreter. In late first-millennium Babylon it is clear that there were many professional dream interpreters who could both arrange for a dream and explain its significance.

Later still horoscopic prediction achieved considerable status. Long after Nebuchadnezzar's time Babylon must have been awash with competing professionals, mystics and charlatans who always knew, in return for a handful of silver, a way to pierce the veil.

Notes: The City of Babylon

45. Reade and Safadi 1986
46. Rich 1839: 187–8, no. 5.
47. Hilprecht 1903: 163.
48. Larsen 1996: 312–15.
49. Oppert 1863: I.
50. Rich 1839: 43.
51. Barnett 1974: 21.
52. Rich 1839: 39–104.
53. Rich 1839: 43–4.
54. Rich 1839: 58–72.
55. Myers 1874: 219.
56. Rich 1839: 65.
57. Rich 1839: 94–5.
58. Koldewey 1914: 181–2.
59. Rich 1839: 73.
60. Selby 1859.
61. Rich 1839: 72–6.
62. Rich 1839: 87–94.
63. Rawlinson 1861: 18.
64. Rich 1839: 107–34.
65. Rich 1839: 135–79.
66. Lloyd 1980: 65.
67. Loftus 1857: 18.
68. Keppel 1827: 208–9.
69. Mignan 1829.
70. Ker Porter 1821–2 II: 379–82.
71. Ker Porter 1821–2 II: facing p. 349.
72. Mignan 1829: facing p. 138.
73. Rawlinson 1862–7 III: 338.
74. Selby 1859.
75. Buckingham 1827: 426.
76. Ker Porter 1821–2 II: 341.
77. Layard 1853: 502–5.
78. Rawlinson 1858 II: 573–6.
79. Koldewey 1914: 7–12.
80. Oppert 1863: 168–82.
81. Reade 1999: 57–8.
82. Rassam 1897: 352–5.
83. Koldewey 1914: vi–viii summarizes the main stages of the excavations up to 1912.
84. Rassam 1897, Reade 1986, 1993, 1999.
85. Key publications for the German excavations are: Koldewey 1911; 1913 (English ed. 1914; revised German ed. Hrouda, 1990); 1918; Reuther 1926; Wetzel 1930; Koldewey and Wetzel 1931; 1932; Wetzel and Weissbach 1938; Wetzel, Schmidt and Mallwitz 1957 and Schmid 1995.
86. Matthews 2003: 10, citing the case of de Sarzec's excavations at Telloh.
87. Koldewey 1914: vi.
88. Bohrer 2003: 280.
89. Matthews 2003: 12; Pollock 1999: 16–19
90. Matthews 2003: 12: 'An extremely important development came in the form of Andrae's deep stratigraphic sounding through the Ishtar Temple at Ashur, representing the first occasion in Mesopotamian archaeology where a chronological sequence of buildings was excavated and recorded through application of the principles of archaeological stratigraphy.'
91. Andrae himself produced some of the most valuable historical resources on his own and Koldewey's work: Andrae 1952, 1961.
92. For Andrae's watercolours and pastels see Andrae and Boehmer 1992.
93. Marzahn 1994; Crüsemann et al. 2000: 23–8; Kohlmeyer, Strommenger and Schmid 1991: 49–64.
94. In January 1927, 536 cases of finds from Babylon reached Berlin. The work of desalinating, sorting and reconstructing the fragments of glazed brick reliefs progressed rapidly thereafter, and the completed reconstructions, together with those of the Pergamon altar, opened to the public in 1930 (Kohlmeyer, Strommenger and Schmid 1991: 53–5).
95. Layard 1849.
96. For the *Babel–Bibel* affair see Larsen 1995; Lehmann 1994, 1999.
97. Koldewey 1913.
98. Koldewey 1914.
99. 'The Archaeological Revival of Babylon Project' (various authors in *Sumer* 35, 1979: 20–253); Ishaq 1979–81.
100. Schmid 1995.
101. Bergamini 1977, 1988.
102. Koldewey famously opened his own book thus: 'It is most desirable, if not absolutely necessary, that the excavation of Babylon should be completed. Up to the present time only about half the work has been accomplished, although since it began we have worked daily, both summer and winter, with from 200 to 250 workmen' (Koldewey 1914: v).
103. Langdon 1912: 114, i 37–41.
104. Koldewey 1911: 35.
105. He refers to himself as the 'son of a nobody'.
106. Berossus (quoted by Eusebius, *Chronicle* 46) tells us that their alliance was sealed by a royal marriage between the Babylonian prince Nebuchadnezzar and Amytis, daughter of Cyaxares the Mede.
107. Nebuchadnezzar Chronicle 5–7 (Grayson 1975a: 99).
108. The recovery of the looted statue of Marduk by Nebuchadnezzar I (1125–1104 BC) was commemorated in *Enuma Eliš*, the literary account of the creation of the world known from its opening words as 'When on high', recited at the beginning of each new year as part of the rituals that reinforced the king's right to rule; see Fig. 61.
109. Lambert 1965: 5–6, 8.
110. Lambert 1965: 5, 8.
111. Langdon 1912: vii 36–9.
112. Yaqut I 447–50; Yaqut III 380.
113. 2 Kings 24:7 records that Nebuchadnezzar was so successful that the pharaoh did not march out of his country because the Babylonians held everywhere from the Wadi of Egypt to the Euphrates.

114. Yaqut explains the name of the Iraqi city Al-Anbar through a story that Nebuchadnezzar locked Arab prisoners in a granary (Yaqut I 368).
115. Grayson 1975a: 21–2. For the judgment against Baba-ahu-iddina see Weidner 1954–6.
116. A. L. Oppenheim in Pritchard 1969a: 308.
117. Josephus, *Against Apion* I 156.
118. Quoted by Josephus, *Jewish Antiquities* X 227. There is no evidence to support these claims, which were perhaps motivated by contemporary political considerations.
119. Quoted by Josephus, *Against Apion* I 146–57.
120. Grayson 1975b: 88–91.
121. A.L. Oppenheim in Pritchard 1969a: 308.
122. A.L. Oppenheim in Pritchard 1969a: 311–12.
123. In another inscription, a basalt stela from Babylon (A.L. Oppenheim in Pritchard 1969a 308–11), Nabonidus refers to himself as the 'legitimate representative of Nebuchadnezzar and Neriglissar', their armies being entrusted to his control (Langdon 1912: v 17–20).
124. The Dynastic Prophecy (ii 14) describes him as the founder of the dynasty of Harran, someone who 'will oppress the land'; Grayson 1975b: 32–3.
125. See Kinnier Wilson and Finkel 2007: 17.
126. Grayson 1975a: 106–8.
127. Berossus (quoted by Josephus, *Against Apion* I 153) records a tradition that Nabonidus was exiled to Carmania. This seems to confirm the cryptic account found in the Dynastic Chronicle, ii 17–21; see Grayson 1975b: 32–3.
128. The Midrash *Shir HaShirim Rabbah* iii 4 records a tradition that Belshazzar was killed by Cyrus and Darius, acting as overzealous doorkeepers.
129. Barnett 1974: 20.
130. Stolper 1999.
131. Rich 1839: 185–6.
132. Barnett 1974.
133. Mignan 1829: 227.
134. Ker Porter 1821–2: 370.
135. Keppel 1827 I: 183–4.
136. Mignan 1829: 228–30.
137. Mignan 1829: 191–2.
138. Keppel 1827 I: 117.
139. Mignan 1829: 74, 189.
140. Mignan 1829: 190, 226, 229–30.
141. Larsen 1996: 294–303.
142. Rawlinson in Bewsher 1867: 157–8.
143. Hilprecht 1903: 262–3.
144. Hilprecht 1903: 263.
145. Reade 1986: xvii.
146. Reade 1986: xvii–xxv.
147. Reade 1993: 50.
148. Rassam 1897: 262–4.
149. Rassam 1897: 348.
150. British Museum, BM 91133.
151. British Museum, BM 90827.
152. British Museum, BM 90834.
153. Peters 1897 I: 14–15, 31.
154. Reade 1986: xxi.
155. From British Museum, BM 38101 (unpublished).
156. Westenholz 2007: 304–5.
157. Geller 1997: 43–95; Westenholz 2007: 274–83.

History
and Legend

History and Legend

The very name of Babylon triggers certain images – above all the Hanging Gardens and the Tower of Babel – that seem likely to live on for ever. Here we consider where these images originate, and why they and their associated ideas still lie so close to the surface of the modern mind when Babylon itself is vanished into dust.

The work of the early explorers and the archaeological reality that has been described in the preceding pages has little part in this consciousness. The remarkable treasures that have come to light are discoveries too recent to have embedded themselves within general culture. On the contrary, our frame of reference here is that of the story-teller, from two of the most potent sources of stories that were ever committed to writing.

The source above all, of course, is the Bible. It is the Old Testament that has given us the great edifice of the Tower of Babel. As we have seen above, virtually nothing visible remained of the structure itself before the work of archaeology. Now, at our vantage point, we can appreciate that the description in Genesis is no flight of ungrounded fancy but derives explicitly from an original Babylonian monument. In Genesis terms the Tower was ineluctably the symbol of foolish human pride, and this theme was to prove a major preoccupation of artists. Nebuchadnezzar was always a familiar figure from the Bible, long before excavation or decipherment recovered ancient Mesopotamian sources. The Bible is also at the root of Babylon's universal reputation as a City of Sin, the golden cup that has made all nations drunk, and this manifestation in time becomes a commonplace of apocalyptic imagery.

In contrast, a completely different stream of tradition has brought us the Hanging Gardens. This paradisiacal delight, a ready source of fantasy on myriad levels, depends on the fragmented accounts of ancient historians who wrote in Greek, recording everything from architecture to folklore. Two of the many accounts are particularly important. First come the long descriptions of Herodotus, who may have visited Babylon personally in the fifth century BC. Then there is the work of Diodorus of Sicily, whose first-century BC description is based mainly on that of the fourth-century BC Ctesias of Cnidus, a physician at the Persian court, and on Cleitarchus, a contemporary and historian of Alexander the Great. Sadly, what was perhaps the most interesting Greek source of all is lost: the *Babyloniaca* of Berossus was the only history of the city to have been written in Greek and for a foreign audience by a native Babylonian. It survives only in fragments quoted by later authors.

Herodotus recorded everything from architecture to zoology, and left us a long chapter on Babylon. He was followed by Ctesias, Cleitarchus, Berossus, Megasthenes, Strabo and Pliny the Elder, Josephus and Quintus Curtius Rufus, a roll-call of painstaking and usually reliable scholars who searched among sources that were already dusty and crumbling, and produced their own colourful digests for posterity. Even these digests sometimes only exist in later works, where they

are copied out, summarized or even misquoted by their later counterparts. Many of these figures are far from household names, but the stories they have transmitted took on a life of their own, and it is because of them that the gardens that were supposedly Nebuchadnezzar's pride and joy can bewitch us even today.

The following chapters thus examine the stories and legends that have grown up around Babylon in later tradition. Some of these are firmly rooted in the history of Nebuchadnezzar's city, others less so, but all have proved influential and none will be readily dislodged. This is all the more true because, long before archaeological excavations, many artists and writers scrutinized the sources available for detail to support their imaginative reconstructions. In the depiction of Babylon in art we see far more than simple fantasy, but rather a complex intertwining of factual knowledge, myth and creativity whose history is as intriguing as that of the city itself.

E FIG. 82
Albrecht Dürer, *The Whore of Babylon, the Destruction of Babylon, and the Knight Called Faithful and True* (detail)

Babylon has been re-imagined in many different forms, sometimes very distantly removed from the ancient city itself.

See Fig. 172

Babylon's Wonders of the World

Classical accounts

Michael Seymour

E FIG. 83
Inscribed eye-stone of Sammu-ramat

This inscribed eye-stone belonged to Queen Sammu-ramat of Assyria, consort of Šamši-Adad V (824–811 BC) and mother of Adad-nirari III (811–783 BC). Exceptionally for a woman, Sammu-ramat had a royal stela at the Assyrian capital Ashur, and even accompanied her son personally into battle. Her name and character probably underlie the later classical Semiramis. The inscription reads:

To Ishtar, her lady.
Sammu-ramat
Consort of Shamshi-Adad
King of Assyria
gave (this) for her health.

Agate. 9th century BC. D 4.5 cm, Th. 1.8 cm.
Private collection. Previously unpublished

E FIG. 84 *opposite*
Mario Larrinaga, *Hanging Gardens of Babylon*

The Seven Wonders as listed by the classical Greek authors, revived during the Renaissance, retain their fascination. This painting was one of a series done by Larrinaga for Lowell Thomas' documentary Cinerama film *Seven Wonders of the World* in 1956. The originals, on glass, were photographed but no longer exist. The surviving versions, on canvas, were commissioned by a Detroit industrialist.

AD 1959-62. Oil on canvas. H 110.0 cm, W 80.0 cm
Private collection, USA. Thomas 1956; Lendemann 2007

Of the Seven Wonders of the World the Hanging Gardens of Babylon are the least understood. The other six were certainly real monuments and their sites can be identified. One wonder, the pyramids at Giza, may still be seen today. By contrast it has only ever been possible to make tentative suggestions for the exact location of the Hanging Gardens, and indeed their very existence remains disputed.

Overshadowed by the Hanging Gardens today, Babylon in many lists laid claim to a second Wonder of the World: the city's massive walls. According to many Greek writers, both the walls and many other monuments were the work of the legendary Semiramis, yet unlike the gardens Babylon's walls have been both identified with certainty and excavated. Their dimensions are hard to reconcile with those of the classical writers, but there is no doubt that the city's huge fortifications and monumental architecture would have left a powerful impression on foreign visitors.

The Colossus of Rhodes and the Pharos at Alexandria were both constructed in the third century BC, and were the last to be included in the canon of wonders we know today. By the end of the third century the Colossus had been destroyed by an earthquake, making this period the most important for the composition of the list: all the wonders (except possibly the Hanging Gardens) could have been seen by a Greek traveller in the mid–late third century BC. The earliest surviving list is that of Antipater of Sidon in the second century BC, and differs from the definitive list (see map on page 107) only in substituting the Walls of Babylon for the Pharos at Alexandria. Despite this continuity, however, many competing lists of wonders exist in the classical sources, usually but by no means always seven in number. The number seven is significant in many religious and mystical contexts,[158] but ultimately its use to classify the Wonders of the World is largely arbitrary. A popular trope has been the addition of an 'eighth wonder', candidates for which have ranged from the Colosseum to the Empire State Building. (New lists of Seven Wonders have included the Great Wall of China, Macchu Pichhu and the Taj Mahal; and lists of seven 'natural wonders' such as the Grand Canyon and Great Barrier Reef have also been compiled.)

A definitive list of wonders crystallized in medieval and Renaissance Europe, despite the fact that most of the seven were by that time in ruins. A series of engravings produced by Philips Galle after designs by Maarten van Heemskerck (see Fig. 97), depicting the Seven Wonders and the Colosseum at Rome, is one of the earliest known representations of the definitive list, but not so early as to be able to draw on contemporary observation; instead, like all depictions since, the series relies heavily on the textual descriptions of the ancient authorities.

Greek accounts of Babylon's wonders

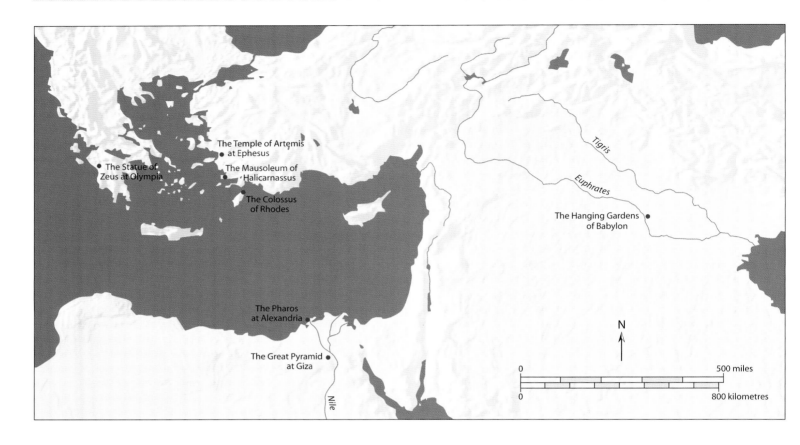

The Hanging Gardens

There was also, beside the acropolis, the Hanging Garden, as it is called, which was built, not by Semiramis, but by a later Syrian king to please one of his concubines; for she, they say, being a Persian by race and longing for the meadows of her mountains, asked the king to imitate, through the artifice of a planted garden, the distinctive landscape of Persia. The park extended four plethra on each side, and since the approach to the garden sloped like a hillside and the several parts of the structure rose from one another tier on tier, the appearance of the whole resembled that of a theatre. When the ascending terraces had been built, there had been constructed beneath them galleries which carried the entire weight of the planted garden and rose little by little one above the other along the approach; and the uppermost gallery, which was fifty cubits high, bore the highest surface of the park, which was made level with the circuit wall of the battlements of the city. Furthermore, the walls, which had been constructed at great expense, were twenty-two feet thick, while the passage-way between each two walls was ten feet wide. The roof above these beams had first a layer of reeds laid in great quantities of bitumen, over this two courses of baked brick bonded by cement, and as a third layer a covering of lead, to the end that the moisture from the soil might not penetrate beneath. On all this again earth had been piled to a depth sufficient for the roots of the largest trees; and the ground, when levelled off, was thickly planted with trees of every kind that, by their great size or other charm, could give pleasure to the beholder. And since the galleries, each projecting beyond another, all received

the light, they contained many royal lodgings of every description; and there was one gallery which contained openings leading from the topmost surface and machines for supplying the gardens with water, the machines raising the water in great abundance from the river, although no one outside could see it being done. Now this park, as I have said, was a later construction.
DIODORUS SICULUS[159]

The Babylonians also have a citadel twenty stades in circumference. The foundations of its turrets are sunk thirty feet into the ground and the fortifications rise eighty feet above it at the highest point. On its summit are the hanging gardens, a wonder celebrated by the fables of the Greeks. They are as high as the top of the walls and owe their charm to the shade of many tall trees. The columns supporting the whole edifice are built of rock, and on top of them is a flat surface of squared stones strong enough to bear the deep layer of earth placed upon it and the water used for irrigating it. So stout are the trees the structure supports that their trunks are eight cubits thick and their height as much as fifty feet; they bear fruit as abundantly as if they were growing in their natural environment. And although time with its gradual decaying processes is as destructive to nature's works as to man's, even so this edifice survives undamaged, despite being subjected to the pressure of so many tree-roots and the strain of bearing the weight of such a huge forest.

FIG. 85 *opposite*
The Seven Wonders

The 'definitive' list of Seven Wonders that has survived into the present is as follows:

The Great Pyramid at Giza
The Hanging Gardens of Babylon
The Statue of Zeus at Olympia
The Temple of Artemis at Ephesus
The Mausoleum of Halicarnassus
The Colossus of Rhodes
The Pharos at Alexandria

It has a substructure of walls twenty feet thick at eleven foot intervals, so that from a distance one has the impression of woods overhanging their native mountains. Tradition has it that it is the work of a Syrian king who ruled from Babylon. He built it out of love for his wife who missed the woods and forests in this flat country and persuaded her husband to imitate nature's beauty with a structure of this kind.
QUINTUS CURTIUS RUFUS[160]

Babylon, too, lies in a plain; and the circuit of its wall is three hundred and eighty-five stadia. The thickness of its wall is thirty-two feet; the height thereof between the towers is fifty cubits; that of the towers is sixty cubits; and the passage on top of the wall is such that four-horse chariots can easily pass one another; and it is on this account that this and the hanging garden are called one of the Seven Wonders of the World. The garden is quadrangular in shape, and each side is four plethra in length. It consists of arched vaults, which are situated, one after another, on checkered, cube-like foundations. The checkered foundations, which are hollowed out, are covered so deep with earth that they admit of the largest of trees, having been constructed of baked brick and asphalt – the foundations themselves and the vaults and the arches. The ascent to the uppermost terrace-roofs is made by a stairway; and alongside these stairs there were screws, through which the water was continually conducted up into the garden from the Euphrates by those appointed for this purpose, for the river, a stadium in width, flows through the middle of the city; and the garden is on the bank of the river.
STRABO[161]

The Hanging Garden [is so-called because it] has plants cultivated at a height above ground level, and the roots of the trees are embedded in an upper terrace rather than in the earth. This is the technique of its construction. The whole mass is supported on stone columns, so that the entire underlying space is occupied by carved column bases. The columns carry beams set at very narrow intervals. The beams are palm trunks, for this type of wood – unlike all others – does not rot and, when it is damp and subjected to heavy pressure, it curves upwards. Moreover it does itself give nourishment to the root branches and

fibres, since it admits extraneous matter into its folds and crevices. This structure supports an extensive and deep mass of earth, in which are planted broad-leaved trees of the sort that are commonly found in gardens, a wide variety of flowers of all species and, in brief, everything that is most agreeable to the eye and conducive to the enjoyment of pleasure. The whole area is ploughed in just the same way as solid ground, and is just as suitable as other soil for grafting and propagation. Thus it happens that a ploughed field lies above the heads of those who walk between the columns below. Yet while the upper surface of the earth is trampled underfoot, the lower and denser soil closest to the supporting framework remains undisturbed and virgin. Streams of water emerging from elevated sources flow partly in a straight line down sloping channels, and are partly forced upwards through bends and spirals to gush out higher up, being impelled through the twists of these devices by mechanical forces. So, brought together in frequent and plentiful outlets at a high level, these waters irrigate the whole garden, saturating the deep roots of the plants and keeping the whole area of cultivation continually moist. Hence the grass is permanently green, and the leaves of trees grow firmly attached to supple branches, and increasing in size and succulence with the constant humidity. For the root [system] is kept saturated and sucks up the all-pervading supply of water, wandering in interlaced channels beneath the ground, and securely maintaining the well-established and excellent quality of the trees. This is a work of art of royal luxury [lit. 'riotous living'], and its most striking feature is that the labour of cultivation is suspended above the heads of the spectators.
ATTRIBUTED TO PHILO OF BYZANTIUM[162]

The walls

The city stands on a broad plain, and is an exact square, a hundred and twenty furlongs in length each way, so that the entire circuit is four hundred and eighty furlongs. While such is its size, in magnificence there is no other city that approaches to it. It is surrounded, in the first place, by a broad and deep moat, full of water, behind which rises a wall fifty royal cubits in width, and two hundred in height. (The royal cubit is longer by three fingers' breadth than the common cubit.)

And here I may not omit to tell the use to which the mould dug out of the great moat was turned, nor the manner wherein the wall was wrought. As fast as they dug the moat the soil which they got from the cutting was made into bricks, and when a sufficient number were completed they baked the bricks in kilns. Then they set to building, and began with bricking the borders of the moat, after which they proceeded to construct the wall itself, using throughout for their cement hot bitumen, and interposing a layer of wattled reeds at every thirtieth course of the bricks. On the top, along the edges of the wall, they constructed buildings of a single chamber facing one another, leaving between them room for a four-horse chariot to turn. In the circuit of the wall are a hundred gates, all of brass, with brazen lintels and side-posts. The bitumen used in the work was brought to Babylon from the Is, a small stream which flows into the Euphrates at the point where the city of the same name stands, eight days' journey from Babylon. Lumps of bitumen are found in great abundance in this river.
HERODOTUS[163]

Babylonian kings and their names

KING KNOWN TODAY AS	REIGNED	REAL BABYLONIAN NAME	GREEK EQUIVALENT
Nabopolassar	626–605 BC	Nabu-apla-uṣur	Ναβοπαλάσαρος (Nabopalasaros)
Nebuchadnezzar II	605–562 BC	Nabu-kudduri-uṣur	Ναβουχοδονόσορος (Nabuchodonosoros)
Amel-Marduk (biblical Evil-Merodach)	562–560 BC	Amel-Marduk	Ἐύειλμαράδοχος (Evilmaraduchos)
Neriglissar	560–556 BC	Nergal-šar-uṣur	Νηριγλίσαρος (Neriglisaros)
Labashi-Marduk	556 BC	Labaši-Marduk	Λαβοροσοάρδοχος (Laborosoardochos)
Nabonidus	556–539 BC	Nabu-na'id	Ναβοννήδω (Nabonnedo)

One Babylonian, Berossus, wrote a history of Babylon in Greek. Through him the names of the Neo-Babylonian kings survived, and were familiar to us long before the decipherment of cuneiform.

Herodotus' fifth-century BC description is the earliest and most famous Greek account of the walls, but later writers disputed the details, especially their massive dimensions (see below).

The Hanging Gardens of Babylon are conspicuous by their absence from Herodotus' otherwise highly detailed account of the city. The earliest known description comes instead from the Greek physician Ctesias of Cnidus, who worked at and travelled with the court of the Achaemenid king Artaxerxes II in the early fourth century BC. His account, known to us through the *Library of History* of Diodorus of Sicily, consists of two basic elements: a detailed description of the gardens' architecture and mechanics; and the story that the king who built them did so for one of his wives, who missed her mountainous home country.[164] These two narratives, which may derive from separate sources, are found also in the accounts of Cleitarchus[165] and Berossus, the latter of whom identifies the king of the story as Nebuchadnezzar and the 'gardens' as his palace:[166] 'within this palace he erected lofty stone terraces, in which he closely reproduced mountain scenery, completing the resemblance by planting them with all manner of trees and constructing the so-called Hanging Garden; because his wife, having been brought up in Media, had a passion for mountain surroundings'.[167]

Although less detailed than others, the *c.* 280 BC account of Berossus is in all probability the most trustworthy. Berossus was a Babylonian priest and, though writing in Greek several centuries after the time of Nebuchadnezzar, he had access to cuneiform written sources that described Nebuchadnezzar's reign and achievements in detail. Fragments preserved by later authors show that he knew seventh- and sixth-century BC names and chronology with an accuracy that would have been impossible without access to Babylonian texts. Drawing on Berossus' account, the first-century AD historian Josephus is able to place the kings Nabopolassar, Nebuchadnezzar, Amel-Marduk, Neriglissar, Labaši-Marduk and Nabonidus in their correct order and with reign-lengths that are shown by cuneiform documents to be impressively accurate. Further the names themselves are not garbled, as often happened with the transmission of Mesopotamian names into Greek.[168]

Berossus claims that Nebuchadnezzar constructed the Hanging Gardens, and his description of them comes during a passage that is otherwise very reminiscent of a Nebuchadnezzar royal inscription[169] (see Fig. 17). The royal gardens described by Berossus may indeed be those of Nebuchadnezzar at Babylon, though there is still the possibility that the relevant passage was placed and integrated – albeit very astutely – by a later author; the best candidate would be the Alexander Polyhistor.[170]

Practical details vary, but perhaps the best-known account is that of Strabo (see page 107), probably based on the now lost fourth-century BC description of Onesicritus. Mechanical considerations obsessed the Greek writers, but they were also fascinated by the romantic tale of the king who built this monumental structure to please his homesick consort. Amyitis, as she is called in Josephus, is a difficult character for historians. Although there is agreement that her mountainous homeland was somewhere in Iran, differing versions of the story identify her as Persian and Median, while her genealogy, available only for the Median version, raises problems of chronology.[171] On the other hand the version of the marriage given by Berossus is plausible: in a passage unrelated to any discussion of Babylon's wonders Nebuchadnezzar (as crown prince) is married to the Median princess Amyitis to cement a political alliance between the Babylonians and Medes against their old enemy Assyria.[172] Political marriage was not unusual, and such an alliance may well underlie the more romantic story that came to be associated with the gardens. Oddly nothing is known about Nebuchadnezzar's wives from contemporary Babylonian sources, and we are forced to accept that, for the present, the existence of Amyitis remains a matter of conjecture.

The search for the Hanging Gardens
Irving Finkel

Gardens of any stature in ancient Iraq were always a luxurious and costly royal prerogative. Elegant irrigation and flourishing greenery in any Mesopotamian palace gave pleasure to the royal family and impressed visitors. Best known is the garden of the Assyrian king Sennacherib (704–681 BC), who arranged for elaborate water supplies and grew his cotton next to imported exotic wildlife at Nineveh. A sculptured panel from Ashurbanipal's palace (Fig. 88) likewise depicts a well-watered garden of luxury and tranquillity. The earlier Babylonian king Marduk-apla-iddina (Merodach-baladan) has even left us a list of the species of plants that grew in his garden in the south (Fig. 87), and there can be no doubt that many other kings celebrated accession or other personal achievements in building or developing their royal gardens. No other has beckoned from Antiquity, however, as that of Nebuchadnezzar of Babylon.

It has sometimes been suggested that the gardens described by the Greek authors were not located in Babylon at all, but in Nineveh to the north, identifying them with the work of Sennacherib.[173] Most writers stick to Babylon itself, and have offered a variety of possible – and some improbable – locations. The most likely candidates have been in or near to Nebuchadnezzar's Southern Palace (Fig. 28).

E FIG. 87

Plants in a royal garden at Babylon

This tablet gives a list of plants in the garden of a Babylonian king from before Nebuchadnezzar's time, Marduk-apla-iddina. This was the biblical Merodach-Baladan, who reigned at Babylon around 700 BC.

While it is clear from the internal arrangement of the list that these plants fall into groups, the identification of the individual names remains extremely difficult. The table below is, therefore, only a guide to recent identifications and suggestions.

Probably 7th century BC
Clay
H. 6.5 cm, W. 4.0 cm
Purchased from J. Shemtob, 1881
British Museum, BM 46226
Meissner 1891; Campbell Thompson 1902: pl. 50; Brinkman 1964: 52; Wiseman 1983: 142–3; Finkel 1988: 47–8

COL. i	COL. ii	COL. iii	COL. iv
garlic (*šumū*)	*šitû*-spice	mangel-wurzel (*silqu*)	'hound's-tongue' plant (*lišan kalbi*)
onion (*šamaškillu*)	*papparhû*-plant	turnip (*laptu*)	*kanašuttu*-plant
leek (*karāšu*)	*mangu*-plant (alkaline)	malt (*buqlu*)	lucerne (?) (*aspastu*)
mirgu-plant (alliaceous)	beetroot (?) *šumuttu*	a type of cucumber (*naṣṣabu*)	fenugreek (*šambaliltu*)
crocus (?) (*andahšum*)	*qaqqullu*-plant	*zassaru*-plant	*niqdu*-plant (a dye?)
šasnibi-vegetable	*hu-* newly broken -plant	*margal...*-plant	fennel (?) (*ṣurbu*)
kuniphu-plant (alliaceous)	*hur-* broken -plant	*nadal*-plant	melon/gourd/cucumber (*qiššû*)
shallot (?) (*zimzimmu*)	*la-bu-uk-* broken -plant	*yaquqānu*-plant	*piqquti*-plant
mint (?) (*urnû*)	*la-an-* broken -plant	*yarqānu*-plant	a palm-leaf basket
ananihu-plant	*ka-ma-a-* broken -plant	sagapenum (?) (*barīrātu*)	a basket
hamuk-plant	*tu-za-ar-* broken -plant	'slave girl-buttock'-plant (*qinnat andi*)	cultivation (?)
cress (*sahlû*)	*asmidu*-plant	*kukku*-shaped plant	a porter
thorny *hispu*-plant	*azupiru*-spice	*kuṣibi*-spice	tamarisk (?)
murzumurza-plant	coriander (*kusibirru*)	'dear horn'-plant (*qaran ayāli*)	you strike!
marrūtu-onion	rocket (*egingīru*)	'bird dung'-plant (*hallā-iṣṣur*)	**The garden of**
lettuce (*hassû*)	rue (?) (*biššu*)	*haltu*-lettuce (?) (*hassuhaltu*)	**King Marduk-apla-iddina.**
suhullatu-vegetable	origanum (*zūpu*)	*haṣuttu*-lettuce	**Written and collated according to its original.**
dill (*šibittu*)	thyme (*zambūru*)	*hambaṣūṣu*-lettuce	**Tablet of Marduk-šuma-iddin.**
ninû-plant	thyme (?) (*hašû*)	*habbaqūqu*-herb	**He who fears Marduk**
	butnānu-plant (aromatic)	*lihburu*-herb	**will never take (this) away!**

ⓔ FIG. 88 *left*
Assyrian landscape

Ironically, we know a good deal more about the gardens of the Assyrian kings than those of their Babylonian successors. This sculptured relief from the North Palace of Ashurbanipal (669–631 BC) at Nineveh shows a luxurious hillside landscape, watered by an aqueduct that was probably built by the king's grandfather, Sennacherib (704–681 BC).

645–635 BC
From Nineveh
Gypsum
H 129.5 cm, L 208.3 cm
British Museum, BM 124939a
Gadd 1936: 196–7; Frankfort 1996: pl. 106; Reade 1964: 5, 11, 13; Barnett 1976: 41, pl. 23

FIG. 89 *top*
Reconstructed colouring

Although much in this experimental reconstruction is necessarily speculative, we are certain that royal Assyrian reliefs were originally brightly painted. Small areas of black and red pigment still survive on some panels, while new techniques of analysis are now recovering microscopic traces of other colours. Colouring also survives on other Assyrian objects, such as painted tiles.

Paul Goodhead, 2008. Digitally coloured photograph of BM 124939a (Fig. 88)

FIG. 90
Artist's impression of the Hanging Gardens in Nebuchadnezzar's Babylon

This reconstruction places the Hanging Gardens within the Western Outwork, between Nebuchadnezzar's Southern Palace and the River Euphrates. Excavation did reveal a building with enormously thick walls, which could have supported terraces of the kind described by the ancient Greek authors. There is not sufficient archaeological evidence, however, to prove that this was the site of the Hanging Gardens. The same structure has also been interpreted as a treasury or citadel.

William Reade, in Chris Scarre *The Seventy Wonders of the Ancient World*, Thames and Hudson 1999: 27.

Early travellers on the wonders: suggested sites

Julian E. Reade

It was obvious that the Hanging Gardens, as indicated by the Greek historians, would have been inside or close to a royal palace, but they remained elusive throughout the nineteenth century and for much of the twentieth. Buckingham not unreasonably wondered, as Niebuhr had done, whether the solitary tamarisk at the Kasr might be descended from a tree in the Hanging Gardens.[174] Keppel agreed, but imagined the tamarisk was a cedar.[175] Oppert believed he had demonstrated that the gardens were located at Amran, apparently because it was an unexplained mound that could have been accessible from the Kasr by a causeway alongside the river.[176] Although Koldewey successfully found not one but two adjacent palaces of Nebuchadnezzar in the Kasr mound, the corner where he proposed to locate the gardens, above a vaulted cellar, has not found favour. A few scholars have even adopted an idea put forward by Wallis Budge[177] that there was no such structure at Babylon at all. Only in 1979 did Wolfram Nagel observe that the 'western outwork', a massive but badly damaged part of Kasr beside the Euphrates excavated by Koldewey, was a suitable location for at least some of the palace gardens; several archaeologists have commented on the question since and have agreed with him. Nagel's suggestion of the western outwork of Nebuchadnezzar's Southern Palace offers a relatively good fit with the classical sources and, if configured as an inward-facing terraced garden, is viable from engineering and defensive perspectives and could conceivably incorporate (though no direct evidence survives) many of the architectural details described by the Greek authors.[178]

Reconciliation of Greek accounts of the walled defences of Babylon with the remains on the ground caused persistent difficulty in the nineteenth century. Herodotus describes the structure of a magnificent outer wall which he or his informant could have seen, but he also gives some information which can only have been derived from hearsay. The city is said to have been a perfect square; each side of the wall was 120 stadia or slightly over 22 km long, with a total circuit of 480 stadia or 89 km. Rich's outer enclosure wall does make a right-angled turn, and Herodotus' description of the structure is compatible with the remains excavated by Koldewey;[179] the wall which encloses part of the city on the west bank is also roughly square. On the other hand no wall around Babylon remotely approaching 89 km in length has ever been found; if such a wall had been built, with the extraordinary square plan, it could hardly have been maintained in this landscape of irrigation canals and swamps fed by the Euphrates. Nineteenth-century scholars were not compelled to suppose that the entire area enclosed by this wall had been occupied, however. As Rawlinson put it: 'The Babylon thus described was not a town, but a great fortified district very partially built upon, and containing within it not only gardens and parks, but numerous fields and orchards.'[180] Nonetheless they usually accepted Herodotus' account in principle.

Their reconstructions of the plan of Babylon are therefore apt to show the city surrounded by an enormous square. Although Captain Frederick had spent six days 'minutely examining' the countryside in search of this square wall without any success, Rich relied on its existence to accommodate Birs Nimrud as the Tower of Babel within the circuit of the city. Buckingham[181] visited the ziggurat of another nearby city, which we now know to have been ancient Kish, and proposed that it and Birs Nimrud represented the extreme north-eastern and south-western corners of the square. Ker Porter thought

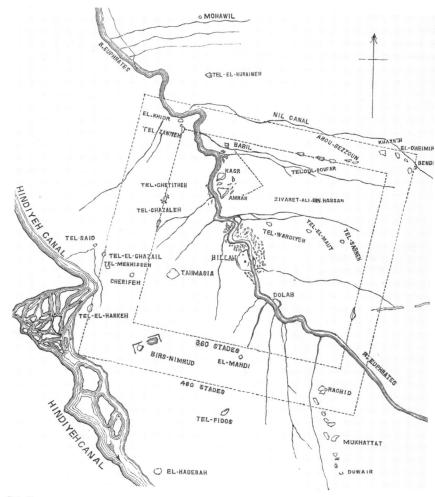

FIG. 91
Babylon as an enormous square

This plan was produced by George Rawlinson, brother of the more famous Sir Henry, following the ideas of Jules Oppert. It shows a proposed square wall of the city based on the vast dimensions given by classical authors. Babylon's city-walls were in fact far smaller, although the city was still the largest in the world.

From Rawlinson 1858: 588.

E FIG. 92
Measurements for the city-wall Imgur-Enlil

This tablet gives remarkably detailed measurements for Babylon's great inner wall, Imgur-Enlil, as it was at the beginning of Nebuchadnezzar's reign. The text names landmarks at Babylon including the Zababa and Uraš gates. Where the figures quoted, given in cubits, can be checked against modern survey and archaeology, they are shown to be extremely accurate.

Reign of Nebuchadnezzar (605–562 BC)
Probably from Babylon; excavated by Hormuzd Rassam before 1882
Clay
H 8.3 cm, W 6.4 cm
British Museum, BM 54634
George 1992: no. 15, pl. 28

the distance between these two sites was too great, but did not question the square shape.[182] Nor did Oppert,[183] who discovered virtual ley-lines of miscellaneous ancient mounds along one of the two alternative courses which he assigned to the outer wall. Layard proposed that the Greeks, in describing such a long wall, might have confused it with other walls 'surrounding the temples and palaces; and that these exterior fortifications were mere ramparts of mud and brushwood, such as are still raised round modern Eastern cities. Such defences, when once neglected, would soon fall to dust, and leave no traces behind.'[184]

One reason for believing Herodotus, at least in principle, was that later Greek historians also referred to what seemed to be the same circuit wall. Theirs was shorter but still of great length. Diodorus quotes 360 stadia (66.5 km) according to Ctesias, and 365 stadia (67.5 km) according to other Greeks who had been there in the time of Alexander the Great; figures of 385 and 368 stadia are given later by the geographer Strabo and the historian Quintus Curtius. Alexander's Greeks were in a good position to collect accurate information. Koldewey, struggling with the problem, claimed that Ctesias' figure was about four times the length of the outer enclosure wall as he himself supposed it to be at the time, and wondered whether there had been some mistake in the Greek calculations.[185] It is notable, however, that Diodorus, although he says that the wall surrounded the city, does not say that it was square; this detail was apparently absent from the books on which he based his compilation.

This leaves open the possibility that the outermost wall of Babylon did not surround the city at all, but was actually a wall, associated with artificial lakes, which stretched from the Euphrates to the Tigris across the territory north of the city itself. The existence of such a wall, which had already been suggested by earlier nineteenth-century historians of the ancient world, was vigorously denied by G. Rawlinson,[186] but traces of it survive near the ancient city of Sippar, and are known as Habl al-Sahr. It was described by Lieutenant J.B. Bewsher,[187] commander of the Indian Navy vessel then renamed the *Comet*. One stretch of the wall was still standing 2 metres high at the time. Part of it was investigated in 1983 by Hermann Gasche and others.[188] It was found to have a mudbrick core faced on both sides with inscribed bricks of Nebuchadnezzar, and was at least 6 metres thick. Its course was traced for 15 km, running alongside an old levee of the Euphrates before presumably cutting across to the Tigris; its original length could have been considerably over 50 km.

The wall is described in inscriptions of Nebuchadnezzar which were not available to the Rawlinsons. Moreover they refer not to one but to two such cross-country walls, a southern one starting at Babylon and passing Kish, and a northern one passing Sippar. Traces of the Kish wall have been tentatively identified.[189] The Sippar wall had a length of 5 *beru*, a figure which is probably greater than 54 km. Xenophon probably passed through this wall in 401 BC, calling it the wall of Media, and it is probably the wall of Semiramis mentioned by Strabo. Berossus, the one ancient author who was thoroughly familiar with Babylon, also refers to defensive walls of Babylon outside Babylon itself.

It is difficult not to conclude that Layard was right in proposing that Herodotus amalgamated features of two walls, thereby creating a spurious Wonder of the World. One was Rich's great outer enclosure wall excavated by Koldewey, only a few kilometres in length, with 'room for a four-horse chariot to turn' (Herodotus) on top and a plan that was, at least in parts, square. The other was Habl as-Sahr, narrower but over 50 km long, forming the outermost defence of the Babylon region. Moreover the region covered by the Sippar and Kish walls on north and south,

The dimensions of Babylon's walls

When are men, living in the same place, to be regarded as a single city – what is the limit? Certainly not the wall of the city, for you might surround all Peloponnesus with a wall. Like this, we may say, is Babylon, and every city that has the compass of a nation rather than a city; Babylon, they say, had been taken for three days before some part of the inhabitants became aware of the fact.
(Aristotle, *Politics* 3.1.12)

Ancient Greek authors offered different dimensions for Babylon's huge walls:

	Wall circuits	Heights
Herodotus:	480 stades = 89 km	200 royal cubits = *c.* 102 m
Ctesias:	360 stades = 66.5 km	50 fathoms = *c.* 91 m
Cleitarchus:	365 stades = 67.5 km	50 cubits = *c.* 23 m

Based on the findings of excavation, Koldewey estimated the circuit of the walls to be much shorter at around 18 km. It is possible, however, that the very large dimensions given by Herodotus may refer to another defensive structure entirely (see page 114).

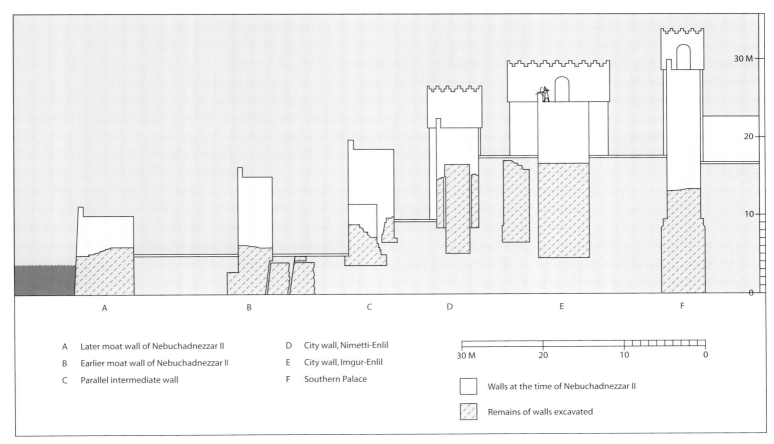

A	Later moat wall of Nebuchadnezzar II	D	City wall, Nimetti-Enlil
B	Earlier moat wall of Nebuchadnezzar II	E	City wall, Imgur-Enlil
C	Parallel intermediate wall	F	Southern Palace

☐ Walls at the time of Nebuchadnezzar II

▨ Remains of walls excavated

FIG. 93
A section through the walls of Babylon

This drawing reconstructs the walls on the northern side of Nebuchadnezzar's Southern Palace, near the Ishtar Gate. Babylon's fortifications and ability to withstand prolonged siege were understandably legendary. The city had large-scale defences on all sides, with diverted river courses and further defensive walls to the north.

Paul Goodhead, after Koldewey 1914: 139, fig. 87

FIG. 94
Paolo Veronese, *The Family of Darius before Alexander the Great*

Alexander III of Macedon was later to have a great impact on Nebuchadnezzar's Babylon, although his dream of rebuilding the ziggurat (by then ruined) was never realized. Among Alexander's works was the funeral pyre for Hephaestion, his closest companion. In this painting Sisygambis, the Persian queen-mother, mistakes Hephaestion for the conqueror, who told her that she was not mistaken, 'for he too is Alexander'. Alexander died in Babylon in 323 BC, at the age of 32.

The lavish Venetian architectural settings employed by Veronese often bore little relation to the subject and narrative of his works. The background here is probably meant on some level to represent Babylon.

AD 1565–70
Oil on canvas
H 236.2 cm, W 474.9 cm
National Gallery. London, NG 294

and by the Tigris and Euphrates on east and west, was roughly tetragonal though certainly not square, so this arrangement could have underlain the statement by Herodotus that Babylon was a perfect square.

Given the problems with the outer wall, there was understandably little discussion in the nineteenth century of the additional walls surrounding the principal remains of Babylon, but both Ker Porter[190] and Buckingham[191] considered the issue, the former with some success. He identified the two main enclosure walls observed by Rich with two described by Diodorus as being 60 and 40 stadia long, or 11.1 and 7.4 km. Koldewey's excavations were to show that the same two walls, if the sections along the river are included, were very roughly 10.5 and 6.3 km long; they were respectively 26.8 and 17.4 metres wide, so that the outer one at least was wide enough for the 'dual carriageway' described by Herodotus. Koldewey's discoveries thus offer some support for the figures offered by Diodorus, but the length of 20 stadia or 3.7 km which Diodorus gives for a third innermost wall is twice what it should be, unless it includes not only the Kasr palaces but also the main city temple of Marduk which Koldewey found in the Amran mound. Diodorus also gives a good figure of 30 stadia or 5.5 km for a wall enclosing an area of Babylon on the western side of the Euphrates; this was about 5.2 km long according to Koldewey. The existence of three city-walls, in addition to three outer or cross-country walls, is confirmed by Josephus (*Apion*). Descriptions by Diodorus, however, of elaborate palaces on both sides of the river connected both by a bridge and allegedly by a tunnel led only to fruitless speculation before Koldewey's excavations. Ker Porter's valid identifications of two walls do not seem to be taken up by later writers.

Oppert made one further observation which he surprisingly failed to develop.[192] Diodorus records that Alexander the Great demolished 10 stadia or nearly 2 km of city-wall to create the base of a massive funeral pyre for Hephaestion.[193] It might therefore have been possible to locate first the mound on which the pyre was placed, and then the wreckage of the city-wall nearby. Oppert proposed, however, that the pyre was represented by an isolated mound near Amran. In the event Koldewey was to discover traces of a pyre on top of one of a group of mounds, called Homera after their distinctive burnt red colour, which lie near the north-eastern corner of Rich's inner enclosure, opposite the Kasr palaces.[194] It is possible that this became a standard place for Greek funeral pyres, and there is no compelling reason to suppose that what Koldewey found was the remains of Hephaestion's pyre; there was another higher mound nearby, and in any case much – though perhaps not all – of the soil of the Homera mounds seems to have been brought not from a city-wall but from the ziggurat of Bel, that is the tower of Belus or Tower of Babel.

It is striking how far the earlier nineteenth-century travellers and scholars discussing the topography of Babylon appear reliant on the Greek accounts, and sometimes seem to be forcing what survived of the ruins into an unnatural mould. Just as in the sixteenth century, when the biblical records were often supposed to be literally true, travellers were apparently willing to believe that they had seen the very Tower of Babel mentioned in the Book of Genesis, so travellers in the enlightened nineteenth century wished to believe the classical records. Although some of these were plainly overimaginative or inconsistent with one another, the problems did not seem serious enough to affect their basic reliability. Babylon, with its biblical and classical associations, was clearly a place of great interest, and had to be studied by use of the best technique available, which was the reconciliation of written and material evidence. A lengthy chapter on the topography of Babylon, however, written by G. Rawlinson at the end of this long period of Greek-oriented research, when altogether relatively little had been added to the discoveries of Rich, does display a distinctly exasperated tone.[195]

Essentially what these men had done was to treat Babylon as a classical Mediterranean ancient site. If they had been studying a ruin in Greece, for instance, they could have taken with them an array of authentic ancient authorities; there were histories describing buildings and sieges and so forth, derived from eye-witness accounts, and there was even a virtual tourist guidebook written by Pausanias in the second century AD. Authentic accounts about Babylon written in Greek did exist, especially those from the period of Alexander the Great and his successors, but they were not numerous. Unfortunately the very earliest available accounts of the city were those of Herodotus and Ctesias, which already had a touch of fairy-tale about them and were beginning to portray that same exotic Orient that ultimately inspired the orientalist fantasies of Enlightenment Europe. It was symptomatic that by the time of Ctesias in 400 BC the legendary Queen Semiramis had appropriated virtually all the achievements of Nebuchadnezzar less than two centuries earlier.

Later in the nineteenth century there was no such problem in interpreting other ancient sites in the region, such as Ur and Nippur, because there were virtually no Greek records about them. Those ruins would have to speak for themselves, but they took time to do so. In Rich's day the existence of some of these other sites was known to the Europeans in Baghdad, but they were far less accessible than Babylon and it cannot have been obvious that they too would have light to throw on ancient history. They succeeded in doing so partly because of other discoveries made at Babylon.

The Hanging Gardens and Walls of Babylon in art and culture

Michael Seymour

Despite their fame today, the Hanging Gardens have been a less popular subject for artists than the Tower of Babel. One reason for this is that Babylon's wonders are known from classical, rather than biblical, sources, and as a result they were relatively neglected prior to the renewed humanist interest in classical Antiquity associated with the Renaissance. Early images are scarce, although some medieval illustrations do show Queen Semiramis among trees to represent a garden.

Representations become more common in the sixteenth and seventeenth centuries. Our earliest known image of the Hanging Gardens and Walls of Babylon specifically as Wonders of the World comes in 1572, in a series of engravings by Philips Galle after designs by Maarten van Heemskerck representing the Seven Wonders of the World and the Colosseum, sometimes suggested as an eighth wonder. Heemskerck gives the walls primacy, and indeed until relatively recently the walls excited just as much interest and speculation as the Hanging Gardens. Although the exotic location is indicated to the viewer by features such as obelisks (which in this case may also refer to the other wonder described only in Diodorus – the black obelisk 'one hundred and thirty feet long and twenty-five feet thick' erected by Semiramis), Heemskerck's Babylon is, naturally enough, very European in appearance, and indeed this can be said of most representations of the city and its wonders prior to the nineteenth century. European pleasure gardens have been a major source of inspiration, as may be seen very clearly in Lievin Cruyl's design, engraved by Conraet Decker for Athanasius Kircher's *Turris Babel* (Fig. 98). Here they are the gardens of Semiramis, whose reputation as a great builder in classical sources has meant that almost all of Babylon's great structures have at some time been attributed to her – in this case in direct conflict with the tradition that the gardens were constructed by a king for his queen. In these illustrations we do not see the trailing foliage of modern imagination; the classical descriptions of the 'Hanging' Gardens themselves imply that 'suspended' would be a better term (for the wonder lay in raising and watering planted terraces at a great height), and indeed this seems the most plausible basis for reconstructions.

The great buildings of Babylon are closely tied in literary and artistic tradition to the identity of Semiramis as their architect. The origins of the tradition are disputed, but may originate in ancient Near Eastern religion and folklore: the existence of such a tradition is noted by Strabo,[196] while Diodorus – who notes that 'many of the works she built throughout Asia remain today and are called Works of Semiramis' – also refers to an existing 'Assyrian' tradition of deifying Semiramis by worshipping the Dove.[197] She is discussed only briefly as a builder by Herodotus,[198] but Ctesias (as preserved in Diodorus) makes her the central figure of his Babylonian history. In his version of events Semiramis is the daughter of the goddess Derceto. She founds Babylon itself, dresses as a man to fight in battles, leads military campaigns eastwards even to India, and though unwilling to risk her position by marrying is possessed of a dangerous sexual appetite, routinely choosing soldiers from her army to sleep with before having them executed the following morning, in order that no husband can usurp her throne.[199] Her character, as well as her name, are thought to derive from the ninth-century BC Assyrian queen Sammu-ramat; see Fig. 83.

Over time the story of the murderous, lust-driven queen, like that of Semiramis the great builder, attracted further elaborations and embellishments. One good example is the legend, first mentioned by the Roman historian Valerius Maximus,[200] that Semiramis was brushing her hair

FIGS 95, 96

95
Master of La Manta, *The Nine Worthies and the Nine Worthy Women* (detail of Semiramis)

AD 1418–30
Fresco
Italy, Saluzzo, Castello della Manta

96
Sandro Botticelli, 'Primavera'

About AD 1482
Tempera on panel
H 203 cm, W 314 cm
Florence, Galleria degli Uffizi

Semiramis figured in late medieval representation as one of the 'nine worthy women', as in the La Manta frescoes (left). It has recently been argued that this more positive tradition is reflected in Botticelli's *Primavera* (left, below), with Semiramis as a secondary identity attached to the central figure of Venus and as part of a disguised portrait of Semiramide Appiani, the wife of Lorenzo di Pierfrancesco Medici.[201]

BABYLONIS MVRI.

IMPERIOSA TVI SECTA CERVICE MARITI, MŒNIBVS INCINGI, LENTOQVE BITVMINE PORTAS
IVSSIT COCTILIBVS BABYLONA SEMIRAMIS ALTAM ADIECIT CENTVM, ET SVPER HIS SIBI NOBILE BVSTVM.

E FIG. 97 *left*

Philips Galle after Maarten van Heemskerck, *The Walls of Babylon*

This sixteenth-century image amalgamates many elements of Babylon's identity, mixing scales and perspectives. The mounted figure is Semiramis, near her own tomb. In the background to the right of the image the Hanging Gardens may be seen. Heemskerck's *Seven Wonders* provided some of the first published reconstructions, and their influence may be seen in many later depictions.

AD 1572. Engraving in series *The Seven Wonders of the World and the Colosseum*
H 21.2 cm, W 26.7 cm
British Museum, 1875, 0508.46
Kerrich 1829: 104–6; Hollstein 1953: no. 363; Hollstein 1993-4: no. 519.I; Bartsch 1987 no. 101.7

E FIG. 98 *below*

Johann Georg Schmidt after Lievin Cruyl and Conraet Decker, *The Hanging Gardens of Babylon*

Loosely based on the descriptions of Diodorus and Strabo, this vision of the Hanging Gardens is largely composed of classical and contemporary European elements. The clearest signs of the ancient Eastern world are the Egyptian obelisks at the corners.

About AD 1730
Engraving after Cruyl/Decker (in Kircher 1679)
H 34.5 cm, W 53 cm
Staatliche Museen zu Berlin, Kupferstichkabinett, KDA 119–123
Wullen 2008: 77, no. 37

Die schwebenden Garten zu Babylon.

Nota SEMIRAMIDIS constructa viraginis altè
MOENIA, quadrato Babylona oheuntia saxo.
Asphalite iubet Regina bitumine necti
Marmora, longævos non formidantia casus.

E FIG. 99 *left*

Antonio Tempesta, *The Walls of Babylon*

The Walls of Babylon were sometimes included among the Seven Wonders as well as, or instead of, the Hanging Gardens. Here Semiramis (silhouetted in her chariot) can be seen directing construction of the famous defences that had in fact been constructed by Nebuchadnezzar. Already in the third century BC the Babylonian historian Berossus complained that too many of Babylon's famous buildings had been attributed to Semiramis by the Greek authors.

AD 1608
Etching in series *Septem orbis admiranda*
H 22.2 cm, W 28.2 cm
British Museum, 1928, 0313.67
Bartsch 1803-21 XVII: 186.1456; Madonna 1976: 54

FIG. 100
Guercino (Giovanni Francesco Barbieri),
Semiramis Receiving Word of the Revolt in Babylon

Hearing of the revolt in Babylon, Semiramis refuses to finish combing her hair until she has led an army to crush the rebellion. The intended significance of the story is disputed. Our earliest source, the Roman historian Valerius Maximus, in considering moral behaviour listed it under de *ira aut odio*, 'of anger or hatred'. Guercino's later treatments of the subject give Semiramis a more composed, classical appearance; this first depiction, by contrast, emphasizes her power and activity. [207]

AD 1624
Oil on canvas
H 112.4 cm, W 154.6 cm
Boston, Museum of Fine Arts 48.1028

when she heard of a revolt in Babylon. Wasting no time, she rushed out personally to put down the revolt, killing its leaders before returning to her palace to finish her toilette. The scene of Semiramis receiving word of the revolt in Babylon has been depicted by several artists, most memorably Guercino. Another story has her tricking Ninus, her husband, out of the throne before having him imprisoned.[202] This bloodthirsty Semiramis is clearly a product of Greek fascination with the exotic rather than real biography, but in terms of impugning Babylonian honour it seems that the portrayal of Semiramis the builder may have been more contentious. Berossus, as a Babylonian contributing to a Greek discourse, was motivated in his account by an awareness that many great Babylonian architectural achievements had already been misattributed to Semiramis by the Greek authors.[203]

When Degas came to depict Semiramis, he looked to her guise as a builder as described by Herodotus (although earlier studies do depict a more war-like queen than the final canvas). It appears that Degas considered other aspects of the Herodotus account; it is certain that he made drawings of Assyrian reliefs at the Musée du Louvre,[204] and reportedly he was inspired by a production of Rossini's *Sémiramide* (whose Semiramis in fact owes much more to Diodorus than to Herodotus) featuring Assyrian costumes.[205] Elements drawn from these may still be seen in detailed preparatory studies for the work (Figs. 102, 104), but the final painting removes them almost completely, replacing them with influences and iconography that are overwhelmingly classical.[206]

This is not to suggest a lack of interest in reconstructing Babylon's real appearance. Prior to the detailed accounts of the late eighteenth and nineteenth centuries, leading eventually to Koldewey's excavations, Babylon's topography had to be derived entirely from classical sources. Considerable ingenuity and great scholarly care was shown in this task, as a number of seven-

FIG. 101 *above*

Edgar Degas, *Sémiramis construisant Babylone (Sémiramis construisant une ville)*

The discovery of Assyrian antiquities by British and French excavators in the mid-nineteenth century did not always have a visible impact on domestic artistic representation of the ancient Near East. His studies and notebooks show that Degas considered and largely discarded available Assyrian iconography. Degas drew his models for depicting the ancient past from other sources of a different character: his experience of Italian art and architecture. The main group of Semiramis and her attendants, in particular, reflects Piero della Francesca's fresco *Queen of Sheba in Adoration of the Wood of the True Cross* in Arezzo.

About AD 1861
Oil on canvas
H 151 cm, W 258 cm
Paris, Musée d'Orsay RF 2207

E FIG. 102

Edgar Degas, *Study for Sémiramis construisant Babylone*

This highly developed study shows quite clearly the Assyrian iconography that Degas was considering, particularly in the horse and chariot. It also shows details of architecture and signs of construction on the near bank of the river that do not appear in the final painting.

AD 1861
Oil on paper laid down on canvas
H 26 cm, W 41 cm
Paris, Musée d'Orsay, RF 2007–2.
Jamot 1924: 131; Lesmoine 1946: vol. II, no. 84, p. 45; Monnier 1978: no. 14, p. 414;
Boggs et al.1988: 90, fig. 44

FIG. 103

Assyrian bas-relief showing horses and harness

Reliefs from the Assyrian palaces of northern Iraq such as this, excavated by Paul-Émile Botta in the mid-nineteenth century and on show in the Louvre, were sources for Degas.

Reign of Sargon II (r. 721–705 BC)
From palace of Sargon II at Khorsabad (ancient Dur-Sharrukin), northern Iraq
Gypseous alabaster
Paris, Musée du Louvre, AO 19883

teenth- and eighteenth-century reconstructions show. The most impressive is that produced by J.A. Delsenbach for Fischer von Erlach's *Entwurff einer historischen Architektur* (1721–3). The large, highly detailed engraving of the city is given a key, and several pages of accompanying text in parallel German and French explain each feature of the scene and its rationale, specifying the underlying Greek and Latin sources. The author even notes those occasions on which he has had to choose between two conflicting accounts in his reconstruction. The resulting picture combines the attention lavished by Herodotus on the long straight roads and massive walls of Babylon (taking literally his rhetorical claim that they contain one hundred gates) with features such as the luxurious Hanging Gardens described by other authors. Comparisons with the descriptions of classical writers remained important for explorers and antiquarians: in the nineteenth century, as we have seen, Claudius Rich made extensive use of Herodotus in his detailed surveys of the ruins, and the descriptions of Greek authors have continued to excite both scholarly and wider interest to the present day.

E FIG. 104

Edgar Degas, Sketch for *Sémiramis construisant Babylone*

This ink sketch suggests that Degas also considered a different aspect of Herodotus' description of Babylon: the specific claim that the city's walls were so thick that two chariots could pass one another on top of them. Although unclear, the ruined building in the background might represent a stepped temple-tower, another feature described by Herodotus.

About AD 1861
Brown ink
H 34.8 cm, W 22.5 cm
Paris, Musée du Louvre, département des Arts Graphiques
RF 43191

E FIG. 105

J.A. Delsenbach after a design by Johann Bernhard Fischer von Erlach, *View of Babylon*

Fischer von Erlach relied entirely on classical authorities including Herodotus, Diodorus Siculus, Strabo, Pliny the Elder and Quintus Curtius Rufus for his careful reconstruction of the city of Babylon. It was not until the excavations of Koldewey in the early twentieth century that any detailed reconstruction from evidence on the ground became possible.

AD 1721–3. Engraving in J.B. Fischer von Erlach, *Entwurff einer historischen Architektur*
Page H 42 cm, W 52.5 cm
British Library, 648.a.3
Kunoth 1956: 29–31; Minkowski 1991: 228, no. 428; Seipel 2003: vol. I, 161, 1.1.37

The Tower of Babel

The hunt for the Tower of Babel only ended with the discovery of the ziggurat at Babylon by modern archaeologists. Early travellers to the site had assumed that the biblical narrative depended on an identifiable building, but the Babylon ziggurat itself – one of the largest buildings of the ancient world – had to all intents and purposes vanished. The ziggurat was an enormous brick tower, square in base and formed of stages of diminishing size, rather like a step-pyramid, and crowned with a small temple. Many cities of ancient Mesopotamia boasted at least one such building. The ziggurat at Babylon, Etemenanki, was dedicated to Marduk, the god of the city. That ziggurat, the glory of Nebuchadnezzar's Babylon, was the inspiration behind the Tower of Babel, but realization of the point involved a colossal effort of scholarship and exploration.

The search for the ziggurat

Julian E. Reade

The mystery of the location of this huge structure, which Herodotus had described in detail, remained unsolved throughout the nineteenth century. Herodotus had said that Babylon was divided into two quarters, on either side of the Euphrates, and that the ziggurat and the palace were in different quarters, which should have meant that they were on opposite sides of the river. If, as Claudius Rich thought, the ziggurat was at Birs Nimrud, there was no difficulty. Birs Nimrud was west of the river, and if the mound of Kasr – which was rightly identified as the palace – was on the east bank of the river, the ancient course of the river seemed clear although it had shifted slightly further west since Antiquity. If on the other hand, as Rennell thought, the ziggurat was at Babil, which is clearly east of the river, then the palace had to be west of the river; in that case it was necessary to suppose that, at least in the time of Herodotus, the Euphrates had followed a different course, circling eastwards so that the palace was on the west bank.

The question generated a fine academic spat between Rich and Rennell. Rich and his friends maintained that he and others had inspected the ground closely and that the Euphrates had never flowed around the palace.[208] Rennell maintained that it must have done, and he could cite John Macdonald Kinneir, who had inspected the ground previously and proposed the very same change of course; R. Mignan was to say the same, and found it 'indeed surprising that this idea did not immediately occur to Mr Rich'.[209] The rival claims of Birs Nimrud and Babil were still being promoted as late as 1897, and it was only in 1901 that the excavators of Babylon solved the problem: they discovered that the ziggurat had actually been located in the middle of Babylon, between Kasr and Amran.[210] It had been invisible because Alexander the Great had demolished much of it with a view to rebuilding, as recorded by Arrian[211] and Strabo,[212] dumping the spoil at Homera.

It is surprising that Rich, Rennell and others, with their great knowledge of the Greek writers, had not apparently considered the implications of this attempt at demolition. J. Baillie Fraser, however, had an answer, pointing out that 'in tracing the progress of its decay, we have witnessed a rapidity of destruction, which is the more impressive as it corresponds so accurately with all the denunciations of divine wrath which were hurled against the sinful and devoted city'.[213]

W.B. Selby was another who relied on biblical authority, but he reached an opposite conclusion. He was still disinclined to accept the identification of the site as Babylon, because:

> we do not find in the face of the country, as it is presented among these ruins, any similarity to the doom foretold of Babylon, in Isaiah xiii, 20th to 22nd verses: 'It shall never be inhabited, neither shall it be dwelt in from generation to generation; neither shall the Arabian pitch his tent there; neither shall the shepherds make their fold there. But wild beasts of the desert shall lie there; and their houses shall be full of doleful creatures; and owls shall dwell there, and satyrs shall dance there. And the wild beasts of the islands shall cry in their desolate houses, and dragons in their pleasant places.' On the contrary, gardens and cultivation extend in places to the very edge and among the ruins, and in the spring the country is covered with flocks of cattle grazing in every direction; nor do we find here more wild animals than in any other part of the country. I was there at one time in April, and, save in some places where the soil is nitrous, the country was covered with vegetation, fruits and flowers abutting close on the 'Amran' mounds, and corn-fields within 100 yards of the 'Mujelibé' itself. [214]

Rich, however, had at least heard of satyrs near Babil:

> The tchoadar [a Turkish officer] ... told me that in the desert to the west animals are found, the upper part of which resembles perfectly a man, and the lower parts a sheep – that the Arabs hunt them with greyhounds, and that when they find themselves close pressed, they utter miserable cries, entreating for mercy – but that the hunters kill them, and eat their lower parts. The tchoadar had evidently not the slightest doubt of the truth of his wonderful story.[215]

Ironically the resolution of the old controversy about the location of the ziggurat failed to resolve the debate about the course of the Euphrates because, in order to vindicate Herodotus, it may still be necessary that the river has shifted eastwards. The problem remains with us in the twenty-first century. The final publications of Robert Koldewey's excavation accept that there was a change of course and it duly appears on the plans, but it has been suggested that the excavators were unduly influenced by their respect for Herodotus, who may himself have been misinformed.[216] The evidence available does not seem decisive. A detailed study has been made of all the records relating to alluviation at Babylon and to structures that adjoined the river and the canals and moats derived from it, and this seems to favour the change in the course of the river,[217] but the records are not comprehensive. It is unclear how the spoil from the demolished ziggurat would have been transported to Homera unless by boat along the new river course. This

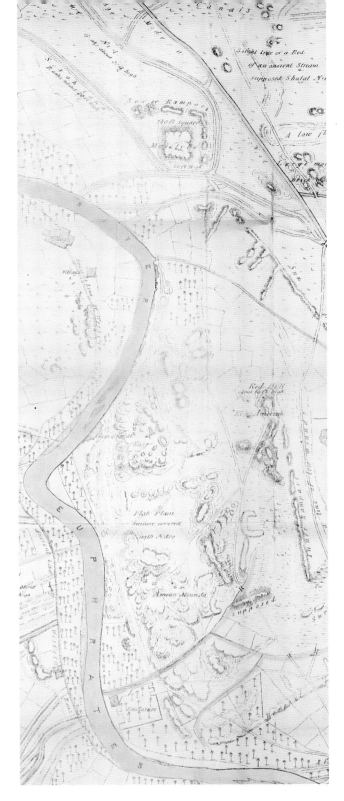

FIG. 106
Finding the Tower

There were several large mounds at Babylon, and the ziggurat was not easily identified. From north to south along the bank of the River Euphrates lay Tell Babil, the mound known as Kasr or Mujellibeh, and Amran ibn 'Ali. To the east of the Kasr mound were Homera and Merkes. These five tells held the remains of palaces, temples and residential areas, but ironically the ziggurat itself did not appear as a mound at all (see Fig. 8). The nearest standing ruin of a ziggurat, at Birs Nimrud, was often suggested as the site, but in fact this lay several miles outside Babylon and was the temple-tower of another ancient city, Borsippa.

Selby 1859: fold-out map (detail of Fig. 20)

Scale model of the ziggurat Etemenanki

We know that the seven stages of
Nebuchadnezzar's ziggurat stood well over 70
metres high, rising from a base measuring 91
metres square. This recent scale model gives a
realistic impression of what the temple-tower may
have looked like when originally complete.

Scale 1:150
H 56 cm, L 97 cm, W 50 cm
Staatliche Museen zu Berlin, Vorderasiatisches Museum,
VAG 1284
Schmid 1991

Cylinder seal depicting a ziggurat

Here a king acting as a priest performs a religious
ritual in front of a five-stage ziggurat. It may
represent either a building or possibly a model,
used as temple equipment. This seal, which was
made long before the Neo-Babylonian period, was
found in a grave in the centre of Babylon.

13th century BC
From Babylon, Merkes
Agate
H 4.7 cm, Th. 1.6 cm
Staatliche Museen zu Berlin, Vorderasiatisches Museum,
VA 7736
Moortgat 1940: no. 592

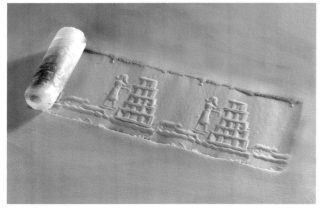

course would have passed through the inner enclosure wall, severely damaging it; Herodotus
indeed refers to demolition of the wall of Babylon by a Persian king,[218] but this could have been
an outer wall; Babylon was one of the most important cities of the Persian Empire and its rulers
surely wished it to remain defensible. Other references to the city in Greek and in local Babylonian
records have so far failed to clarify whether the river changed its course. Anyway, the palace
would sometimes have been a virtual island because of the spring floods from the Euphrates,
which could have made it appear to lie on the other side of the river from the ziggurat without
the river having changed its main course at all. Rich remarked how 'in January the river is high,
and then a great part of this plain is overflown, which renders many of the ruins inaccessible'.[219]

The truth about Etemenanki, the ziggurat of Babylon

Andrew George

The great ziggurat of Babylon was dedicated to Marduk, the god of the city and head of the pantheon. The temple at its summit supplemented Marduk's main sanctuary, Esagil, which lay at
ground level 200 metres to the south. The ziggurat served not only a religious purpose but also,
unintentionally, a military one. As the highest structure in Babylon the tower provided a vantage
point in times of war. This made it vulnerable to reprisals. The siege of Babylon by the army of
the Assyrian king Sennacherib ended with the sack of the city in 689 BC. It is clear that the ziggurat was damaged beyond repair, for Sennacherib's successors spent many years rebuilding it
from the foundations up. Xerxes of Persia disabled this new ziggurat on suppressing the
Babylonian revolt of 484 BC. The ruined superstructure was cleared 150 years later by Alexander
the Great and his successors in preparation for its rebuilding, but the project did not progress
beyond levelling the site. The plot was put to good use in the Sasanian period (AD 224–651),
when a mansion was built on it. This building was subdivided by later inhabitants but finally abandoned in the early Islamic period. The true site of the ziggurat was then hidden from history. Its
memory lived on in Genesis and in the accounts of such classical historians as Herodotus and
Strabo, who reported its dimensions often with much exaggeration.

As we have seen, early modern adventurers in the Middle East came
across ruined ziggurats that had fared less badly at other Babylonian cities,
notably Borsippa (Birs Nimrud, the tower of Nimrod) and Dur-Kurigalzu ('Aqar
Quf), both of which had been claimed as ruins of the Tower of Babel. The true
location of Babylon was always remembered by local people, however, for the
name Babil survived among Abbasid and later geographers and came to refer
especially to Babylon's most impressive landmark, the mound that concealed
Nebuchadnezzar's Summer Palace. Already in the seventeenth century the
Italian traveller Pietro della Valle identified Babil with the Tower of Babel and
the structure described by Herodotus and Strabo. Although he was in the
right vicinity, he was misled by the archaeological remains.

The growing interest in ancient Mesopotamia in the early nineteenth
century led to the first attempts at reconstructions on paper of the Tower of Babel, based on
the ruins at Birs Nimrud. Early archaeological excavations of sites in what is now northern Iraq
quickly threw up the remains of Assyrian ziggurats and bas-reliefs depicting temple-towers.

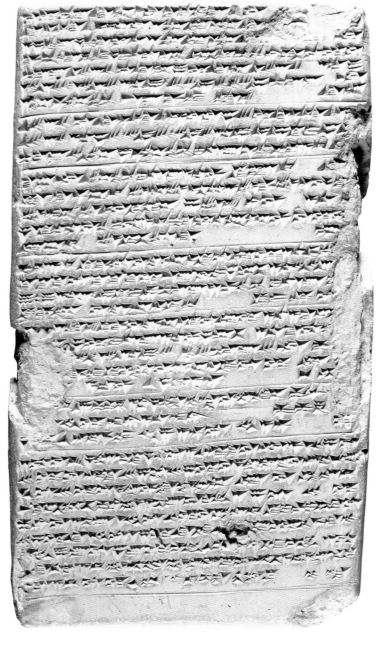

ⓔ FIG. 109
Measuring a ziggurat: the Esagil Tablet

Here the ziggurat and its enclosure become the subject of mathematical exercises in which the student is to calculate areas. The tablet first gives the dimensions of two courtyards and six shrines in the Esagil temple complex. It then lists the length, breadth and height of each of the seven stages of the ziggurat Etemenanki. Measurements are quoted in *nindanus* – a unit of 6 metres – as well as other units from an earlier system.

This famous tablet was found in a scholar's library in the ancient city of Uruk (in southern Iraq). It is dated to 229 BC, but the scribe tells us that he had carefully copied it from an older manuscript from Borsippa, near Babylon.

229 BC. From Uruk. Baked clay
H 18 cm, W 10 cm, Th. 2 cm
Paris, Musée du Louvre, département des Antiquités orientales, AO 6555
Thureau-Dangin 1922: 32; Weissbach 1939: 49ff; André and Ziegler 1982: 336, no. 284; George 1992: 109–19, no. 13 source a

These discoveries led to fresh attempts to reconstruct the Tower of Babylon, often in accordance with the accounts of classical historians, but there was still no genuine evidence at this time.

The ruined ziggurat of Babylon began to emerge in the late 1880s, when locals digging a well two miles south of Babil – in the low ground that separates the mounds of Amran ibn 'Ali and Kasr – discovered a few feet below the surface a massive structure of baked brick. What they had found was the subterranean part of the baked-brick mantle of the ziggurat levelled in Antiquity, but no one realized this at the time. Brick is easy to make in lower Mesopotamia but – because fuel is in short supply – expensive to fire, so the ziggurat's baked-brick infrastructure was rapidly removed and reused to build houses. As the bricks were dug out, the voids filled with groundwater to form a square pond encircling a square island (Fig. 8).

During the course of the quarrying inscribed barrel cylinders fell out of cavities in the brickwork where they had rested for nearly 2,500 years and found their way on to the antiquities market. These were foundation deposits left by the ziggurat's builders, the kings of Babylon Nabopolassar (626–605 BC) and Nebuchadnezzar II (605–562 BC), inscribed with cuneiform writing that recorded their construction and completion of Etemenanki, the ziggurat of Babylon. The cylinders were bought by the British Museum, the Louvre and the University Museum in Philadelphia, and the better preserved exemplars were quickly published. However knowledge of their exact provenance had been lost, so the true significance of these inscriptions for the identification of Etemenanki on the ground was not immediately grasped.

Another cuneiform inscription, which had appeared on the antiquities' market a decade earlier, was a clay tablet summarized in 1876 by George Smith in an article for the *Athenaeum*.[220] Smith worked for the British Museum but was unable to acquire the tablet. He recognized that it described Marduk's cult-centre at Babylon, and from that time the text has been called the Esagil Tablet after Marduk's main sanctuary (Fig. 109). Part of the text gave the dimensions of the ziggurat, already translated by Smith as the 'temple tower'. The Esagil tablet was then lost from sight for nearly forty years and several late nineteenth-century scholars who tried to reconstruct the ziggurat in drawings took no notice of Smith's contribution.

At the very end of the nineteenth century controlled excavation began at Babylon under Koldewey. At first the excavators followed Pietro della Valle's idea, that the temple-tower of Babylon survived as a ruin under the mound Babil. However when they discovered Marduk's main temple under the mound Amran ibn 'Ali, they knew that the ziggurat had to be nearby. The Assyriologist Bruno Meissner quickly asserted that the square pond just to the north of Amran ibn 'Ali must be the building's true location,[221] but the team had to wait twelve years before Meissner's proposal could be tested. In 1913 the groundwater was low enough to permit an exploration of the pit left by the removal of baked bricks in the 1880s. The project was led by Friedrich Wetzel, who reported that the main pit measured 91 metres square. A trench of 51 by 9 metres leading from the middle of the south side of the main pit was quickly identified as the site of a great staircase that projected from the tower's south façade at right angles. Traces of two further staircases, attached to the same façade, were found at the south corners of the square island. The island was identified as the tower's core, made of earth and mudbrick and measuring 61 metres on each side.

By chance the same year saw the re-emergence of George Smith's Esagil Tablet, which was quickly bought by the Louvre and republished in a full scholarly edition by Vincent Scheil.[222] The tablet turned out to be a beautiful copy of a text from Borsippa, written out by an apprentice scribe in the southern city of Uruk in 229 BC. Scheil's understanding of the text was far superior to Smith's, for knowledge of Babylonian language and grammar had greately improved in the interval.

The simultaneous publication of the dimensions recorded by Wetzel on the ground and those given in the ancient Esagil Tablet meant that suddenly there were good documentary and archaeological data available to would-be reconstructors. Many new drawings and models were made. There were still some, including Koldewey himself, who obstinately ignored the new understanding of the Esagil Tablet and came up with alternative reconstructions, but most scholars took both sets of evidence seriously. Many reconstructions thus looked rather similar because they took account of the same data concerning the size of the tower's base and the heights of its stages. But there were disagreements as to where the three staircases landed and the number of stages.

During the remainder of the twentieth century research on the ziggurat of Babylon rested soundly on the twin bases of archaeological survey and philological study. Both were revisited. Wetzel's definitive account of his excavation was delayed by the First World War but finally published in 1938.[223] In the same volume F. H. Weissbach gave an improved edition of all the cuneiform sources relating to Babylon's ziggurat, including the Esagil Tablet.[224] In 1962 the architect-archaeologist Hansjörg Schmid led a team that explored the remains of the ziggurat using modern techniques.[225] Another manuscript of the Esagil Tablet, this time from Babylon, was identified in the

FIG. 110
Second copy of the Esagil Tablet

This fragmentary copy is of earlier date than the famous Uruk manuscript in Fig. 109, and is from the city of Babylon itself.

6th–4th century BC
From Babylon
Clay
H 6.8 cm, W 5.4 cm, Th. 2.2 cm
British Museum, BM 40813
George 1992: 109–19, no. 13 source b

British Museum (Fig. 110). This led to the correction of previously unrecognized errors on the apprentice's copy and a new edition, published by the writer in 1992.[226] This edition also identified the text as essentially mathematical in outlook, raising the question of how far it matched any historical reality, as opposed to an academic ideal of Babylon's ziggurat.

A new element in the discussion of iconography comes in the form of a further monument[227] in which a carved relief depicts a Babylonian king standing in profile opposite a seven-staged ziggurat. The tower is clearly labelled with a cuneiform caption, 'Etemenanki, the ziggurat of Babylon.' The king is not identified by a caption, but the inscription carved in three columns underneath the relief is so similar to known inscriptions of Nebuchadnezzar II that there can be no doubt that the monument depicts him. It was Nebuchadnezzar who completed the ziggurat, in about 590 BC. The obvious conclusion is that this stele was prepared to commemorate his work on the tower. Probably it was once embedded in the tower's brickwork as part of a ritual deposit. A word of caution might be opportune: ancient images do not belong to a tradition of realism but tend towards the depiction of ideals. The ziggurat here is thus the Babylonians' ideal image of Etemenanki, just as the figure of Nebuchadnezzar is their ideal of a king; in both cases the reality may have been different.

The Genesis account

Irving Finkel and Michael Seymour

> Now the whole world had one language and a common speech. As men moved eastward, they found a plain in Shinar[228] and settled there.
>
> They said to each other, 'Come, let's make bricks and bake them thoroughly.' They used brick instead of stone, and tar for mortar. Then they said, 'Come, let us build ourselves a city, with a tower that reaches to the heavens, so that we may make a name for ourselves and not be scattered over the face of the whole earth.'
>
> But the Lord came down to see the city and the tower that the men were building. The Lord said, 'If as one people speaking the same language they have begun to do this, then nothing they plan to do will be impossible for them. Come, let us go down and confuse their language so they will not understand each other.'
>
> So the Lord scattered them from there over all the earth, and they stopped building the city. That is why it was called Babel – because there the Lord confused the language of the whole world. From there the Lord scattered them over the face of the whole earth.[229]

The folly of human ambition, the confusion of languages and the scattering of cultures embodied in the stark biblical passage above have lost none of their potency today. Yet it is interesting to look again at this familiar wording from a new standpoint. On one level the story is probably an answer to the natural enquiry as to why there are so many languages in the world. But the answer surely reflects familiarity with the ziggurat at Babylon. Basing a didactic narrative on a familiar icon is a hallmark of effective teaching, and the case here tends to support the idea that the Genesis passage took its form during the period of the Babylonian Captivity.

Complementing this is the text's curious focus on the building material. What does this point serve of itself? Bricks of baked clay with bitumen instead of stone and mortar reflect exactly the practice of Nebuchadnezzar's builders and, to the audience, can only have been understood that way. One can be sure that building a city that would last for ever was a conscious ambition in Nebuchadnezzar's mind. He had personally witnessed the downfall and destruction of an Assyria

– with its great stone palaces – that must have seemed certain to last for eternity. At the same time his lavish, upward-looking work on the ziggurat, if not symbolizing personal pride, was certainly designed to bridge the human and divine worlds, as well as to create an unforgettable impression on those who saw it for themselves.

Josephus, quoted below, records a curiously apposite prediction from the Sibylline oracle:

When all men spoke a common language, certain of them built an exceeding high tower, thinking thereby to mount to heaven. But the gods sent winds against it and overturned the tower [230]

In the light of this, we bring in the following prediction from within the cuneiform world itself, in the form of one highly abnormal omen in a collection of highly abnormal omens:

If a city rises to the interior of heaven like a mountain peak, that city will be turned to rubble[231]

Is it then thinkable that there were spasmodic rumblings of anti-tower building operations in Babylon itself from time to time?

Our understanding of the biblical story as one of the punishment of pride owes much to Flavius Josephus, the first-century AD historian of the Jews.[232] Josephus also includes the physical destruction of the tower, an event not explicitly described in the Genesis account, and transforms the identity of Nimrod, naming him as the tower's architect and making him a hubristic advocate of defiance of God's will. [233]

They were incited to this contempt by Nebrodes [Nimrod], grandson of Ham the son of Noah, an audacious man of doughty vigour. He persuaded them to attribute their prosperity not to God but to their own valour, and little by little transformed the state of affairs into a tyranny, holding that the only way to detach men from the fear of God was by making them continuously dependent upon his own power. He threatened to have his revenge on God if He wished to inundate the earth again; for he would build a tower higher than the water could reach and avenge the destruction of their forefathers.

The people were eager to follow this advice of Nebrodes, deeming it slavery to submit to God; so they set out to build the tower with indefatigable ardour and no slackening in the task; and it rose with a speed beyond all expectation, thanks to the multitude of hands. Its thickness, however, was so stout as to dwarf its apparent height. It was built of baked bricks cemented with bitumen to prevent them from being washed away. Seeing their mad enterprise, God was not minded to exterminate them utterly, because even the destruction of the first victims had not taught their descendents wisdom; but He created discord among them by making them speak different languages, through the variety of which they could not understand one another. The place where they built the tower is now called Babylon from the confusion of that primitive speech once intelligible to all, for the Hebrews call confusion 'Babel.'

In this guise Dante describes Nimrod as one of the giants chained in the deepest levels of the Inferno, among those who have made war against God:[234]

He told me: 'He condemns himself in speech.
This is the Nimrod, through whose evil spurred,
We cannot speak one language, each to each.
Let's leave him standing there, nor waste a word
For every language is the same to him,
As his own to us, senseless, absurd.'

The Tower of Babel in art

Michael Seymour

 FIG. 111

The Tower of Babel in *La Bouquechardière*

This image comes from the fifteenth-century universal history of Jean de Courcy.

Although both King Nimrod, the legendary builder of the Tower, and the Tower itself appear European at first sight, an effort has been made by the artist to give the scene an exotic 'Eastern' flavour. Nimrod wears a scimitar, a curved, typically Middle Eastern sword, and the spires of Babylon are apparently intended to resemble minarets. At the top angels hurl stones at the Tower, thereby halting construction. Whether they herald the confusion of languages or the destruction of the Tower itself is unclear.

In the Bible Nimrod is not specifically described as the architect of the Tower but as the founder of Babylon and other Mesopotamian cities. He is also described as a 'mighty hunter before the Lord', an epithet that supports the identification of Nimrod with Ninurta, the chief Mesopotamian god of hunting and war.

About AD 1460–70
Full-page manuscript miniature in the universal history of Jean de Courcy, *La Bouquechardière*.
Page H 43 cm, W 32 cm
British Library, Harley 4376, f. 206v
De Chancel 1987

Our earliest visual representations of the biblical Tower of Babel come from the European Middle Ages; from the eleventh century the Tower is to be found in both architectural decoration[235] and manuscript illumination.[236] The surviving images suggest an emphasis on building materials and techniques, with the subject of the tower taken as an opportunity to represent contemporary carpentry and masonry in detail. The Tower itself tends to be depicted as a recognizably European medieval building, always in the process of construction. Its scale, shape and setting varied considerably, not least because there was no clear architectural model available.

The Tower became an important icon in medieval histories, taking prominent position as a full-page miniature in the manuscripts of Jean de Courcy's universal history, known as *La Bouquechardière*. In the example shown here Nimrod – the Tower's architect – stands in the foreground of a scene showing both the city of Babylon and the Tower of Babel. The relationship between city and Tower posed a problem for artists, as for antiquarians, until well into the nineteenth century. Attempts to resolve the incomplete or even destroyed tower in Genesis with the eye-witness accounts of classical Greek authors often led to the conclusion that there must have been two towers, the first constructed by Nimrod, the second by Semiramis. This line of thinking lies behind the occasional representation in art of two coeval towers: a Temple of Bel (Marduk) based on the account of Herodotus, and a great Tower of Babel based on Genesis.

Another spectacular late medieval depiction of the Tower is to be found in the *Bedford Hours*, where it forms part of an unusual cycle of four full-page illustrations to Genesis.[237] The *Bedford Hours* tower is fantastic in its appearance and setting, but also shows meticulously observed detail in portraying construction techniques (this use of the theme as a vehicle for representing contemporary masonry and carpentry is widespread in medieval depictions). At the top of the Tower two angels begin its physical destruction. The improbable external staircase in the *Bedford Hours* tower bears a resemblance to that of the colossal Malwiya minaret of the Great Mosque at Samarra; however there are no surviving texts to suggest that medieval travellers mistook this minaret for the Tower of Babel, nor that their written travel accounts conveyed details of its architecture to Europe. Such external staircases in later depictions (e.g. that of the *Breviarium Grimani*, 1508–20) owe much to the description of Herodotus, but it is highly unlikely that the artists working on the *Bedford Hours* miniatures would have consulted this source, or equated the stepped temple tower it describes with the Tower of Babel of Genesis.

Much in the Tower's representation changes in the sixteenth century, and for a number of reasons. Certainly humanism and a renewed interest in classical authors created new avenues for the representation of the ancient past, but in the case of the Tower of Babel other factors were to prove far more powerful. The most important changes of all were those wrought, directly and indirectly, by the Reformation. The sixteenth century was to be a period of profound religious and moral upheaval in northern Europe, and it is in this light that many works of Pieter Bruegel the Elder and other leading artists of the Northern Renaissance, and particularly the sudden popularity of the Tower of Babel as a theme, can best be understood.

Pres que
des twyre
ations de
nant pse
et comme
seur ate
fut iadis
destruitte.
mesmement comme de la ligne
qui de enls yssi suuent apres
pluseurs sermes peuplez. Me
comment il des assuriens dire
somme premier ourent come
tement. et comme seur sernie su
a pluseurs roys depluseurs se
rnies z peuples par force comis
Et aueques de la trant babi
lone comme en son premier su

edissice n des principaulx rops
qui iller habiterent. Car tout
en la maniere que fortune twne
et au monde somme puis Joye
puis douleur. ne se peut on to
iours en vnch estat ester. Ains
nous commient pluseurs choses
natuuellement souffrir. Car to
ainsi que la comonction de la
lune. qui de moys en moys ad
nient nous somme obscurte en
la moictie de la superficie. pour
la cause quelle est separtique
Iusques a ce que par son tinne
oppositement contre elle Iette.
si clarte. ce qui la fait sur latie
kiyer. Et par son mouuemet
celle clarte nous rendre. estoit

FIG. 112
The Tower of Babel in *The Bedford Hours*

The Tower of Babel appears here as one of a series of full-page Genesis miniatures, most unusual in a book of hours and the last illustrations to be added to this famous manuscript. It has been argued that the miniatures were intended to have had some didactic function for the 9-year-old Henry VI, to whom the book was given in AD 1430, between his coronations as king of England (in 1429) and of France (1431). The explanatory captions in French at the bottom of the pages were probably also added for the young king's benefit.

Produced in several stages from about AD 1410–30.
This fol. AD 1430
Bedford Master (probably Haincelin of Haguenau) and Parisian studio
Page H 26.3 cm, W 18.4 cm
Miniature in the *Bedford Hours*
British Library MS Add. 18850, f. 17v

FIG. 113 *below*
Malwiya minaret, Great Mosque of Samarra, Iraq

Because of its unusual shape this ninth-century AD minaret has frequently been mistaken for a pre-Islamic tower. The tower may have inspired artists in Europe, but early travellers to the region more often identified surviving ziggurat ruins, albeit not those of Etemenanki at Babylon, as the biblical Tower of Babel. This photograph was taken in 2005; the top of the minaret has since been severely damaged.

FIG. 114 *above*
The Tower of Babel in the *Grimani Breviary*

This highly original manuscript illustration is an important link between medieval depictions of the tower and that of Bruegel, containing precursors of the latter's colossal scale and depth of landscape. Bruegel would have known the image through working with the miniaturist Giulio Clovio in Italy; Clovio's tower in the *Farnese Hours* (1546) is itself closely based on that of the *Grimani Breviary*.

AD 1508–20. Miniature in the *Grimani Breviary*. H 28 cm, W 19.5 cm
Biblioteca nazionale Marciana, Venice

E FIG. 115 *left*
Cornelis Anthonisz Teunissen, *Fall of the Tower of Babel*

The Colosseum in Rome became a template for the Tower of Babel's architecture in hundreds of artworks, of which this may be the first. The engraving shows the tower's violent destruction, an event not described in the Bible, but added to the story by later historians and commentators. The inscription in the top right has been emended from 'Genesis 11' (the Tower of Babel) to 'Genesis 14'. This is probably a cryptic reference to Revelation 14, which contains the passage: 'Fallen! Fallen is Babylon the Great'.

AD 1547. Engraving. H 32.3 cm, W 38.3 cm
British Museum, 1871, 1209.4631
Nagler 1860: vol. 2, no. 23; Passavant 1862 no. 2; Nijhoff 1933–9: pp. ; Hollstein 1986 no. 1; Armstrong 1990: 105–14; Minkowski 1991: 36, no. 169, pl. 11

FIG. 116
Pieter Bruegel the Elder, *The Tower of Babel*

By using Antwerp as the setting for his painting, Bruegel set out to demonstrate the relevance of the Tower to his contemporary world. The painting is enormously detailed, particularly in its depiction of building technologies and of vast numbers of people on and around the Tower. The use of the Colosseum as an architectural model for the Tower, although not original to Bruegel, was to be particularly influential through his pictures.

AD 1563
Oil on panel
H 114 cm, W 155 cm
Kunsthistorisches Museum, Vienna, GG inv. no. 1026

Bruegel and his legacy

Pieter Bruegel the Elder's extraordinary paintings of the Tower of Babel are probably the best-known images of Babylon today. Painted in the late sixteenth century, Bruegel's images have visibly influenced almost every artistic representation of the tower produced since, and indeed sparked an immediate spate of similar works on the theme by leading Flemish and Dutch artists of the late sixteenth and early seventeenth centuries.[238] Bruegel is known to have produced three paintings on the subject, of which two survive. The religious, political and social meanings of the works have long been debated. While they certainly show the traditional biblical story of the Tower (perhaps with a particular emphasis on the folly of pride and the Confusion of Tongues), some authors have seen more utopian ideas at work. It has also been strongly argued that the two surviving paintings contain veiled attacks on Philip II of Spain and on the power and wealth of the Catholic hierarchy.[239]

Although the central feature is the fantastic, Colosseum-like tower, the landscapes and people

represented in Bruegel's paintings are those of his contemporary world. The same is true of his other treatments of historical and biblical themes.[240] This approach reflects contemporary humanist thought: Erasmus, a strong influence in many of Bruegel's works, criticized attempts merely to imitate the past rather than to transfer the substance of ancient texts thoughtfully and creatively into contemporary context, thus 'making the ancient past live in the present'.[241] Bruegel's settings do not merely incorporate contemporary architecture for want of an alternative; here the Tower of Babel looms very deliberately over sixteenth-century Antwerp.

Except through his works themselves very little is known of the religious and political views of Pieter Bruegel the Elder, and what information there is seems somewhat contradictory.[242] Though their symbolism is rarely straightforward, Bruegel's paintings are more revealing of the artist and his beliefs than the scanty biographical information. As 'peasant' Bruegel his work sometimes seems to celebrate everyday life, but this simplistic view of his work is no longer accepted: closer inspection frequently reveals a deeply pessimistic focus on human folly and weakness. Other works are more explicitly negative; some notable examples among the latter are

FIG. 117
Pieter Bruegel the Elder, *The Tower of Babel*

The political meaning of Bruegel's *Tower of Babel* paintings has been much disputed. The Tower refers to the folly of pride, but may also contain specific attacks on the Catholic hierarchy (a tiny detail on the Tower has been interpreted as a cardinal's procession, for example). It is also possible to discern a more optimistic, utopian element: some allusion to what might be achieved if human, and particularly religious, differences could be overcome.

AD 1564–8
Oil on panel
H 60.5 cm, W 74.5 cm
Museum Boijmans van Beuningen, Rotterdam, inv. 2443

The Triumph of Death, *The Blind Leading the Blind* and *The Land of Cockayne*. To some extent the *Tower of Babel* paintings must be seen as belonging to the same category, although this hardly precludes a second, more utopian meaning: if discord and separation foil the builders, perhaps unity and communication could one day succeed?[243] It is worth noting that those works of Bruegel generally agreed not to have a satirical intent often relate to productive work,[244] and it has been argued that the effort of construction, if not the hubristic project of the Tower itself, was seen by the artist as positive and worthwhile.

Bruegel's paintings were hugely influential, and dozens of major works following their format were produced by leading artists in the Low Countries in the later sixteenth and early seventeenth centuries. Particularly notable among these many images are the works of Lucas van Valckenborch,

Ⓔ FIG. 118
Lucas van Valckenborch, *The Tower of Babel*

Like Bruegel, Lucas van Valckenborch paid meticulous attention to architectural detail. A less obvious inheritance from Bruegel is his mastery of landscape painting. As in Bruegel's Vienna tower there is a suggestion that the great building is partly hewn from an enormous natural rock.

Valckenborch, a Protestant who had to leave his native Mechelen due to religious persecution, was directly affected by Reformation conflicts and, as with Bruegel, the figure of Nimrod in the foreground here may have political significance. Valckenborch's depictions vary (indeed, Nimrod is not always represented at all), but in this case a soldier in distinctively Spanish costume – behind the king in red – supports a possible identification

with the rule of Philip II and more broadly with the Spanish army and Inquisition.

AD 1595
Oil on panel.
H 42.0 cm, W 68.0 cm
Mittelrhein-Museum Koblenz, Germany, MRM M 31
Wied 1990: 31ff., 44, no. 82; Minkowski 1991: no. 199
(attributed to Paul Bril); Gall 1994: 120, no. 4/16; Wegener 1995: 47, pl. 20, 224; Stutenbrock 1997: 74; Seipel 2003: 142, no. 1.1.21; Kramp 2005: 35, no. 10.

E FIG. 119 *above*
Flemish School, *The Tower of Babel*

This vision of the tower was reproduced almost identically in nine different paintings by several artists of the late sixteenth century. Although artists did not aim to re-create a known ancient building, strong conventions developed to govern the Tower of Babel's appearance. This extremely fine version may be the earliest, although this is impossible to establish in the absence of a lost work by Abel Grimmer, known today only through photographs.

The town and landscape are European, in the world-landscape tradition. Most important, however, is the embodiment of the passage of time within the architecture itself: the lower, medieval levels give way to Renaissance classicism. The incomplete summit is likely, therefore, to represent both the biblical confusion of tongues and the cultural and religious conflicts of the artist's contemporary world.

Late 16th century AD. Oil on panel. H 49.5 cm, W 66.5 cm. Pinacoteca Nazionale di Siena, N. 534
Torriti 1978: 258–60, no. 534; 1990: 458, no. 534; Minkowski 1991: 172, no. 202

E FIG. 120 *left*
Dutch School, *Tower of Babel*

This scene makes clear reference to the tower's imminent destruction and shows the city of Babylon itself on fire, introducing the apocalyptic themes of Revelation into the Genesis story. The notion that the tower had been struck by lightning was supported by the observations of visitors to Babylon: not only did the desolation of the area feature in all their accounts, but several also observed that large parts of Birs Nimrud (ancient Borsippa) appeared to be vitrified. It was a natural conclusion that this was caused by lightning that struck the tower.

Late 16th century AD. Oil on canvas. H 62.0 cm, W 56.0 cm
Broelmuseum, Kortrijk, MSK 12
Minkowski 1991: 170, no. 193; Seipel 2003: 136, no. 1.1.17

🄴 FIG. 121

Philips Galle after Maarten van Heemskerck,
Tower of Babel

Although, like his peers, Heemskerck could have had no direct knowledge of Babylonian architecture, his Tower of Babel bears a striking resemblance to an ancient ziggurat. The artist achieved this through close reference to the description of the 'Temple of Zeus Belus' [245] by the ancient Greek historian Herodotus, which in fact described the ziggurat Etemenanki at Babylon and whose account implies (though not unambiguously) a square base. Heemskerck's treatment of Semiramis and Babylon's wonders (Fig. 97) shows his familiarity with this and other classical sources.

AD 1569
Engraving
H 12.3 cm, W 19.7 cm
Paris, Bibliothèque nationale de France, RB 17 Ancien Testament Tome II: M 60623
Minkowski 1991: 68, 164–5; Hollstein 1993-4: no. 240; Martin-Jaquemier 1999: 97; Hollstein 2001: no. 106

En molem ædificant animisque, opibusque parati, Vertice quæ nubes, et vertice tangeret astra.

*Alta cadit Babylon multa constru
cta virum vi, Contutit hæc terras, mortalia pectora sternit*

🄴 FIG. 122

Philips Galle after Maarten van Heemskerck, *Destruction of the Tower of Babel*

This engraving of the tower's sudden destruction shows more clearly that Heemskerck imagined the top levels to be cylindrical. We know today that this was not the case, but archaeologists have consistently found the lost top levels of the ziggurat the most difficult to reconstruct.

AD 1569
Engraving
H 13.8 cm, W 20.0 cm
Paris, Bibliothèque nationale de France, RB 17 Ancien Testament Tome II: M 60624
Minkowski 1991: 688, 164–5; Hollstein 1993-4: no. 241; Martin-Jaquemier 1999: 97; Hollstein 2001: no. 107

who varied his depictions of the Tower across several paintings. Both Bruegel's sons, Jan Brueghel the Elder and Pieter Brueghel the Younger,[246] produced depictions of the Tower, as well as Maarten van Valckenborch, Hendrik van Cleve, Abel Grimmer and others.

Pieter Bruegel's achievement and influence had another interesting effect. At around the same time as Bruegel was producing his Tower of Babel paintings, Maarten van Heemskerck produced a pair of designs showing the destruction of the Tower of Babel at its beginning and its climax. Although they contain many ancient Roman motifs, Heemskerck's pictures show a tower that is not based on the Colosseum. In fact, they bear a surprising resemblance to an actual Mesopotamian ziggurat – an architectural form that was, of course, completely unknown to sixteenth-century Europe. It seems that the artist achieved this uncanny likeness by close reference to the description of Herodotus. Although the idea that the building described by Herodotus somehow related to the tower of Genesis was developed later (see below), Heemskerck's interpretation was all but forgotten amid the profusion of Bruegel-inspired towers of the late six-

Ⓔ FIG. 123 *left*
Athanasius Kircher, *Turris Babel*

In this unique work the scholar Athanasius Kircher attempted to bring together all existing knowledge of the Tower of Babel, from studies of Genesis to drawings recently made at the site of Babylon. Kircher was particularly interested in the confusion of languages, and attempted to discover something of the universal language he believed was spoken before the tower was built.

AD 1679
Engraving by Conraet Decker after Lievin Cruyl in Athanasius Kircher, *Turris Babel* (p. 41)
British Library 213.f. 5
Closed: H 53 cm, W 30 cm
Godwin 1979: 37–8; Minkowski 1991: 40–1; Wegener 1995: 150–5; Seipel 2003: no. 1.1.32

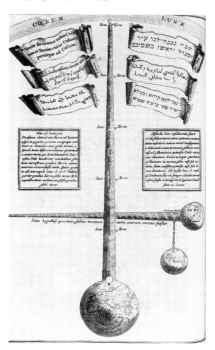

Ⓔ FIG. 124
Conraet Decker after Lievin Cruyl, *Demonstration of the Impossibility of Building a Tower to scale Heaven*

Kircher set out to solve many problems stemming from the different sources for the Tower of Babel and ancient Babylon. Among the most remarkable aspects of the work are his attempts to bring scientific and humanistic analysis to bear on the Genesis Tower of Babel. This image graphically demonstrates the difficulty of building a tower to reach heaven. Kircher calculated that to reach the moon (and thus the first level of heaven) the tower would require 3 million tonnes of material, stand 178,672 miles high, and as a result tip the Earth off balance. For Kircher the problem of scaling heaven, while insurmountable, was to some extent a mechanical one.

AD 1679. Engraving in Athasius Kircher, *Turris Babel* (p. 38)
British Library 213.f. 5. Closed: H 53 cm, W 30 cm
Godwin 1979: 36; Minkowski 1991: 40–1

teenth century. Bruegel, as noted above, had no intention of accurately representing a scene from the past, but his is undoubtedly the image of the Tower of Babel that has survived best in the artistic and popular imagination. The effect of so much copying and referencing of Colosseum-like towers was to reinforce a general idea of what a Tower of Babel 'should' look like. This idea is still with us today, since paintings like these remain more familiar to most people than images of Mesopotamian ziggurats.

Athanasius Kircher and 'Turris Babel'

Religious and artistic interests in the Tower met with antiquarian concerns in Athanasius Kircher's *Turris Babel*. Published in 1679, this unique work attempted to synthesize all existing knowledge of the Tower, or more properly of the two towers. Kircher, a polymath, is sometimes described as the 'last Renaissance man', and his work on the Tower of Babel treats theological, antiquarian and linguistic questions[247] in a single encyclopaedic treatise. Images of the Tower(s) in *Turris Babel* reflect this diversity: they vary considerably, few being compatible with one another. Two images are particularly remarkable. The first shows a curiously literal and rational–empirical approach to the question of building a tower to scale heaven, while the second, based on drawings by an artist accompanying the Italian traveller Pietro della Valle, shows two views of Tell Babil, part of the ruins of Babylon itself. This was the first time Babylon had been depicted through first-hand observation of the site, and though perhaps dull in contrast to the more fantastic images of *Turris Babel*, these images and the site description of della Valle (also reproduced by Kircher) mark the beginning of a new and very different approach to Babylon: one based on close study of the city's physical remains themselves.

The Babylonian Captivity

Babylon, Jerusalem and the Jewish Exile

Jonathan Taylor

Babylon and the Bible are inextricably mixed. Despite the varied media through which the city makes its name felt today, many individuals' first encounter with the name of Babylon will have come from the Old Testament. Of the momentous events that took place in the city, not the least concerned the Judaean exiles taken from Jerusalem by Nebuchadnezzar as part of a conventional military campaign. The repercussions of the Babylonian Captivity in theology, culture and art are still with us, while our knowledge of the historical events has been enhanced by some of the world's most important cuneiform texts.

During campaigns to secure the western borders of his empire, Nebuchadnezzar II deported Jehoiachin, king of Judah, and a large number of prisoners to Babylon in 597 BC. Further problems with the new Judaean king Zedekiah led Nebuchadnezzar to attack Jerusalem again in 587 BC, destroying the Solomonic temple and deporting even larger numbers of people to the imperial capital in Babylon. The Babylonian Captivity, as the subsequent period of exile became known, came to an end in 539 BC with the Persian conquest of Babylon, when the new policies of the Achaemenid king Cyrus II enabled populations deported by the Babylonians to return to their own lands. A large number of Judaeans did return but more stayed, their descendents forming a substantial Jewish community in the land of Iraq almost until the present day.[248]

It was during and immediately after the period of Jewish exile in Babylon that large parts of the Old Testament narrative are likely to have taken on their final forms. The biblical picture of Babylon is informed primarily by the events of this period, with the result that the city encountered in later art and literature is specifically that of Nebuchadnezzar's time.

Assyria: the wolf on the fold

Israel to the north and Judah to the south were always overshadowed by their more powerful neighbours Egypt, Assyria and later Babylonia. Successive conquerors imposed vassallage, extracting relentless tribute to swell their own coffers while sometimes forcibly relocating native populations to prevent recurrent insurrection. Israel had fallen under Assyrian control during the ninth century, and was finally annexed once and for all in 721 BC. Many Israelites were deported to other parts of the Assyrian Empire, where their integration into the general population was such that we lose sight of them as an entity. Israel's territory meanwhile seems to have been settled by deportees from the east. Through such campaigns the much-vaunted cruelty of the Assyrians on the battlefield became a legend in its own right.

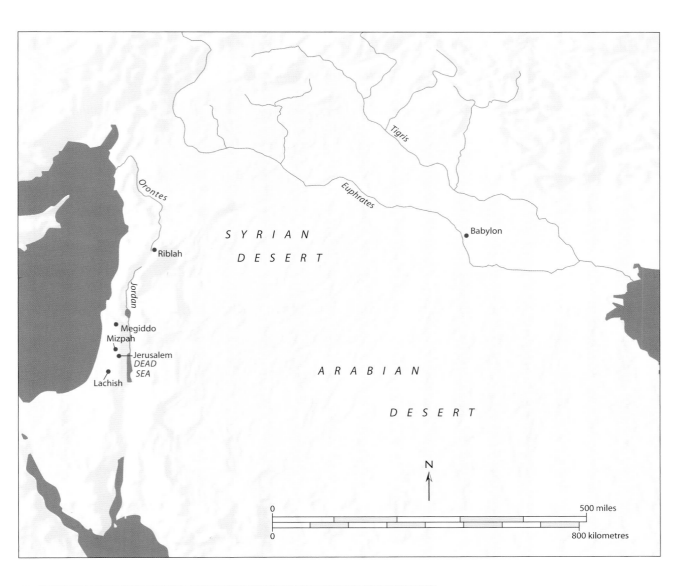

FIG. 125
Map showing Babylon, Jerusalem and other sites significant in the fall of Judah
***c.* 610–581 BC**

FIG. 126
Relief panel from the South-West Palace, Nineveh

This typical scene from the 'palace without rival' of the Assyrian king Sennacherib shows captives from an unidentified city being deported to Assyria. In 701 BC Sennacherib launched a punitive raid on Judah. His capture of the city of Lachish is depicted in a series of relief panels in the palace. Hezekiah, king of Judah, had allied himself with a rebellion and imprisoned Padi, king of Ekron. Sennacherib trapped Hezekiah in Jerusalem, as he describes it, 'like a bird in a cage', forcing him to release Padi and pay tribute to Assyria. Many Judeans were deported at that time. The Babylonian approach to unrest in Judah was a continuation of this Assyrian policy.

About 700–692 BC.
From Nineveh, South-West Palace
Gypsum
H 99.1 cm, W 101.6 cm
British Museum, BM 124947

143

The fall of Jerusalem

The sudden collapse of the Assyrian Empire at the end of the seventh century put Judah and the other Levantine states in a dangerous position. Assyrian domination had at least offered protection and stability, but nothing now would act as a buffer against invasion by new armies. In 610 BC Judah's king, Josiah, took the field in an attempt to stop the Egyptian army from marching to the aid of the last outpost of Assyria, based at the city of Harran. At the Battle of Megiddo Judah's army was soundly beaten and Josiah himself killed. The following year Jehoahaz became king by popular acclaim, but was soon ousted by the Egyptians in favour of his half-brother Jehoiakim. In 605 BC the Egyptian army was defeated by Nebuchadnezzar.

After three years as Babylon's vassal Judah again attempted to throw off imperial control. Fierce clashes between Egypt and Babylon left both weakened, but Jehoiakim had miscalculated. Nebuchadnezzar moved against Judah and in 597 BC captured the capital, Jerusalem. The famous *Nebuchadnezzar Chronicle*[249] (Fig. 127) describes these fateful events.

The king captured by Nebuchadnezzar was not Jehoiakim, who had died shortly before, but his son Jehoiachin. To put an end to the troubles Nebuchadnezzar deported Jehoiachin, his family and the upper stratum of the Judaean population to Babylon,[250] although Judah itself was largely spared. Thus began the Babylonian Captivity.

As part of his foreign policy Nebuchadnezzar installed Zedekiah as the new king in Jerusalem. In 594 BC the latter visited Babylon, manifesting allegiance, but it was not long before he too broke his oath of loyalty, fomenting a revolt among Babylon's Levantine subject states. Information about these events comes not from the Babylonians, whose histories here fragment, but from the Old Testament, supplemented by Josephus. In 587/6 BC the Babylonian king crushed this latest rebellion, this time sacking Jerusalem and looting the temple.[251] A second round of deportations took place. According to the Bible Zedekiah himself escaped through the royal gardens as the city fell, but was captured and taken to Nebuchadnezzar's camp at Riblah: 'where sentence was pronounced on him. They killed the sons of Zedekiah before his eyes. Then they put out his eyes, bound him with bronze shackles and took him to Babylon.'[252]

Through these events the Israelite line of kings reckoned to stretch back to King David came to an end, and the Babylonians installed a puppet king, Gedaliah. With Jerusalem in ruins Gedaliah set up camp in the town of Mizpah, supervised by a resident Babylonian garrison.[253] He and the Babylonians were later murdered in a coup by a rebel general, Ishmael, who claimed royal descent for himself. The survivors of Gedaliah's court (including the prophet Jeremiah) were rescued by a loyal general, Johanan, who – fearing Babylonian vengeance – led them to Egypt. Nebuchadnezzar's reactions are unknown, although it is unlikely that this massacre would have gone unpunished. Jeremiah warned that the flight to Egypt was against God's will and would be punished by sword and famine, with captivity in Babylon for the survivors. The same prophet records further deportations in 582/1 BC, but thereafter the biblical sources fall largely silent. Josephus records that Judah was not resettled with deportees from elsewhere in the Babylonian realm but the land cannot have been literally deserted, as one might assume from some Old Testament accounts.[254]

 FIG. 127
Nebuchadnezzar captures Jerusalem

This historical chronicle covers the period of twelve years from the twenty-first year of Nabopolassar (Nebuchadnezzar's accession year) through to Nebuchadnezzar's eleventh regnal year. It includes Nebuchadnezzar's first capture of Jerusalem in 597 BC.

The seventh year: in the month Kislev the Babylonian king
mustered his army and marched to Hattu.
He encamped against the city of Judah [Jerusalem] and on the second day
of the month Adar he captured the city and seized its king [Jehoiachin].
He appointed a king of his own choice in the city, and,
taking vast tribute, he brought it into Babylon.

Reign of Nebuchadnezzar (605–562 BC)
From Babylon
Clay
H 8.25 cm, W 6.12 cm
British Museum, BM 21946
Wiseman 1956: 66–75, pls 5, 14–16; Grayson 1975: 99–102; Glassner 1993: 198–200

 FIG. 128
An administrative text naming Nabu-šarrussu-ukin

Jeremiah had long prophesied Babylonian victory over Judah, seeing this as a punishment for the people's failure to observe divine law. A group of high officials in Judah threw him into a cistern, intending him to sink slowly to his death beneath the mud. But King Zedekiah gave permission for Jeremiah to be rescued, and had him imprisoned instead near the palace. The victorious Babylonians freed Jeremiah, clearly approving of his efforts to end resistance to their advance. The Book of Jeremiah records that after the fall of the city Babylonian officials set themselves up at the Middle Gate of Jerusalem. The men in question were Nergal-sharezer the *samgar*, Nebu-sarsekim the *rab saris* and Nergal-sharezer the *rab mug*.

The Babylonian identities of two of these men can now be independently verified. The first is *Nergal-šarra-uṣur*, governor of *Bît-Sin-magir* and future king of Babylon, as found in a list of Nebuchadnezzar's court personnel. The second can be recognized as Nabû-šarrūssu-ukin, the *rab sa rêšu* ('chief eunuch'), who is recorded several years earlier on this tablet as having made a gold payment to the main temple in Babylon.

595 BC
Purchased from E. Géjou, 1920
Clay
H 3.5 cm, W 5.4 cm
British Museum, BM 114789
Jursa 2008

Babylonian chronology and Nebuchadnezzar's destruction of Jerusalem

C.B.F. Walker

Tradition had it that the Babylonian Captivity lasted seventy years. In fact the dates concerned are from 597 to 539 BC – fifty-eight calendar years. The precise date of Nebuchadnezzar's capture of Jerusalem can be read off the chronological tables produced by R. A. Parker and W. H. Dubberstein,[255] where the first day of Addar (Adar) for Nebuchadnezzar's seventh year is given as 15 March 597 BC. This precise date (as all of their calendrical tables) depends on modern computer calculation of the day on which the new moon would be expected to have been visible at Babylon, and the authors point out:[256]

it is possible that a certain number of dates in our table may be wrong by one day ... It should be noted that there is an additional element of uncertainty for biblical dates given in the Babylonian calendar, since the new moon was visible at Jerusalem thirty-seven minutes before it was visible at Babylon and therefore upon occasion the new month could begin a day earlier at Jerusalem.

Babylonian days begin at sunset, so if the 1st of Addar is listed as 15 March this actually means 15/16 March, and the 2nd of Addar will be 16/17 March 597 BC.

The date of Nebuchadnezzar's second capture of Jerusalem is not recorded in currently available Babylonian records, so its date has to be calculated on the basis of the biblical record (in the eleventh year of Zedekiah, so July 587 BC).

The relative chronology of the kings of the Neo-Babylonian and Achaemenid Persian dynasties has long been known from Claudius Ptolemy's *Canon Basileon*.[257] Since the list was presumably compiled for the purpose of controlling astronomical records, short reigns of less than a year, such as that of Labaši-Marduk and the various rebels against Darius and Xerxes, are ignored. The number of regnal years

assigned to each king in the canon is confirmed in the case of all kings from Nabopolassar down to Darius II from contemporary economic documents. Thus Ptolemy credits Nebuchadnezzar with forty-three years and we have many economic documents dated in each of those years; the same applies to his successors. The relevant figures in regnal years are:

Nabu-kudurri-uṣur (Nebuchadnezzar) II 43 years (604–562 BC)
Amel-Marduk (Evil-Merodach) 2 years (561–560 BC)
Nergal-šar-uṣur (Neriglissar) 4 years (559–556 BC)
Nabu-na'id (Nabonidus) 17 years (555–539 BC)
Cyrus 9 years (538–530 BC)[258]

Modern Assyriologists follow the Babylonian system in which the regnal year begins sometime around the spring equinox, but tend to ignore the overlap to the following year. So Cyrus having captured Babylon in October 539 BC, his first full regnal year would have run from March 538 to March 537, but Assyriologists tend to call it just 538 BC. The precise date of the return of the Jews from exile in Babylonia will depend on whether one assumes the first chapter of the biblical Book of Ezra uses the Babylonian or the Jewish calendar. In any case Babylonian chronology certainly does not support the idea of a seventy-year exile of the Jews in Babylonia if that is to be counted from the second capture of Jerusalem to the first year of Cyrus.

Although precise dates in Babylonian chronology can be derived from a combination of Ptolemy's *Canon* and contemporary economic documents, there is a further source of dates in the Babylonian astronomical texts. From about 747 BC (the beginning of the reign of the Babylonian king Nabu-naṣir (Nabonassar) Babylonian astronomers were keeping regular records of astronomical observations. These observations survive in the

(incomplete) series of what are now called 'astronomical diaries' and in other astronomical texts probably derived from these diaries. There also survive fragments of tables for such events as eclipses of moon, the eighteen-year cycles of which became well understood by the Babylonians. Thus there are in the British Museum fragments of a table of successive lunar eclipse possibilities arranged in eighteen-year cycles in twenty-four columns, starting apparently in 747 BC, which if complete would have given 18 x 24 = 432 years of eclipse data from 747 to 315 BC. It seems probable that such tables of Babylonian data were available to Ptolemy (whose *Almagest* refers to a few dated Babylonian lunar eclipse observations), and this may explain how it is that the chronology embodied in his *Canon Basileon* has survived the test of 150 years of excavation of contemporary Babylonian sources.

It should be pointed out that the chronology of the Achaemenid kings of Persia is also tied in to a well-established Greek chronology by numerous events recorded by Greek historians.

In general for Assyriologists and others engaged in studying the available source material for the Neo-Babylonian and Achaemenid periods, the chronology is secure and needs no further discussion. But there are two groups who may take a different view. First, the Jewish Talmud contains some chronological remarks which have been understood to imply a significantly shorter chronology (by several decades) for the Achaemenid dynasty; but in general Talmudic scholars have been ready to accept this as a mistake. Secondly, the Jehovah's Witnesses, apparently on doctrinal grounds, seek to establish a date for the second fall of Jerusalem some ten years later than would be accepted by mainstream historians.[259]

FIG. 129
Letter from Lachish

A group of letters written on potsherds at this time was found near the main gate of the Judean outpost of Lachish. They offer a poignant record of the city's last days. In one of these letters a military officer writes to his commander, despite the imminent defeat:

To my lord Ya'osh. May Yahweh cause my lord to hear the news of peace, even now, even now.

586 BC. Baked clay ostracon. H 9.0 cm, W 9.90 cm, Th. 0.4 cm. From Tell ed-Duweir (ancient Lachish), Israel
British Museum, BM 125702

 FIG. 130 *left*

Rations for Jehoiachin, exiled Judaean ruler in Babylon

Tablets excavated at Babylon record rations from Nebuchadnezzar's palace for the support of workers, such as carpenters or boatmen, including individuals from across the Babylonian empire. This example includes the name of the Judaean king Jehoiachin as well as other Judean deportees resident in Babylon. It dates to the thirteenth year of Nebuchadnezzar (592/1 BC):

30 litres (of oil) for Ja'ukin, king of Ja[hudu]
2½ litres for the 5 [son]s of the king of Jahudu
4 litres for the 8 Jahudeans, ½ litre for each

592/1 BC. From Babylon
Clay. H 20 cm, W 13 cm
Staatliche Museen zu Berlin, Vorderasiatisches Museum,
VAT 16283
Weidner 1939: Texts B and C; Borger 1975: 92; Pedersén
2005a; Pedersén 2005b: nos 1.97, 1.99, pl. 60

 FIG. 131 *below*

The Chronicle of Jerachmeel

The Book of Jeremiah tells us that during Jehoiachin's thirty-seventh year Amel-Marduk became king of Babylon and gave the exiled Judaean ruler his freedom. The medieval Hebrew 'Chronicle of Jerachmeel', written down almost eighteen centuries after the event, suggests a possible explanation for this compassion: it describes Jehoiachin and Amel-Marduk being in prison together. It is the only source to do so, but 'The Lament of Nabu-šuma-ukin' (Fig. 132 below), suggests that this much later European chronicle records a genuine historical event. (Prince Nabu-šuma-ukin later took the throne name Amel-Marduk.)

12th century AD
Ink on parchment
H 22.7 cm, W 34 cm (open)
Bodleian Library, University of Oxford, MS Heb d.11
Gaster 1899; Finkel 1999

 FIG. 132 *left*

'The Lament of Nabu-šuma-ukin'

At the break of day,
During siesta time, while sleeping,
In the evening, at dusk,
Throughout the night, during the dawn watch,
The wretched, weary person weeps;
The wretched, unseeing person sheds tears.
He sheds tears because of the tricks of mankind;
He weeps in his prison because his situation is so
grievous.
He sheds tears over matters not to be spoken, the
evil done him …

This poetic and tortured appeal to Marduk was composed by Nabu-šuma-ukin, son of Nebuchadnezzar, who was languishing in prison in Babylon. This Nabu-šuma-ukin is thought to be the crown prince, and thus Nebuchadnezzar's successor, who later took the throne name of Amel-Marduk (the biblical Evil-Merodach). The poem is remarkable for its obsessive and modern-sounding expressions.

Reign of Nebuchadnezzar (605–562 BC)
From Babylon
Clay
H 17.1 cm, W 9.2 cm
British Museum, BM 40474
Finkel 1999

The Jews in Babylon and the return to Jerusalem

Those deported to Babylon included many experts or craftsmen whose skills were prized in their new homeland.[260] Certain well-placed deportees were marked out for patronage and promotion, as is expressly described in the Book of Daniel, when Daniel and his fellow-exiles were inducted into the mysteries of cuneiform reading and writing as part of the standard court programme of cultural indoctrination. They were selected as:[261]

> young men without any physical defect, handsome, showing aptitude for every kind of learning, well informed, quick to understand, and qualified to serve in the king's palace. He was to teach them the language and literature of the Babylonians. The king assigned them a daily amount of food and wine from the king's table. They were to be trained for three years, and after that they were to enter the king's service.

This process had the effect of making the inherited lore of the Babylonians – theological and literary as well as medical and divinatory – directly available to these favoured exiles. There can be no doubt that it is through this conduit that diverse Babylonian influences could and did make themselves felt, with – in some cases – lasting consequences. Many priests, for example, were among the exiles, and they must have been directly influenced by their time in Babylon, especially in view of the prevailing tendency to monotheistic thinking that was in the air throughout the exilic period. The text of the Bible contains certain elements that are commonly accepted as having been influenced by Babylonian culture, as we have already seen with the Tower of Babel narrative. The most commonly cited example is the Flood story: the account of Genesis 6–8 is startlingly close to the text of the Babylonian Epic of Gilgamesh, still certainly alive in Babylon's scribal schools at this time.

Not all the Jewish families in Babylon did, in fact, return to their ancestral homeland. Cyrus' conquest of Babylon in 539 BC led him to institute a number of internal reforms, as touched on in the famous cylinder that bears his name (Fig. 161). The restitution of local cults followed, such as that of Yahweh in Jerusalem. Sheshbazzar (possibly one of Jehoiachin's sons) would journey to Judah and make preparations for the Second Temple. But by no means all Jews accompanied him; a great many remained in Babylonia where, by this time, their families had been living for three generations, although links were always maintained between the two communities and individuals went to and fro. The extent to which the communities that remained in Babylonia continued to influence Jewish culture as a whole is strongly manifested in the Babylonian Talmud, a vast compilation in Aramaic incorporating disparate traditions from the cuneiform environment, especially in the fields of magic, medicine, dream interpretation and religious textual commentary. Much of this content had its roots in older Babylonian scholarship, and in this way too Nebuchadnezzar's profound influence on the history and culture of Judaism was to continue long after his own empire had vanished.

Ⓔ FIG. 133

Bukhtnassar (Nebuchadnezzar) destroying Jerusalem

This unusual miniature in a fourteenth-century Arabic manuscript depicts Nebuchadnezzar destroying the city of Jerusalem.[262] The Dome of the Rock can easily be recognized, although this was a much later construction; the association followed the idea that the rock itself had formed part of the Solomonic temple.

The author, renowned Persian scholar and polymath al-Biruni (AD 973–1048), was conscious of the symbolic importance of Nebuchadnezzar's conquest and the captivity in Jewish culture. When discussing the sack of Jerusalem by Titus in the first century AD he observed, 'it seems that the people of Jerusalem call everyone who has destroyed their city Nebuchadnezzar'.

AD 1307 / 707 AH
Miniature in manuscript copy of Abu-Raihan Muhammad ibn `Ahmad al-Biruni, *'al-Athar al-Baqiya' (Chronology of Ancient Nations)*
University of Edinburgh Library, MS 161, f. 134b
Soucek 1975: 145–7

The Babylonian Captivity in art and culture

Michael Seymour

The primacy of the Bible in Western culture has left us with a specific view of the Babylonian Captivity, but one that archaeology and Assyriology are in a unique position to complement.[263] We now know that from a Babylonian perspective the significance of the kingdom of Judah was merely that of a rebellious border state in an area contested with rival Egypt. On the other hand, the Old Testament narratives themselves have had an enormous impact over the subsequent two and a half thousand years of cultural history. Whatever the immediate significance of Nebuchadnezzar's deportations from Jerusalem in the sixth century BC, therefore, their influence in defining the Babylonians' later reputation and our understanding of cultural displacement has been overwhelming.

The Old Testament passages describe a specific historical event, and in very powerful terms. The best known of all is Psalm 137: [264]

> By the rivers of Babylon we sat and wept when we remembered Zion.
> There on the poplars we hung our harps,
> For there our captors asked us for songs, our tormentors demanded songs of joy;
>   they said, 'Sing us one of the songs of Zion!'
> How can we sing the songs of the Lord while in a foreign land?

As well as such emotive passages, the biblical books of 2 Kings, 2 Chronicles, Jeremiah, Isaiah, Daniel and others contain much detailed historical information about the period. In recent times, as the Babylonian sources themselves have become available to scholars, some remarkable links have been drawn between the two literatures, including the identification of the same events and even named individuals in the two sets of sources (see Figs. 128, 130).

The Old Testament sources certainly give a particular history of a specific experience of exile in the sixth century BC. That experience, however, was transferred to and reworked in other contexts in early Christianity. The Old Testament rhetoric associated with the exile remains very powerful politically. In the twentieth century it has been adopted by many causes, most famously the Zionist and Rastafarian movements. In the latter particularly, 'Zion' and 'Babylon' are not physical places or are only loosely attached to physical geography.

The exile in art

Artistic representations of the Jewish Exile have most commonly taken their inspiration from Psalm 137, whose text they often represent quite literally. Eugène Delacroix, the leading history painter of his age, epitomizes this approach in his 1843–5 pendentive for the library of the Palais Bourbon (which at that time had recently become the Assemblée Nationale), Paris. The inclusion of the scene is significant in itself: the event merited a place in the very grandest of nineteenth-century conceptions of human history and culture. Another celebrated depiction of the subject is that of Eduard Bendemann. Bendemann was one of a group of Düsseldorf-based history painters who challenged Delacroix's practice of focusing always on the moment of crisis itself, preferring instead to portray the moment of tension immediately before or after an event.[265] The Babylonian Captivity is a subject particularly suited to such treatment, since it is the period of exile itself on which the biblical texts and later culture have focused. That Delacroix represents the same

E FIG. 134 *above*

Eugène Delacroix, *Study for The Babylonian Captivity*

The design is for part of Delacroix's complex decorative scheme for the Bibliothèque du Palais-Bourbon.[266] *The Babylonian Captivity* was one of four images representing theology in a scheme for the southern apse that also includes science, history, legislation and poetry. Earlier in his career Delacroix had produced one of the most famous representations of ancient Assyria in art, *The Death of Sardanapalus* (1827).

Before AD 1845
Watercolour, gouache and pencil on brown paper
H 24.9 cm, W 31.3 cm
Paris, Musée du Louvre, département des Arts Graphiques, RF 4774
Sérrulaz 1984: no. 298; Johnson 1989: vol. 5, 54; Louvre 1997: no. 443

FIG. 135 *left*

Eugène Delacroix, *Theology*

The completed pendentive for *The Babylonian Captivity* forms part of the cupola representing theology. The other subjects depicted within the theme of theology are *Adam and Eve after the Fall*, *The Death of St John the Baptist* and *The Tribute Money*.

AD 1843–5
Ceiling decoration
Each composition H 291 cm, W 221 cm
Bibliothèque du Palais Bourbon, Assemblée Nationale de France, Paris

FIG. 136
Eduard Julius Friedrich Bendemann,
Die trauernden Juden in Exil

Bendemann's famous composition presents a variety of personal responses to the experience of exile. The artist followed the example of the earlier Nazarene painters in Germany by concentrating on what were seen to be the weightiest and most emotionally complex of biblical subjects. Exhibited to critical acclaim, this image established Bendemann's reputation as a great history painter and has achieved a lasting iconic status.

AD 1831–2
Oil on panel
H 183 cm, W 280 cm
Walraf-Richartz-Museum, Cologne, WRM 1939

FIG. 137 *right*
Jean Fouquet, *The Siege of Jerusalem by Nebuchadnezzar*

From a Babylonian perspective Jerusalem was of only limited importance, yet it was Nebuchadnezzar's treatment of this city that would subsequently define both him and Babylon itself.

About AD 1470–6
Manuscript illumination in Josephus, *Jewish Antiquities*
Paris, Bibliothèque nationale de France, Ms Fr 247 fol. 213

Ⓔ FIG. 138 *left*
Dalziel Brothers after Edward John Poynter, *By the Rivers of Babylon*

Produced for *Dalziel's Bible Gallery*, this vision of the Babylonian Captivity takes advantage of recent discoveries in Assyria as sources for costume and architecture. Poynter was noted for his efforts to achieve archaeological accuracy in his work, most famously drawing on ancient Egyptian architecture for *Israel in Egypt* (1867). The more conventional depiction of the exiles themselves, typical of a Victorian neo-classical taste for drapery and for beautiful female figures, may be compared with

the depiction of the same subject by Evelyn De Morgan (Fig. 139), who had studied under Poynter at the Slade School of Art.

AD 1865
Wood engraving heightened with Chinese white, produced for *Dalziel's Bible Gallery*, published 1881
H 22.4 cm, W 18.1 cm
British Museum, 1913, 0415.201.669
McCall and Tubb 2003: 12, no. 17; Esposito 2006: 284, fig. 34

'moment' highlights that in this case the moment of crisis and that of emotional response are one and the same. Nebuchadnezzar's capture of Jerusalem, though frequently represented in medieval manuscripts, was not a popular theme in later ages, for the principal reason that the crucial 'event' was that of exile, not military defeat. Alongside the Egyptian exile of Exodus, the Babylonian Captivity came to stand in Judeo-Christian culture for the experience of worldly constraints and oppression.

The sense of loss and longing for salvation so powerfully evoked by Psalm 137 was the focus for Victorian British artists' representations of the Captivity, and depictions of the subject by Sir Edward John Poynter and Evelyn De Morgan are good examples of this interest. Poynter was a leading neo-classical artist, but also known for his interest in depicting the ancient past accurately. In his *By the Rivers of Babylon* he employs the iconography of recently discovered Assyrian antiquities, particularly noticeable in the costumes of the Babylonians. These ancient Mesopotamian motifs are not drawn upon by Evelyn De Morgan, although a more contemporary Middle Eastern setting may be intended. Her work frequently concentrated on forms of mental or spiritual constraint or imprisonment, and her treatment of the Babylonian Captivity certainly fits within this category. The concentration on female figures is also a constant in De Morgan's painting. Politically she was a prominent campaigner for women's democratic rights, but the kind of imprisonment on which her art focuses is principally spiritual.

E FIG. 139
Evelyn De Morgan, *By the Waters of Babylon*

De Morgan's painting is particularly striking because it brings the biblical story together with the artist's own views on constraint of the spirit.

AD 1882–3
Oil on canvas
H 88.9 cm, W 167 cm
De Morgan Centre for the Study of 19th Century Art and Society, London
Smith 2002: 81–2

The 'Babel–Bibel' crisis

One very important aspect of Babylon's legacy has been the impact of Babylonian culture upon the Old Testament. Cuneiform literature contains many texts with links to biblical passages. While the 1870s discovery of the Mesopotamian story of the Flood was largely celebrated in Victorian Britain, however, the public reaction to the news elsewhere was not always positive.

With the German excavations at Babylon achieving spectacular results, Friedrich Delitzsch, professor of Assyriology in Berlin, gave a series of high-profile lectures entitled 'Babel und Bibel' to an audience of scholars, industrialists and others backing the Deutsche Orient-Gesellschaft. Kaiser Wilhelm, who had a keen interest in the ancient history of the Near East, attended the first lecture on 13 January 1902. Delitzsch spoke not about the excavations at Babylon, but about the discovery over the previous fifty years of many cuneiform texts with strong links to the Old Testament. His lectures contained very little that was new for specialists but much that came as a shock to a wider public, combined with a fierce insistence on the primacy of Babylonian literature as the direct source for many biblical passages. His lectures were seen as blasphemous and attacked in the press; while many of the links Delitzsch discussed were already well known, at least to scholars, his insistence that the moral and ethical precepts of the Old Testament were inferior to those of Mesopotamian religion went too far for German media and public alike.[267] Just as importantly Delitzsch's strident if not confrontational tone is evident in the published versions of the *'Babel–Bibel'* lectures.[268]

Towards the end of his life Delitzsch's work took on a strongly anti-Semitic character, and he joined some radical German pastors in declaring that the Old Testament was not revealed wisdom, that Jesus was not himself a Jew, and that Germany should establish a new German Christianity rooted only in the New Testament. His work on the subject – his final book before his death in 1927 – was called *Die Grosse Täuschung*.[269] The 'great deception' to which the title referred was the Hebrew Bible.

Daniel

Daniel the seer

Irving Finkel and Michael Seymour

The Book of Daniel, largely written in Aramaic, is thought in modern scholarship to have taken its finished form during the reign of Antiochus Epiphanes (168–164 BC), although it consists of two primary sections. The first of these describes with some conviction the world of Nebuchadnezzar's court, especially with regard to dream interpretation, despite a parallel emphasis on miracles and wonders. As has been shown above, Babylon was a cultural environment in which dream omens, solicited and unsolicited, were taken very seriously. Daniel found himself competing with the professionals who were answerable to the king in crucial cases of uncertainty.

The later chapters are concerned with apocalyptic visions in which the rise and fall of empires, including those of Cyrus and Alexander, are prophesied by Daniel in graphic terms:[270]

> Three more kings will appear in Persia, and then a fourth, who will be far richer than all the others. When he has gained power by his wealth, he will stir up everyone against the kingdom of Greece. Then a mighty king will appear, who will rule with great power and do as he pleases. After he has appeared, the empire will be broken up and parcelled out towards the four winds of heaven. It will not go to his descendants, nor will it have the power he exercised, because his empire will be uprooted and given to others.

Such passages contain more than an echo of certain Babylonian writings of similar preoccupation, as in the famous cuneiform *Dynastic Prophecy*:[271]

> A rebel prince will arise … the dynasty of Harran … for 17 years he will exercise kingship and will prevail; over the land. The festival of Esagil(?) … the wall in Babylon … he will plot evil against Babylonia. A king of Elam will rise up, the sceptre … he will remove from his throne … he will seize the throne.

The 'rebel prince' and 'king of Elam' here are Nabonidus and Cyrus respectively, and the prophecy as a whole deals with kings from Nabopolassar to Alexander, who is also the 'mighty king' of the prophecy of Daniel.

The Book of Daniel as a whole covers the prophet's deeds in the successive courts of Nebuchadnezzar, Belshazzar and 'Darius the Mede'.[272] To all these kings Daniel proves his worth as a prophet and wise man. Whether Daniel himself will ever be shown to be a historical figure in Nebuchadnezzar's court is unforeseeable; it is quite possible that he was, but there is also a case for a pre-exilic tradition of a wise man named Daniel, to whom many stories attached.[273]

🅔 FIG. 140
A Babylonian manual for soliciting dreams

This manual describes the procedures a professional would perform in order to allow a private individual to obtain a prophetic dream. The first two sections outline the ritual and quote the titles of the necessary incantations, which are then written out in full on the rest of the tablet.

[When you perform the ritual for a dream oracle]

[On a propitious day …], you set up a censer on its left-hand side. [You put … (and)] mountain buṣinnu *in it (as a wick); you light the lamp; [you set up] the censer […]; [you recite] the incantation 'Mamu, god of dreams' three times [before the st]ars(?). You crush(?) magnetite and add it to oil; you recite the incantation 'Enmesharra' and the incantation '…' three times over it and you anoint your face. [You …]* atāišu *plant, myrrh, juniper balsam (and) tamarisk seeds […]; he should place coals on the censer [(and) set it up] in front of your bed. [You recite] the incantation ['…]s' (and) 'Oh wind, be present! Oh wind, be present!' three times each over the […] aro[matics]. [You lie down(?) and] recite the incantation 'You roam about, Shedu and Lamassu' three times (and) [you will see the oracle.]*

[Its ritual: … …, you light] the 'star'(?) torch. You crush anamīru *plant (and) magnetite (and) throw (them) into oil.] You recite the incantation 'Enmesharra' three times over it, and you anoint your face as if [at night(?)] [you sprinkle] … aromatics. You lie down and [you will see] an oracle.*

The ritual takes place on the roof during daylight hours. The atmospheric effects of the lamp and the brazier are enhanced by application of the plant *anamīru*, crushed in oil, to the client's face. The client then lies down, and experiences a dream oracle, which they will know to be reliable. The choice of

this unidentified plant involves a pun, in which the Akkadian word *anamīru* is understood as two separate words, *ana āmiru*, 'for the seer'. Other contemporary manuscripts reveal that the order of these incantations at Babylon, and the individual lines, were not rigidly established, as is usually the case with Mesopotamian magical sources. The god of dreams is then addressed:

*Mamud, god of dreams, god of dreams, messenger of the great gods,
He who delivers their cry, are you, he who carries their words, are you. Do you grant me a vision!
Let me see a dream of good import! Let the dream I am about to see [bode well!]
Let the dream I am about to see be reliable! Let the dream I am about to see be rendered of good import! May Mamud, god of dreams, be steadfast at my head! Spell.*

In another tablet the dream messenger ascends by means of a miniature ladder that has to be prepared in advance. The compiler of this tablet also included an ancient one-line spell in Sumerian: *zi hare zi hara zi Ninurta hara*. This spell is also found in unrelated magical compositions and on cylinder seals and amulets, and was valued for its protective power against evil forces. It was no doubt included within the dream manual as a safety precaution in case the client's experience or vision became too alarming.

About 4th century BC.
Clay
H 11.2 cm, W 88.9 cm, Th. 2.4 cm
From Babylon
British Museum, BM 45637
Previously unpublished

Cultural reception and art

Michael Seymour

One episode from Daniel – Shadrach, Meschach and Abednego in the Fiery Furnace – is depicted, remarkably enough, in one of the earliest surviving Christian paintings: a third-century AD fresco in the catacombs of Rome (Fig. 10). In this story Nebuchadnezzar condemned three Hebrews to death by fire for refusing to worship an idol, only to see them unharmed by the flames and a fourth, apparently divine, figure appearing in the furnace. The Fiery Furnace and Nebuchadnezzar's prophetic dreams were both regularly depicted in medieval manuscript illustration.

Daniel is important not only for his acts as a prophet and diviner but also for his exemplary life, during which he responds with grace and forbearance to the caprice of kings and jealousy of his fellow courtiers. Through the Book of Daniel we are also presented with an unusual version of Nebuchadnezzar – not simply as a tyrant and oppressor, but as a king who comes to respect the wisdom of Daniel and the power of his God. In other stories, such as the Lions' Den, Daniel continues in his role under the Persian kings of Babylon.

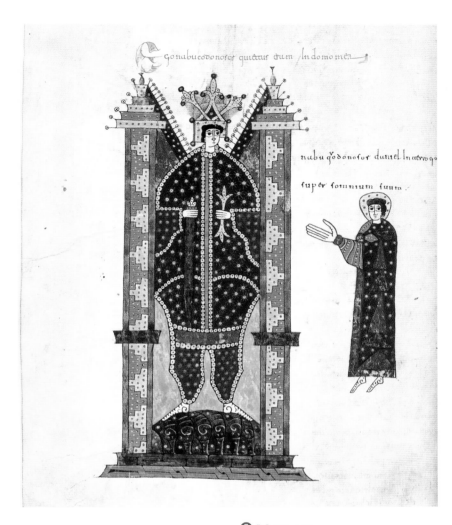

Ⓔ FIG. 141 *above*
Daniel and Nebuchadnezzar

Writing in the late eighth century, Beatus of Liébana synthesized existing works to produce his influential *Commentary on the Apocalypse*. This copy takes its name from the monastery of Santo Domingo de Silos, Cantabria, two of whose monks copied the text of Beatus into the manuscript. A later prior, Petrus, produced the vivid miniatures showing scenes from the books of Daniel and Revelation. Colophons added to the manuscript confirm that its production took place over several decades. The bold and distinctive style of illustrations is generally thought to reflect North African influence in Spanish manuscript art.

Manuscript completed early 12th century AD
Manuscript illumination in the *Silos Apocalypse*
H 38.0 cm, W 25.0 cm
British Library Add. MS 11695, f. 232v
Williams 1994–2002: vol. 4, MS no. 16, pp. 31–40, fig. 333

Ⓔ FIG. 142 *left*
Daniel in the Lions' Den

Here, the king who first punishes Daniel and repents overnight must be Darius.

See Fig. 141: ff. 238v–239
Williams 1994–2002: vol. 4, MS no. 16, pp. 31–40, figs 335a–b

fierra cul deorum tradidi omni poteftaqm
noscerecur qsqd in teale loseph te tu puo
fuctu onem teadeipeu fuceru leguni te
In mardocesu a puo u fucretu uali suatoqc
gentat hauct in te ea pa uni teapere, sin ae
aet te la uat et so la cia ut de ci as hominem
genuisse te ipagotum tse prinapem
ut cal deoqc; Daniel aum por cau la
bia et fie te te consecta cui ta cu su po peri
prouinqe e babi lonis reddit uc mi sac
te ru bdi na co; Ho nobli bis ei au st teoqc
cu igis dnim depreca cau s et te sec uni
peri cle u ca cui fuctu na len si fu ci e st ct
ludica prou ni eqa cum Ipse au in
uc te quis lu caere non fe ce di a;

EXPLICET VISIO
SECVNDA

INCIPIT VISIO
TERTIA

Nabu q do no sot rex fecu sta cua su
au su m alci cu di ne m cubi couc u
sex pa cu e quin cu lu ci cu di ne m
cubi couc sex;

Daniel is a skilled interpreter of dreams (a profession well attested in Babylonian texts), and helps Nebuchadnezzar to understand several of his visions. The king's experiences and dreams have provided a rich source of inspiration for artists. One such subject is that of Nebuchadnezzar's madness, famously depicted by William Blake, another the statue with 'feet of clay' symbolizing the succession of empires that would follow the Neo-Babylonian, a vision which archaeological discoveries enabled George Rochegrosse to represent through ancient Near Eastern imagery. Daniel is also the interpreter of the Writing on the Wall foretelling the doom of Belshazzar (see p. 170).

Perhaps the best-known Daniel story is that of the Lions' Den, in which Babylonian courtiers jealous of Daniel force the Persian king Darius to throw him to the lions. After a night Darius, regretting his action, opens their den to find Daniel unharmed. He has been protected by God because of his piety and innocence. Recognizing this, Darius issues a proclamation: [274]

> Then King Darius wrote to all the peoples, nations and men of every language
>   throughout the land:
> 'May you prosper greatly!
> 'I issue a decree that in every part of my kingdom people must fear and reverence
>   the God of Daniel.
> 'For he is the living God and he endures forever;
>   his kingdom will not be destroyed, his dominion will never end.
> 'He rescues and he saves; he performs signs and wonders
>   in the heavens and on the earth. He has rescued Daniel
>   from the power of the lions.'

This is one of several instances in the Book of Daniel of Babylonian and Persian kings acknowledging the power of Daniel's God. Daniel in the Lions' Den has been portrayed by many artists, and not always as a calm and dignified prophet (see Fig. 146). In the nineteenth century Briton Rivière and Georges Rochegrosse were both able to draw on ancient Mesopotamian (though Assyrian) imagery for their depictions of the subject. Rivière looked to the great archaeological discoveries of the mid-nineteenth century to give his work an authentic ancient Near Eastern setting. The crucial point here, however, and one that is relevant to all depictions of the ancient past, is that subject matter and historical detail need not be drawn from the same source. New discoveries in Mesopotamia had changed the visual setting for the depiction of stories from Daniel and for the Babylonian Captivity, but their narratives and meaning were still drawn from the Old Testament alone. In these fundamental respects Rivière's painting of Daniel in the Lions' Den is no more or less historically accurate than that of Rubens, or even of the *Silos Apocalypse* miniature of the same subject produced by the monk Petrus more than seven hundred years before.

E FIG. 144
George Rochegrosse, *Le rêve de Nabuchodonosor*

In the Book of Daniel Nebuchadnezzar demands of his wise men not only that they interpret his dream but that they tell him what the dream itself was. Only Daniel, aided by prayer, succeeds. The dream is of a statue with a head of gold, a torso and arms of silver, stomach and thighs of bronze, legs of iron and feet of iron and clay. Daniel explains that the golden head is Nebuchadnezzar himself, and that the other body parts represent kingdoms that will follow his. The feet of iron and clay represent the fragmentation of empire following the death of Alexander the Great in 323 BC.

Rochegrosse uses a figure from an Assyrian relief as the model for the statue, but also incorporates one of the glazed-brick lion reliefs from Babylon itself, excavated by Koldewey the very same year. This is probably the first time that finds from the site of Babylon appear in art.

AD 1899
Photogravure; printed by Lemercier & Co.
H 45.2 cm, W 35.7 cm
Bibliothèque nationale de France, AA–3 Rochegrosse
Bohrer 2003: 261–2, fig. 68

E FIG. 143 *opposite*
Worship of a Statue and the Burning Fiery Furnace

The Book of Daniel recounts how three Hebrews are thrown into the Fiery Furnace for refusing to worship an 'image of gold', probably a statue of the god Marduk. This manuscript illumination comes from the *Silos Apocalypse* (see also Figs 141, 142).

See Fig. 141: ff. 228v–229
Williams 1994–2002: vol. 4, MS no. 16, pp. 31–40, figs 332a–b

FIG. 146 *left*

Peter Paul Rubens, *Daniel in the Lions' Den*

The morning after reluctantly consigning Daniel to the Lions' Den, King Darius has the stone door sealing removed. Unlike Rivière, Rubens does not show Daniel as calm and composed; rather he looks gratefully to heaven as the stone above him

is rolled away. The lions themselves are modelled on (now extinct) Moroccan lions, which Rubens studied in the menagerie at Brussels.

AD 1614/16
Oil on canvas. H 224.2 cm, W 330.5 cm
National Gallery of Art, Washington, DC, 1965.13.1

E FIG. 145 *above*

Briton Rivière, *Daniel in the Lions' Den*

Briton Rivière treated historical and religious subjects, but is particularly remembered as an animal painter. On the walls of the den he incorporates a real Assyrian relief from the palace of Ashurnasirpal II (884–859 BC), now on display at the British Museum, in which the king may be seen pouring a libation over dead lions at his feet.

The focus of Rivière's image is overwhelmingly upon the lions themselves. Lions were certainly common in ancient Mesopotamia (they became extinct in Iraq only in the twentieth century), and it is quite possible that some were kept in captivity. Reliefs from the palace of the Assyrian king Ashurbanipal at Nineveh show clearly that lions there were caught and caged before being released for royal hunts, although the Book of Daniel remains our only source describing the grisly punishment of feeding prisoners to lions at Babylon. Rivière reprised the theme in 1890, with *Daniel's Answer to the King*, now held by Manchester City Art Gallery.

AD 1872
Oil on canvas
H 66.3 cm, W 101.6 cm
National Museums Liverpool, Walker Art Gallery
Bohrer 2003: 201–3, fig. 47

The End of the Dynasty

The madness of Nebuchadnezzar and the sins of Nabonidus

Irving Finkel

The Book of Daniel brings us face to face with the madness of Nebuchadnezzar:[275]

> All this happened to King Nebuchadnezzar. Twelve months later, as the king was walking on the roof of the royal palace of Babylon, he said, 'Is this not the great Babylon I have built as the royal residence, by my mighty power and for the glory of my majesty?'

> The words were still on his lips when a voice came from heaven, 'This is what is decreed for you, King Nebuchadnezzar: Your royal authority has been taken from you. You will be driven away from people and will live with the wild animals; you will eat grass like cattle. Seven times will pass by for you until you acknowledge that the Most High is sovereign over the kingdoms of men and gives them to anyone he wishes.'

> Immediately what had been said about Nebuchadnezzar was fulfilled. He was driven away from people and ate grass like cattle. His body was drenched with the dew of heaven until his hair grew like the feathers of an eagle and his nails like the claws of a bird.

What lies behind this famous degradation? By his own lights and by any precedent Nebuchadnezzar was the most effective and laudable of the ancient kings of Babylon. His economic, political and religious policies brought lasting wealth and security to the empire. Nebuchadnezzar himself, however, has suffered at the hands of history. Daniel's description has its roots in the opprobrium that had been heaped not on him but on the later Neo-Babylonian king Nabonidus (556–539 BC).

Nabonidus had been exposed since childhood to the idea that Sin, the Moon god, was all powerful and merited exclusive worship. As his reign unfolded, this personal commitment came to result in far-reaching consequences which embroiled his family, the dynasty and the country at large. In native terms Nabonidus failed badly in his duties as reigning Babylonian king. He neglected the cult of Marduk completely, turned his back on Babylon, and travelled for his own reasons to distant Teima in Arabia, where he lived for ten years. Modern scholars have many interpretations for this unexpected behaviour. Nabonidus himself is unabashed in recounting how he left Babylon for Teima, for he had good reasons – and Sin himself instructed him:

> for, being unaware that it would arouse the anger of Nannar, the king of the gods,
> they had neglected his rites and spoken profanely and falsely, so they brought upon themselves heat stress and famine. They even ate one another like dogs, for the famine diminished in their number the people of the land. But, as for me, (Sin) commanded me to flee from my city of Babylon on the road to Teima.·

E FIG. 147 *above*

The daughter of Nabonidus

A foundation cylinder in cuneiform relating the story of En-nigaldi-Nanna, daughter of Nabonidus. On the afternoon of 26 September 554 BC an eclipse was visible in the city:

On 13th of Ululu, the month of the work of goddesses, the Fruit [= moon] became eclipsed and set while eclipsed. 'Sin [the Moon god] requests a high priestess' – such was his sign and decision.[276]

Because for a very long time the office of high priestess had been forgotten and her characteristic features were nowhere indicated, I bethought myself day after day. The appointed time having arrived, the doors were opened for me; indeed I set eyes on an ancient stele of Nebuchadnezzar, son of Ninurta-nadin-shumi, an early king of the past, on which was depicted the image of the high priestess; moreover they had listed and deposited in the Egipar her appurtenances, her clothing and her jewellery. I carefully looked into the old clay and wooden tablets and did exactly as in the olden days. A stele, her appurtenances and her household equipment I fashioned anew, respectively inscribed upon it, and deposited it before my lord and lady Sin and Ningal.[277]

Long before Nabonidus' time it had been the practice of kings to install a daughter as high priestess of the Moon god in Ur. The practice – if not the office itself – had fallen out of favour. The discovery of the stele and ancient records was an important omen, to which the king was deeply attentive.

Reign of Nabonidus (556–539 BC)
From Babylonia
Clay
L 18 cm, D 9.2 cm
Paris, Musée du Louvre, département des Antiquités orientales, AO 6444
Schaudig 2001: 362–70

FIG. 148

Map showing Teima and Harran

It is interesting here to compare the ancient Aramaic composition of the first century BC entitled the Prayer of Nabonidus (Fig. 150), which came to light among the Dead Sea Scrolls:[278]

> An account(?) of the P[ra]yer of Nabonidus, king of Babylon, the [great] king, [when he was smitten] with the evil bušahna-disease by the agency(?) of a dem[onic spi]rit(?) in Teman.
>
> [I, Nabonidus], was (there) smitten with [the evil bušahna-disease] for seven years, and when, from [that] time, I became as [a dying man(?), I prayed to the Most High] and he forgave my sin. (Thereupon) a holy man who was a Judean fr[om the Exiles, came to me saying], 'Proclaim (your forgiveness) and write it down so as to give honour and glo[ry] to the name of [the Most High].'
>
> [So thus I wrote: 'I, (Nabonidus)], was smitten with the evil bušahna-disease in Teman [by the agency(?) of a demonic spirit(?)], and for seven years I prayed [to] gods of silver and gold, [of bronze and iron], of wood, stone and clay, because [I thought] that they were [life-saving] gods.'

Here Nabonidus of Babylon was visited with an evil disease that drove him from his capital city. A Judean 'holy man' – surely Daniel – explains this as punishment for the king's idle worship of false gods, and the text teaches that it was only when Nabonidus turned to the Most High that he regained his health. The disease in question has been thought to be scurvy, unpleasant and anti-social, a consequence of the protracted deprivations induced by famine. Nabonidus' self-imposed exile in Teima was no doubt driven by a combination of factors; but unpleasant physical disfigurement that would exclude him from the central rites of the Marduk cult, coupled with his desire to re-establish his former intimacy with Sin in a foreign cult-centre, could have been decisive.

ℰ FIG. 149
A drawing of an ancient sage

This unique illustration is the central panel in a magical compendium that belonged to a professional Babylonian healer. The illustrated figure, who is shown facing right, is labelled in cuneiform *Abaknana*. He is portrayed as a conventional late Babylonian king, seated on an elaborate throne, wearing a cup-shaped crown and long-fringed robe, and holds before him the symbolic ringed staff and another item of unidentified regalia.

This *Abaknana* is unknown, but is likely to be some legendary ruler renowned for his wisdom and power. The drawing, however, closely resembles the figure of King Nabonidus on the British Museum stela (Fig. 152). This shows that, in visualizing a venerable king from the most remote times, the artist has depicted a figure that closely matches the contemporary ruler that he might once have glimpsed at court, in street procession, or on public monuments in Babylon.

About 500 BC
Clay
H 17.0 cm, W 10.0 cm, Th. 2.0 cm
From Ibrahim al Khalil, Iraq
British Museum, BM 40183+
Unpublished

FIG. 150
Dead Sea Scroll: 'Prayer of Nabonidus'

This fragmentary document in Aramaic shows that the story of Nebuchadnezzar's madness originates in traditions about Nabonidus. It contains the words of a prayer supposedly uttered by Nabonidus when afflicted with a serious illness. A Jewish exorcist aided in his recovery, pointing out the error of his ways. The king's prayers to gods of silver and gold, bronze and iron, wood, stone and clay were of no avail, but a cure came when he approached the 'Most High'.

Before AD 100
Ink on parchment
From Qumran, Cave 4
Israel Antiquities Authority, Jerusalem DSS 4Q242

Nabonidus was reviled for this behaviour. Anti-Nabonidus feeling from within Babylon itself is embodied explicitly in the remarkable *Persian Verse Account* (Fig. 151). His disastrous reputation was compounded by the clear-headed policy of Cyrus' intelligence units, who seized on the abandonment by Nabonidus of his traditional Marduk-centred role as a telling indication that their own regime was destined to take over.

The great malignment suffered by Nabonidus that left him despised and unforgiven was later transferred to the much more famous and magnetic name of his great predecessor Nebuchadnezzar, and thus incorporated into the Book of Daniel and many later Jewish writings. This phenomenon was accelerated by the hostility felt towards the latter for his conquest of Jerusalem, sacking of the temple and exporting of the population to his own territory. By this deed, as pointedly elaborated in the hands of agenda-laden writers, his name suffered irreparable harm, culminating in the iconic image of the king at his lowest possible ebb immortalized by William Blake.

Ⓔ FIG. 151
'Verse Account of Nabonidus'

King Nabonidus' fanatical promotion of the Moon god, his anti-Marduk activities and his prolonged absence from Babylon were unforgivable to many of his subjects. The pro-Persian faction in Babylon created this remarkable poem which ridicules the king:

He had made the image of a deity which nobody had ever seen in this country
He introduced it into the temple; he placed it upon a pedestal
He called it by the name of Nanna ...
As to the effigies in Esagil – effigies which Ea-Mummu had fashioned – he looks at those effigies and utters blasphemies ...

Nabonidus is made to say:

'Till I have obtained what is my desire,
I shall omit all festivals; I shall order even the New Year Festival to cease!'

There was no stopping Nabonidus:

Himself, he started out on a long journey,
The forces of Akkad marching at his side.
He turned towards Teima, deep in the west ...

Reign of Nabonidus (556–539 BC)
From Babylon
Clay
H 12.4 cm, W 12.2 cm
British Museum, BM 38299
Smith 1924: 83–91, pls 5–10; Pritchard 1969a: 312–15;
Beaulieu 1989: 4; Schaudig 2001: 563–78

 FIG. 152
Stela of Nabonidus from Babylon
Reign of Nabonidus (556–539 BC)
Stone
H 58 cm, W 46 cm, Th. 25 cm
From Babylon
British Museum, BM 90837
Rich 1839: 192 pl. 8 no. 2a; Börker-Klähn 1982: 230–1 no. 266; Berger 1973: 382; Schaudig 2001: 530–2.

E FIG. 153
Stela of Nabonidus from Teima
(With drawing by T. Rickards)
Reign of Nabonidus (556–539 BC)
Sandstone
H 50 cm, W 60 cm, Th. 11 cm
From Teima, Saudi Arabia
Deputy Ministry of Antiquities and Museums, Ministry of Education, Saudi Arabia
Eichmann et al. 2006

These two stelae are eloquent survivors of the many that must have been erected during the reign of Nabonidus.

Fig. 152 shows the king under the eye and the protection of his gods – the Moon, Sun and Ishtar. He is clad in a long robe, and holds before him a long staff with rings surmounted by a moon symbol. The symbol in the other hand remains unidentified. Nabonidus wears the conventional contemporary crown of a Neo-Babylonian king.

Fig. 153, recently discovered at Teima, is badly eroded, and so the excavators' own description of the king is quoted:

'The king is standing on the left looking to the right, and from the top centre to the right three symbols are depicted. Of these only the sun disc (centre) and the star (right) show traces of their detailed rendering, the moon crescent [and disc?] (left) is only preserved in its outline. … The king-figure wears a long garment of which very little is preserved. The contour line of parts of the front, the back and the long trailing element of the

headdress can still be identified. Traces of the shoes or details of the garment are not preserved. The same goes for the staff. …. Although nothing of his face is recognizable, there are traces of the headdress, again with similarities to the other known representations of Nabonidus … Some remains of the beard and the hair may be partly preserved but they cannot be clearly distinguished from the unevenly worn sandstone. The same applies to the right arm (or elbow), which may possibly be identified as well as some traces of the left arm.'[279]

In the case of Fig. 152, a long official inscription has been deliberately erased without damaging the adjacent relief carvings. The once-inscribed area to the right has been rubbed completely clean, although the inscription on the right-hand edge has not been effaced and speaks of how the gods put an end to a period of drought in response to the king's own good deeds. Underlining the returned prosperity in the country are details of the new prices of grain, dates and sesame seed.

The 'Verse Account of Nabonidus' (Fig. 151) describes a particular aspect of the behaviour of the conquering Cyrus:

He destroyed the … of his deeds to nothing;
[As for his …] they tore out its image;
[From all mon]uments his name was obliterated;
[Whatever h]e had created, they burned in fire;
[The … which he] had created he had the fire consume

This passage bears directly on the condition of this hard-stone Babylon stela. Great pains were taken to efface all the *writing*, while not destroying the monument outright and leaving the image of the king of Babylon untouched. This raises the question of whether the same might have happened to the even more damaged Teima stela (Fig. 153). This is made of much softer sandstone, and the whole surface has been eroded although fragments of the inscription are still readable.

The artistic legacy: Blake's Nebuchadnezzar

Michael Seymour

The best-known image of a king of Babylon today is that of a haunted and terrified man crawling on all fours, his nails grown into claws, his long beard trailing on the ground and his face a mask of horror and revulsion. William Blake's *Nebuchadnezzar* shows the king's madness described in Daniel 4, the result of the conflation of Nebuchadnezzar with Nabonidus. This conflation was by now two thousand years old, and all European representations of Nebuchadnezzar were affected by it to some degree.

Although more visibly based on a Hans Weiditz woodcut illustration in a 1531 edition of Cicero's *Officia*,[280] the pose of Nebuchadnezzar originates with an Albrecht Dürer engraving, *The Penance of St John Chrysostom* (*c*. 1496).[281] The ascetic St John Chrysostom's mythologized penance was in turn partly based on Nebuchadnezzar's years in the wilderness, making Dürer's figure particularly suitable as a reference. In Blake's religious schema, however, the king and his story took on new significance, and the resulting images are a great departure from all that had gone before.

The figure of Nebuchadnezzar was first conceived by Blake as an illustration to *The Marriage of Heaven and Hell*. In this image he wears a crown, and is depicted above the caption 'One Law for the Lion & Ox is Oppression'. The maxim refers to Blake's ideas on the freedom of the spirit, and seems also to relate to his attitude toward the recent French Revolution.[282] It has been argued

 FIG. 155
Hans Weiditz, *A Man Transformed into a Brute by his Passions*

This image, printed in Augsburg as an illustration to Cicero's *Officia*, does not refer to Babylon, but it was appropriate for Blake's purpose because it depicts a man reduced by base passions to the state of a beast. Blake made a distinction between the damaging worldly desires of 'Experience' and the free expression of human senses and desires of 'Innocence', and believed that the latter would bring about the New Jerusalem.

AD 1531
Woodcut
H 9.5 cm, W 15.5 cm
British Museum, E,7.70
Dodgson 1911: 177, no. 20

 FIG. 156
Albrecht Dürer, *The Penance of St John Chrysostom*

The figure crawling in the background of this engraving appears to have been a key source for Blake's *Nebuchadnezzar*. Dürer shows the mythologized penance of St John Chrysostom. In life the saint was Patriarch of Constantinople and a revered theologian. In the myth he is supposed to have violated a princess and, as penance for his sin, to have taken himself into the wilderness for so long that, like the biblical Nebuchadnezzar, he came to resemble an animal in appearance.[283]

About AD 1496
Engraving
H 18.0 cm, W 11.7 cm
British Museum, E,4,143
Meder 1932: 54; Dodgson 1926: no. 12; Bartsch 1803–21
VII: 79.63; Schoch I.7

FIG. 154 *opposite*
William Blake, *Nebuchadnezzar*

AD 1795 / about 1805
Colour print finished in ink and watercolour on paper
H 54.3 cm, W 72.5 cm
Tate: Presented by W. Graham Robertson, 1939, N05059
Bindman 1977: 98-100; 1978: no. 332; Butlin 1981: no. 301;
1990: no. 28; Myrone 2008: 82, fig. 55. See Butlin 1990 for
full bibliography.

FIG. 157
William Blake, Nebuchadnezzar in
The Marriage of Heaven and Hell

In Blake's first image of the mad king, Nebuchadnezzar is not named. 'One Law for the Lion & Ox is Oppression' refers to Blake's belief that worldly constraints prevented people from acting virtuously. Asserting that Christ broke the Ten Commandments, he wrote, 'Jesus was all virtue, and acted from impulse.'[284]

AD 1790
Page H 26.9 cm, W 17.9 cm
Pl. 24 in *The Marriage of Heaven and Hell*. Copy C, Pierpont Morgan Library, New York

that the image of Nebuchadnezzar was intended as pro-French republican, and even as a thinly veiled attack on King George III. The first part of this interpretation is extremely plausible (Blake's support for the French Revolution, at least prior to the Reign of Terror, is well known),[285] but specific reference to George III seems highly unlikely. It could not refer to the latter's own 'madness' (probably the blood disease porphyria) as that did not begin until 1810, and in any case such direct political satire would be uncharacteristic of Blake.

All this is not to suggest that the artist's sentiments were entirely egalitarian: 'One Law' can also be understood to express an elitist, aristocratic principle. Nebuchadnezzar suffers precisely because he is not a mere animal but a great king. In much the same way Blake seems to regard

FIG. 158
William Blake, *Newton*

Blake aimed to contrast the tyranny of the senses
in *Nebuchadnezzar* with that of reason in Newton.
Believing that excessive reason closed the mind to
a larger world and to Innocence, Blake depicts
Newton as blind to his surroundings. The pose and
compasses closely resemble those of Urizen, a god
governed by reason invented by Blake to show the
same flaws. Blake depicts Newton as engaged in
trying to measure the Holy Trinity, an impossible
and meaningless task.

AD 1795 / about 1805
Colour print with ink and watercolour on paper
H 46.0 cm, W 60.0 cm
Tate, N05058

the laws and norms of society as constraining all, but particularly his own, energy and vision. In
one letter of 1804 Blake explicitly compares his personal experience of social constraint to that
of Nebuchadnezzar in his madness,[286] and in the *Marriage* uses a devil to voice his own view that
'The worship of God is: Honouring his gifts in other men, each according to his genius, and lov-
ing the greatest men best. Those who envy or calumniate great men hate God, for there is no
other God.'[287]

Three versions survive of the large colour print *Nebuchadnezzar*,[288] each quite different owing
to the varying degrees of printed ink and hand finishing involved.[289] The 1795/*c*.1805 prints retain
most elements of the *Marriage of Heaven and Hell* composition, although significantly the crown
and caption are both removed. The order and overall meaning of the twelve pictures in the series
is disputed,[290] but most scholars agree that *Nebuchadnezzar* and *Newton* are paired, representing
excesses of the senses and of reason respectively.[291] Although *Newton* is sometimes seen as a
positive symbol of learning,[292] Blake actually intended the figure as an attack on rationalism,
which he saw as humanity's great barrier to 'Innocence' and the creation of the New Jerusalem.
Where Nebuchadnezzar's expression vividly depicts the horror of madness, Newton is represented as myopic, staring at a small drawing on the floor, oblivious to the world around him.

Belshazzar's Feast and the Fall of Babylon

'Belshazzar, son of the King'

In this administrative document dated to the '24th day of Kislimu in the eleventh year of Nabonidus, King of Babylon', mention is made of a 'slave of Bel-šarra-uṣur, [i.e. Belshazzar] son of the King'. Although Belshazzar was then acting as regent, the dating formula shows that Nabonidus was still considered as the reigning king.

545 BC
From Borsippa
H 4.0 cm, W 5.5 cm, Th. 2.0 cm
British Museum, BM 26740
Previously unpublished

ⓔ FIG. 160 below right
Barrel cylinder of Nabonidus

Nabonidus' ongoing preoccupation was with the cult of Sin, the Moon god. In this foundation inscription he records the rebuilding of Sin's ziggurat at the city of Ur. Nabonidus entreats the Moon god to safeguard both him and his son, Belshazzar, from committing sin.

Reign of Nabonidus (556–539 BC)
From Ur
Clay
L 10.2 cm, Th. 5.1 cm
British Museum, BM 91125
Langdon 1912: 250–2, no. 5

Cuneiform and biblical evidence

Irving Finkel

Belshazzar's Feast is described in the Book of Daniel:[293]

> King Belshazzar gave a great banquet for a thousand of his nobles and drank wine with them. While Belshazzar was drinking his wine, he gave orders to bring in the gold and silver goblets that Nebuchadnezzar his father had taken from the temple in Jerusalem, so that the king and his nobles, his wives and his concubines might drink from them. So they brought in the gold goblets that had been taken from the temple of God in Jerusalem, and the king and his nobles, his wives and his concubines drank from them. As they drank the wine, they praised the gods of gold and silver, of bronze, iron, wood and stone.

Belshazzar, whose name has rung through history as having staged the fateful feast, was, as we have seen, also a historical figure. He was not the son of Nebuchadnezzar, but rather crown prince under the wayward Nabonidus, and he was left by his father as regent to look after affairs in Babylon during the latter's decade of absence at Teima. It appears that Belshazzar was left more or less undisturbed, but he never called himself 'king', always 'son of the king'. Documents from this period were consistently dated by the given year of Nabonidus, who was thus always perceived to be the reigning king.[294] This plan was expected to meet with the Moon god's approval. Meanwhile the crucial New Year festival in Babylon was cancelled, and it was only resumed on the king's return. A fair number of contemporary sources survive from Belshazzar's years, including private contracts and building inscriptions, mostly devoted to Marduk.

In the seventh year of Nabonidus (550 BC) an astrologer reported a dream which conveys something of the balance of the co-regency:[295]

In the month Tebitu, on the fifteenth day, the seventh year of Nabonidus, king of Babylon, Šum-ukin speaks as follows: 'I saw a meteor, Venus, Sirius, the moon and the sun in my dream, and I prayed to them for the well-being of Nabonidus, king of Babylon, my lord, and for the well-being of Belshazzar, the son of the king, my lord.' On the seventeenth day of the month Tebitu, the seventh year of Nabonidus, Šum-ukin speaks as follows: 'I saw a meteor and prayed to it (for) the well-being of Nabonidus, king of Babylon, my lord, and for the well-being of Belshazzar, the son of the king, my lord.'

Ⓔ FIG. 161
The Cyrus Cylinder

This object is one of the most famous cuneiform inscriptions ever discovered. A small fragment of the cylinder, detached at the time of excavation, came into the collection of Yale University (NBC 3504) and was rejoined in 1971. The cylindrical form is typical of Babylonian royal inscriptions, and the text shows that the cylinder was written to be buried in the foundation of the city-wall of Babylon. It was deposited there after the capture of the city by Cyrus in 539 BC, and presumably written on his orders.

The text, written in Babylonian script and language, claims that Nabonidus had perverted the cults of the Babylonian gods including Marduk and had imposed labour-service on its free population, who complained to the gods. It then explains how Cyrus came to take Babylon so successfully. The text ends with food offerings in the temples of Babylon, and an account of the rebuilding of Imgur-Enlil, the inner city-wall of Babylon, during the course of which an earlier building inscription of Ashurbanipal, king of Assyria (669–631 BC), was found.

The whole document is written from a purely Babylonian point of view in traditional terms, and it has been suggested that its author took the Ashurbanipal inscription as his literary model. Cyrus, whatever his own religious beliefs, is portrayed as the tool of Marduk, just as in the biblical Book of Ezra he is presented as the servant of the god of Israel who is instructed to rebuild the temple in Jerusalem and allow the Jews deported by Nebuchadnezzar II to return home.

Because of its reference to just and peaceful rule and the restoration of displaced peoples and their gods, the cylinder has in recent years been referred to in some quarters as a kind of 'Charter of Human Rights'. Such a concept would have been quite alien to Cyrus' contemporaries, and indeed the cylinder says nothing of human rights; but the return of the Jews and of other deported peoples that took place at this time was a significant reversal of the policies of earlier Assyrian and Babylonian kings.

About 539 BC
Found in March 1879 at Amran, Babylon, during the excavation of Hormuzd Rassam, and acquired in 1880.
Clay
L 22.86 cm, Th. 10.0 cm
British Museum, BM 90920
Pritchard 1969a: 315–16; Walker 1972; Berger 1975; Schaudig 2001: 550–6.
Ezra 1:2, 7; 3:7, 5:13; 6:3–4; see also 2 Chronicles 36:22–3

Nabonidus returned from Arabia in 544 BC with elaborate plans to supplant further the worship of Marduk by promoting that of the Moon god. In time, aware of the increasing threat from Persia, he took care to bring many of the gods from outlying cities to sanctuary in Babylon. But by 539 neither prayer nor politics could save his empire; Cyrus II had arrived at the gates.

Cyrus had already established a large and powerful kingdom to the east of the Babylonian Empire. His victory over the Babylonian forces at Opis confirmed his control of the vast holdings that had belonged to Nabonidus. The famous Cyrus Cylinder, perhaps originally one of many such carefully worded documents, was discovered at Babylon in March 1879 by Hormuzd Rassam and swiftly made available to scholars. It is a fine example of contemporary political propaganda in which Nabonidus is mercilessly derided, and the Babylonians given what they want to hear:

> [When ...] ... [...wor]ld quarters [...] ... a low person was put in charge of his country, but he set [a (...) counter]feit over them. He ma[de] a counterfeit of Esagil [and ...] ... for Ur and the rest of the cult-cities. Rites inappropriate to them, [impure] fo[od- offerings ...] disrespectful [...] were daily gabbled, and, intolerably, he brought the daily offerings to a halt; he inter[fered with the rites and] instituted [...] within the sanctuaries. In his mind, reverential fear of Marduk, king of the gods, came to an end. He did yet more evil to his city every day; ... his [people ...], he brought ruin on them all by a yoke without relief.

Marduk accordingly selected the Persian king Cyrus to become the ruler of all the world and set things to rights in Babylon. The actual entry into the city was, we are told, effected without conflict:

> His vast troops whose number, like the water in a river, could not be counted, marched fully armed at his side. He had him enter without fighting or battle right into Shuanna; he saved his city Babylon from hardship. He handed over to him Nabonidus, the king who did not fear him. All the people of Tintir, of all Sumer and Akkad, nobles and governors, bowed down before him and kissed his feet, rejoicing over his kingship and their faces shone. The lord through whose trust all were rescued from death and who saved them all from distress and hardship, they blessed him sweetly and praised his name.

This narrative finds its echo too in the *Persian Verse Account* (Fig. 151), which is correspondingly appreciative of Cyrus' behaviour:

> [To the inhabitants of] Babylon a (joyful) heart is given now
> [They are like prisoners when] the prisons are opened
> [Liberty is restored to] those who were surrounded by oppression
> [All rejoice] to look upon him as king!

Historically speaking, therefore, there was no Fall of Babylon as such. Under this new regime the Jewish Captivity came to an end and many, although by no means all, of the exiles returned to Judah to usher in a new era in their history, the Second Temple period.

For the biblical prophets, however, the Persian conquest marked forever the Fall of Babylon, with Nebuchadnezzar's wickedness finally punished as Isaiah had prophesied:[296]

> She will never be inhabited or lived in through all generations; no Arab will pitch his tent there, no shepherd will rest his flocks there. But desert creatures will lie there, jackals will fill her houses, there the owls will dwell, and there the wild goats will leap about. Hyenas will howl in her strongholds, jackals in her luxurious palaces.

Representations in art

Michael Seymour

Old Testament accounts placed the Persian conquest of Babylon in a decidedly moral context, presenting Cyrus as a great liberator – very much as he portrayed himself in the text of the Cyrus Cylinder. They also show the last kings of Nebuchadnezzar's dynasty in a negative light that fits well with the Persian view of Nabonidus. In the Book of Daniel particular kings and their personalities are shown in some detail, but Nabonidus himself is not mentioned. Instead the role played by Nabonidus in the Persian version of events is divided between his famous forebear Nebuchadnezzar[297] and his son Belshazzar, regent at Babylon during Nabonidus' years at Teima.

As we have already seen, the biblical Nebuchadnezzar's experiences of prophetic dreams and of madness are actually related to events in the life of Nabonidus. What then of Belshazzar, ruling at Babylon in his father's absence?

The biblical account

Although Nabonidus returned to Babylon to face the Persian conquest, in Daniel 5 it is Belshazzar, as king in his own right, who finally presides over the collapse of the Neo-Babylonian Empire. Once again the prophet Daniel plays a pivotal role in the narrative. Belshazzar holds a great feast for a thousand guests. He flaunts the gold and silver goblets taken by Nebuchadnezzar from the Temple in Jerusalem and he, his nobles, his wives and even his concubines drink from them. The moment of the feast is the peak of impious luxury in the Babylon of the Old Testament, and divine retribution is swift: [298]

> Suddenly the fingers of a human hand appeared and wrote on the plaster of the wall, near the lampstand in the royal palace. The king watched the hand as it wrote. His face turned pale and he was so frightened that his knees knocked together and his legs gave way.

Belshazzar summons his wise men, but only Daniel can read the mysterious writing. The characters are Hebrew, the language Aramaic: *MENE MENE TEKEL UPHARSIN*. The words refer to currency weights: *mene* = mina; *tekel* = shekel; *peres* = half (-shekel). The half-measure is the singular of *parsin*; the 'u' of *uparsin* simply means 'and'. *Peres* may also refer to Persia. Daniel interprets them through their secondary meanings of 'numbered, numbered, weighed and divided': [299]

> 'This is what these words mean:
> Mene: God has numbered the days of your reign and brought it to an end.
> Tekel: You have been weighed on the scales and found wanting.
> Peres: Your kingdom is divided and given to the Medes and Persians.'

Belshazzar's Feast, with its themes of divine punishment and the retribution of the righteous, became a very important religious allegory and played a significant part in the apocalyptic Fall of Babylon in the Book of Revelation. For artists, however, the theme posed considerable problems: first, the political pitfalls involved in representing material (and particularly royal) wealth and luxury as sinful; and, secondly, the depiction of the mysterious Writing on the Wall itself.

As a result of Daniel's account Belshazzar has been remembered as the last ruler of Babylon, the name of Nabonidus surviving only through the history of Berossus. Josephus wrongly conclud-

FIG. 162
Rembrandt, *Portrait of Menasseh ben Israel*

Rabbi Menasseh ben Israel, depicted by Rembrandt. Menasseh's ideas about the Writing on the Wall are reflected in Rembrandt's *Belshazzar's Feast*.

1636. Etching. H 14.9 cm, W 10.3 cm
British Museum, 1967,1209.9
Hind 1923: no. 146.(a)1; White and Boon 1969: no. 269

FIG. 163
Menasseh ben Israel, *Arrangement of the Writing on the Wall*

The arrangement of the letters that evidently influenced Rembrandt was one of several solutions to the problem of the Writing on the Wall proposed by Menasseh ben Israel.

1639
Page H 12.5 cm, W 7. 4 cm
Illustration in Menasseh ben Israel, *De Termino Vitæ, libri III. Quibus veterum Rabbinorum ac recentium doctorum, de hac controversia sententia explicatur.*
British Library, 1020.a.19 (1&2)

ed that Belshazzar and Nabonidus must have been the same person,[300] but some awareness of the two as separate figures nonetheless survived into pre-modern scholarship. As described above, however, much of Nabonidus' identity became subsumed within that of the more famous Nebuchadnezzar.

Rembrandt's Belshazzar

The most compelling visual representation of the moment is Rembrandt's *Belshazzar's Feast*, painted *c*. 1636–8. This spectacular large canvas, now held by the National Gallery, London, illustrates both the fleeting nature of earthly power and the drama of the event itself. The image is full of movement, Belshazzar and his companions recoiling from the mysterious hand and its writing. This falling to the left would originally have seemed even more pronounced; the canvas has been trimmed and reoriented slightly anti-clockwise in relation to its original position.[301] In a foreshadowing of his later more introspective and psychological biblical paintings,[302] Rembrandt does not attempt to represent the vastness of Belshazzar's palace or his thronged guests, but concentrates intently on the king himself. Belshazzar shares the shock and incomprehension of the other figures, but through his tense expression and fixed stare shows a more complicated reaction and specifically a deeper unease, as though aware of his guilt in the eyes of God and already suspecting that his hour has come.

Rembrandt was not concerned with providing a historically accurate setting for his work. Authenticity for him lay in the expert rendering of emotions and the creation of an exotic yet believable setting through the careful rendering of materials and textures. Persian costumes and settings had recently begun to figure significantly in Dutch art, but Rembrandt's use of such features was always limited and somewhat arbitrary.[303] The most prominent features here are King Belshazzar's high, crowned turban and his elaborate (but basically European) cloak. The orientalizing features are not extended to the whole painting; like a contemporary wearer of oriental costume the king is surrounded by figures in European dress.[304]

Although Rembrandt was well versed in existing iconographic traditions and themes (and made more use of them in his paintings than has sometimes been suggested[305]), his approach to the subject of Belshazzar's Feast is highly original and relies on textual scholarship as much as artistic tradition. There had always been a problem with the Writing on the Wall as to why neither the king nor his advisers could read the Aramaic inscription – which is in block-letter Hebrew characters – since all in Belshazzar's court could read and write the Aramaic language. Here Rembrandt was able to turn to Rabbi Menasseh ben Israel, who suggested that it be written in vertical columns as opposed to horizontally, right to left, which would suffice to confuse any normal reader. Menasseh's proposal evidently underlies Rembrandt's portrayal of the ominous message, as can clearly be seen from the printed version of his thesis, in which the same arrangement is illustrated. It has been argued that the final character in the painted inscription was a mistake on Rembrandt's part: a *zayin* ('z') rather than a final *nun* ('n'). An X-ray, however, reveals that the character was originally drawn correctly. The most likely explanation for the change in the finished painting is that Rembrandt depicts the final *nun* as incomplete, with the divine hand seen writing the last stroke.[306]

FIG. 164

Rembrandt Harmenszoon van Rijn,
Belshazzar's Feast

The Book of Daniel describes a huge feast at which the king and his guests eat and drink from the gold and silver vessels taken from the temple in Jerusalem. Rembrandt's masterpiece shows only a few figures around the king, and captures the moment at which the feast is interrupted by the appearance of the mysterious writing on the wall.

About AD 1636–8
Oil on canvas
H 167.6 cm, W 209.2 cm
London, National Gallery NG6350

 FIG. 165

A 1-minah weight

A stone minah weight in the shape of a sugar loaf. The inscription states that it was a copy of a weight that Nebuchadnezzar II had made after the standard of Šulgi, the Old Sumerian king. The object itself belonged to one Marduk-ša-ilani, and weighs 978.3 g.

Reign of Nebuchadnezzar (605–562 BC)
From Babylonia, donated in 1892 by Reverend Greville Chester
Stone
H 8.7 cm, W 6.2 cm
British Museum, BM 91005
Belaiew 1927–8: 121; Pritchard 1969b: 118; Powell 1987–90: 510

E FIG. 166

Babylonian duck weights

A group of seven duck-shaped weights of between 8.7 and 24.7 g – that is, between 1 and 3 Babylonian shekels. Weights had been made in this characteristic Mesopotamian form since the second millennium BC.

About 700–500 BC
From Babylonia, purchased in 1928 from Major V.E. Mocatta
Banded agate
Lengths between 2.5 and 3.9 cm
British Museum, BM 128487–128493
Unpublished

E FIG. 167
John Martin, *Belshazzar's Feast*

John Martin's grand historical pictures give an epic
sweep to the destruction of Babylon. The artist
creates a massive and sprawling city, whose impact
on Victorian viewers would have been heightened
by the contemporary tendency to condemn
London as a modern Babylon.

From the left of the picture, the Writing on the Wall
illuminates the entire scene. Daniel stands in the
centre foreground, and spread before him are the
gold and silver from Jerusalem. These biblical
features are supplemented by others drawn from
classical sources: the Tower of Babel is imagined
as a separate structure from Herodotus' temple of
Zeus Belus (both are now understood to refer to
the ziggurat Etemenanki), and the signs of the
zodiac visible on the walls of the grand hall are
inspired by the fourth-century BC Greek description
of Ctesias of Cnidus, who described the zodiac
as Babylonian in origin. Martin had no Babylonian
sources to help his reconstruction, and indeed
the appearance is far from that of any ancient
Mesopotamian architecture, but Ctesias' point
about the zodiac has since been proved correct.

After AD 1821
Oil on canvas, H 152.5 cm, W 222.0 cm
Newcastle City Council, The Laing Art Gallery, Tyne and
Wear Museums, TW CMS:C6999
Feaver 1975: pl. 3, nos 32, 33, 60

John Martin's apocalyptic vision

At the other extreme from Rembrandt's intense focus on the king, John Martin's nineteenth-
century Belshazzar is all but lost in the epic sweep of the artist's vision of Babylon immediately
before (*Belshazzar's Feast*) and during (*The Fall of Babylon*) the Persian conquest. The scale is enormous, with great crowds and architecture of gigantic proportions. Despite its fantastic appearance, however, Martin's work was based on historical architecture, albeit without the aid of any
evidence from ancient Mesopotamia itself. In a guide accompanying the painting of *Belshazzar's
Feast* the viewer was led on a 'tour' through elements of the composition, explaining the meaning and origins of different parts of the image, and particularly of the architecture: [307]

> The immense quadrangle of the Atrium is enriched with the happy combination of the three orders of architecture
> supposed to have been known at the time; the Indian, most likely the origin of the two others, the Egyptian next,
> and the Babylonian. The stupendous peristyles are crowned by galleries, filled with musical performers; above are
> seen the famous gardens as if suspended in the air, and in the gloom of the background the temple of Belus and
> the Tower of Babel; objects of awful grandeur which strike the eye with wonder, and revive classical and solemn
> reflections in the soul.

Martin worked out the scale and proportions of the architecture carefully, following the
description of Herodotus for the scale of the ziggurat. The halls of the palace recede into the distance; in fact Martin's description notes that, using human figures to suggest scale, he has made
the depth one mile.

Like many of his contemporaries John Martin saw direct parallels between the fates of past

FIG. 168 *above*

John Martin, *The Fall of Babylon*

The Fall of Babylon shows the scene only hours after *Belshazzar's Feast*. Belshazzar is betrayed and murdered by his courtiers while the battle for the city rages below. Martin turned with great effect to Egyptian and Indian architecture and the descriptions of ancient Greek authors, as in the case of the Hanging Gardens shown to the right of the scene.

Mezzotint was perfectly suited to the apocalyptic biblical scenes for which Martin was most famed: the medium's great tonal range allowed him to produce dramatic light effects, as in the raging sky and bolts of lightning over Babylon.

AD 1831. Mezzotint with etching
H 46.4 cm, W 71.9 cm
British Museum, Mm. 10–6
Johnstone 1974: 51; Feaver 1975: 40–6 (see also for Martin's 1819 painting of the same subject); Campbell 1992: no. 88; Carey 1999: 264, no. 5.38a

FIG. 169 *left*

Jonathan Martin, *London's Overthrow*

John Martin's brother Jonathan, who spent the last decade of his life in Bedlam, made explicit the link to London in his brother's work. Members of the clergy can be seen in the foreground – Martin held their corruption and vice responsible for London's fate, and intended his arson attack on York Minster, inspired by a dream, as a warning to them. He describes the invading army as that of the 'son of Bonaparte'.

AD 1832
Pen and ink on paper. H 66 cm, W 98 cm
Bethlem Royal Hospital Archives and Museum, London

empires and those of the present. Although it was his brother, the religious fanatic Jonathan, who made explicit the link between Martin's epic, apocalyptic cityscapes and London,[308] the contemporary resonance of John Martin's work had a great deal to do with millenarian ideas and fears engendered by rapid social and economic changes. Not least among these was the rapid expansion of London itself; the battle for the soul of this changing city was often expressed in antique terms, with the ideal that the Victorian city could escape the fate of sinful, doomed Babylon and emerge instead as a New Jerusalem.

E FIG. 170
J.M.W. Turner, *Babylon*

Babylon was indeed a deserted and desolate place. This illustration was reproduced for a popular volume of *Landscape Illustrations of the Bible*.[309] Turner himself never visited Babylon, but he worked from a watercolour sketch by the traveller Sir Robert Ker Porter.

Seventy years later the area pictured here would be excavated by Robert Koldewey, and German archaeologists would reveal the palaces, temples and houses of Nebuchadnezzar's city.

AD 1835–6
Watercolour after a sketch by Sir Robert Ker Porter
H 14.0 cm, W 20.6 cm
Victoria and Albert Museum, 982–1900
Omer 1981: 18

Babylon deserted

When European travellers did visit the site of Babylon, they were struck by the apparent fulfilment of prophecy that met them. All that was left was a shapeless ruin, as seen in Turner's melancholy watercolour of the site. The transience of a great city and empire was a subject worthy of attention in itself, since it provided a strong lesson on the ephemeral nature of worldly power and a demonstration of God's ability to destroy it. Wordsworth noted the totality of this destruction, and especially of the city's voice:[310]

> … Babylon,
> Learned and wise, hath perished utterly,
> Nor leaves her Speech one word to aid the sigh
> That would lament her

These lines were written in around 1821–2, only a few decades before the spectacular successes of, principally, Edward Hincks and Sir Henry Rawlinson in deciphering the languages and scripts of ancient Babylon. Perhaps, though, Wordsworth's point still stands: unlike Judah and Israel, Greece or Rome, Mesopotamia could not be known through indigenous sources, and so could offer no parallel to the influence of the Bible and the Classics on knowledge of the ancient past in European culture. It is arguably as a direct result of this difference that the world of ancient Mesopotamia remains unfamiliar to most people today, and that its kings have acquired their reputations as corrupt, cruel and despotic. In historical terms the archaeological excavation of ancient Mesopotamian cities and the decipherment of cuneiform scripts and languages are recent, and only since these watersheds have we begun to discern something of the Babylonian voice on the world of the Neo-Babylonian dynasty and this most remarkable phase in Babylon's history.

Revelation and the Whore of Babylon

Babylon in the Book of Revelation

Michael Seymour

Babylon's association with pride and lust originates in the Old Testament, but in shaping the later image of the City of Sin no source has been as powerful as the Book of Revelation, the only apocalyptic text to gain a place in the canon of the New Testament.[311] By the time of its composition in the late first century AD Babylon had already fallen, or rather faded, and was no longer a great earthly power of the kind suggested by St John's vision of the Apocalypse. Instead, the Babylon of Revelation is a cipher for imperial Rome, and draws on the language with which Old Testament prophets cursed Nebuchadnezzar's city to prophesize Rome's downfall without incurring reprisal. This is the first of many instances in which the name of Babylon has been transferred to other locations and used to attack the vices of other great sinful cities.

The language of Babylon's destruction in the Book of Revelation grows out of that of the Old Testament prophets, particularly Daniel, Jeremiah and Isaiah. In the evolution of this literature can be seen something of a circle, whereby the apocalyptic visions of Revelation are informed by those of Daniel, while these, as we have seen, are themselves informed by Babylonian ideas. The result, however, is a radically new vision of the Apocalypse, centred on an almost abstract City of Sin.

Among the host of new images introduced is that of the Whore of Babylon. The Old Testament prophets addressed 'Babylon' and 'Daughter of Babylon' as feminine in their tirades against the city, but it is only here that Babylon takes on a form of flesh and blood:[312]

> Then the angel carried me away in the Spirit into a desert. There I saw a woman sitting on a scarlet beast that was covered with blasphemous names and had seven heads and ten horns. The woman was dressed in purple and scarlet, and was glittering with gold, precious stones and pearls. She held a golden cup in her hand, filled with abominable things and the filth of her adulteries. This title was written on her forehead:
> MYSTERY
> BABYLON THE GREAT
> THE MOTHER OF PROSTITUTES
> AND OF THE ABOMINATIONS OF THE EARTH.
> I saw that the woman was drunk with the blood of the saints, the blood of those who bore testimony to Jesus.

Both the woman herself and the beast on which she sits represent Babylon, specifically as Rome and more broadly as earthly luxury, corruption and sin. The seven heads of the beast refer to Rome's seven hills (but are also part of Revelation's complex use of traditional sacred numbers throughout), while the golden cup surely echoes Jeremiah:[313]

Babylon was a gold cup in the Lord's hand;
she made the whole earth drunk.
The nations drank her wine;
therefore they have now gone mad.

This resonance with the Old Testament prophets is rhetorically powerful, and the substitution of Babylon for Rome is far more than a politically necessary mask to protect its early Christian audience from persecution. Revelation makes something transcendent out of the specific Babylon of the sixth century BC: a city that can exist, in some sense, in any time or place. The many modern cases in which the name of Babylon has been attached to other cities or cultures all stem ultimately from Revelation, and the language of those associations often directly reflects this.

The abstraction of the City of Sin from Babylon itself continues with St Augustine's *City of God*. Here the contrast between the earthly and heavenly cities was also a contrast between the worldly Babylon and the heavenly New Jerusalem that would follow the Last Judgement.[314] The 'City of God' in life was rather a path, as was the Earthly City. 'Following our Scriptures,' St Augustine argued, 'we may well speak of them as two cities. For there is one city of men who choose to live carnally, and another who choose to live spiritually, each aiming at its own kind of peace, and when they achieve their respective purposes, they live such lives, each in its own kind of peace.'[315]

Representing the Babylon of Revelation in art and culture

Michael Seymour

The imagery of Revelation is extremely complex. The Apocalypse has, of course, been a perennially important theme in Christian art, and medieval depictions of scenes from Revelation abound. The *Silos Apocalypse* (Figs 141–3) is a particularly impressive medieval manuscript depiction of the events of Revelation, and one that achieves a remarkable fidelity to the difficulties of the received text.

One particularly grand medieval conception of the Apocalypse is to be found in a series of large late fourteenth-century tapestries at the Loire valley Château d'Angers, namely the *tapisseries de l'Apocalypse* executed by Nicolas Bataille and Robert Poinçon and based on cartoons by the painter Jean de Bondol. Completed in about 1382, the tapestries were commissioned for Louis I d'Anjou.[316] Despite their scale and naturalism the scenes depicted are closely related to manuscript traditions, and it is generally agreed that thirteenth-century manuscript miniatures lie behind Jean de Bondol's designs for the huge Angers scenes.[317]

The late sixteenth century sees a radical development. Revolutionizing both the technical scope of their medium and the visual representation of the text of Revelation, Albrecht Dürer's fifteen woodcuts of the Apocalypse are among his most important and influential prints. Dürer worked ingeniously to achieve a close adherence to the text. As mentioned above, this was a far from simple matter in the case of Revelation, and the resulting images constantly juxtapose a plausible material world with fantastic visions and catastrophic events. A single intense scene contains the Whore of Babylon, the city's destruction, angels proclaiming Babylon's fate and the vision of the knight called Faithful-and-True leading the armies of heaven. Although their costumes are extremely varied, both the Whore of Babylon herself and her crowd of admirers wear contemporary dress.[318] Dürer's iconography provided strong models for printed illustrations of Revelation in Germany and further afield.[319] Revelation was often the only book to be illustrated

at all in early printed Lutheran Bibles. Luther himself acknowledged the usefulness of illustrations both because of the difficulty of the text and of Revelation's then slightly uncertain status as a fully recognized part of the New Testament canon. For Protestants fiercely debating the appropriate role of images within religion the dangers did not seem as great as those of illustrating the Gospels.

Moving forward in time, William Blake's *Whore of Babylon* presents a deeply unpleasant and lurid vision. She is a major theme in Blake's literary/theological work, representing one of the great barriers to innocence and salvation.[322] Blake's millenarian beliefs made the Fall of Babylon and the coming of a New Jerusalem urgent themes in his writing. The Whore of Babylon is a distillation of all those vices he labelled 'experience', the worldliness that would eventually be overcome by 'innocence'. Where perhaps Blake differs from his predecessors is that, despite the lascivious appearance of the Whore of Babylon in his depiction, his attitude to sexuality was far from a puritanical dismissal. Rather, Blake believed that an unrestrained sexuality would form a key aspect of innocence; something liberating rather than sinful.[323] The sexuality his Whore of Babylon represents is something specifically worldly – a context in which her identity as a prostitute takes on greater significance. She also represents many worldly 'sins' that have nothing to do

FIG. 171
The Whore of Babylon in the *Apocalypse of Angers* [320]

This scene illustrates a moment in the Book of Revelation, in which an angel shows St John 'the verdict of the Great Whore, she who is enthroned over many waters'. This description echoes Jeremiah's much older warning to Babylon:[321]

You who live by many waters
and are rich in treasures,
your end has come …

Instead of a golden cup the woman here holds a mirror and comb, referring both to vain pride and to her role as seductress.

Completed about AD 1382
Section of tapestry executed by Nicolas Bataille and Robert Poinçon after designs by Hennequin de Bruges
H 6 m, in six sections each W 23.5 m
Château d'Angers, France

FIG. 173 *left*

Hans Burgkmair, *The Whore of Babylon*

In early Lutheran New Testaments, Revelation was commonly the only book that was illustrated. In this image St John himself is depicted, with an angel revealing and interpreting the vision of the Whore of Babylon and the Seven-headed Beast. This echoes the strange hybrids seen by Daniel, but also symbolizes the seven hills of Rome: 'the seven heads are seven hills on which the woman sits'. [324]

AD 1523
Woodcut
H 16.0 cm, W 12.9 cm
From a series of 21 woodcuts illustrating the Apocalypse for Martin Luther's translation of the New Testament, published by Sylvan Otmar, Augsburg, 1523–4
British Museum, 1909,0403.43.

E FIG. 174
William Blake, *The Whore of Babylon*

In Blake's schema the Whore of Babylon was conflated with another biblical harlot, Rahab. In this image she engenders violence and war; in Blake's Jerusalem she also stands for the 'twenty-seven Heavens' of false religious doctrine. [325] Despite her appearance, the Whore of Babylon here also represents the authorities of Church and State, whose suppression of human energy and 'natural' law and religion Blake deplored.

AD 1809
Pen and black ink and watercolour
H 26.6, W 22.3 cm
British Museum, 1847, 0318.123.
Binyon 1898: 1; Butlin 1981: no. 523; Carey 1999: 258, no. 5.34

E FIG. 172 *opposite*
Albrecht Dürer, *The Whore of Babylon, the Destruction of Babylon, and the Knight Called Faithful and True*

Albrecht Dürer's uniquely influential representations of the Apocalypse show the tumult of the many visions described in the Book of Revelation. One of Dürer's many innovations in treating this subject was the combination of fantastic imagery from the biblical text with prosaic details of the material world. These details, and his use of contemporary costume, do everything possible to render the visions of Revelation physical and immediate.

About AD 1496–7
Presented by William Mitchell
Woodcut
H 39.1 cm, W 28.2 cm
British Museum, 1895, 0122.577
Bartsch 7.129.73; Dodgson 1903: 272; Meder 1932: 177ff; Schoch II: 125; Carey 1999: 138, no. 4.19

with sexuality: the laws, customs and social norms that Blake despised.

Alongside all these images there has developed a tradition of depicting or suggesting Babylon's destruction in other contexts, notably the Tower of Babel itself (see Fig. 115). John Martin's interest in the Fall of Babylon was closely linked to his belief in a coming Apocalypse, and the dramatic skies of *Belshazzar's Feast* and *The Fall of Babylon* suggest an event more final than the mere entry of an invading army. As Martin knew, Babylon was not destroyed but remained an imperial capital under the Achaemenid kings and Alexander (the latter died there in 323 BC); so powerful is the language of the Old Testament prophets, however, that in Western culture the Persian conquest of Babylon has become the supreme example of a civilization's sudden and total destruction.

FIG. 175
John Martin, *The Fall of Babylon* (detail)

John Martin's picture nominally depicts the Old Testament Persian conquest of Babylon, but his works on the destruction of great ancient cities were recognized as referring also to the Apocalypse. A millenarian, Martin himself believed that the Last Judgement was close at hand, and saw in modern cities, particularly London, the Babylon referred to in the Book of Revelation.

AD 1831
See Fig. 168

Notes: History and Legend

158. '[L]ike number three, indivisible, it has assumed a role of importance through its use in magic and religious thought. It is unique in that it is neither a factor nor a product of any of the first ten numbers, a virgin number labelled by the Greek philosopher-mathematician Pythagoras and his followers with the name of the virgin goddess, Athena' (Clayton and Price 1988: 4).
159. Diodorus Siculus II.10.1–10.
160. Quintus Curtius Rufus V.1.31–5.
161. Strabo XVI.1.5.
162. Attributed to Philo of Byzantium; quotation after David Oates in Finkel 1988: 45–6. This author is now thought not to be Philo the Engineer of Byzantium, but either a later rhetorician using the name because of the subject matter, or specifically Philo the Paradoxographer of Byzantium (Dalley 2002: 70).
163. Herodotus I.178–9.
164. Diodorus II. 10, in which the gardens are built 'not by Semiramis, but by a later Syrian king to please one of his concubines; for she, they say, being a Persian by race and longing for the meadows of her mountains, asked the king to imitate, through the artifice of a planted garden, the distinctive landscape of Persia'. There is an interesting parallel here with Assyrian landscape engineering, where royal inscriptions clearly convey the intention of re-creating the hilly and forested environments of north Syria in the Assyrian heartland (Thomason 2001).
165. Known through Diodorus and Quintus Curtius Rufus. Writing in the late fourth century, Cleitarchus was a historian of Alexander, although it is disputed whether he travelled to Babylon with Alexander's army himself. His account seems to a large extent to be based on that of Ctesias; however the question of attributing specific details to either author is complicated by the fact that Diodorus used both accounts in his *Bibliotheca Historica*.
166. The location Berossus gives corresponds with the main or Southern Palace of Nebuchadnezzar. This identification is supported by recent research showing a close relationship between Berossus' description of Nebuchadnezzar's building works and the East India House inscription of Nebuchadnezzar (Fig. 17); see Van der Spek 2008.
167. Josephus, *Against Apion* I 19; cf. the very similar account at Josephus, *Jewish Antiquities* X 11.
168. Josephus *Against Apion* I 20 (= Eusebius *Praeparatio Evangelica* IX).
169. Reade 2000: 199; Van der Spek 2008 argues in detail that the relevant text is specifically that of the East India House inscription.
170. Van der Spek 2008.
171. Again the story is complicated by the absence of Berossus' original text. It is possible that parts of his account of the gardens as we read it today were added by a later redactor, Alexander Polyhistor, who may also be responsible for naming the Median wife Amyitis and for making Astyages (rather than his father Cyaxares) the Median king at the time of the alliance.
172. Eusebius, *Chronicle* 46.
173. Dalley 1994; 2003; Foster 2004.
174. Buckingham 1827: 437.
175. Keppel 1827 I: 206–8.
176. Oppert 1863 I: 156–67.
177. Budge 1920 I: 298.
178. Reade 2000: 208–13.
179. Koldewey 1914: 1–6.
180. Rawlinson 1858 II: 570.
181. Buckingham 1827: 490.
182. Ker Porter 1821–2 II: 397.
183. Oppert 1863: 220–3.
184. Layard 1853: 494.
185. Koldewey 1914: 2
186. Rawlinson 1858 I: 521–2.
187. Bewsher 1867: 160–82.
188. Gasche et al. 1987.
189. Gibson 1972: 50.
190. Ker Porter 1821–2 II: 373–4.
191. Buckingham 1827: 433.
192. Oppert 1863: 183.
193. Diodorus XVII 115.
194. Koldewey 1914: 309–11.
195. Rawlinson 1862–7 III: 337–75.
196. Strabo, *Geography* XVI 1 2.
197. Diodorus II 14 2; II 20 2. In this connection it has been argued that the name and mythology of Semiramis are linked not only to the Assyrian queen Sammu-ramat but also to the Syrian Astarte (see Weinfeld 1991). For a recent discussion of the Semiramis myth see Dalley 2005.
198. Herodotus I 184–5.
199. Diodorus II 3 4–II 13 4.
200. Valerius Maximus IX 3 4.
201. Michalski 2003.
202. The story is attributed by Diodorus to one 'Athenaeus' (Diodorus II 20 3–5).
203. Josephus, *Against Apion* I 142.
204. Among other 'exotic' or oriental sources. Sketches survive in Notebook 18, Bibliothèque nationale de France Dc 327d réserve, Carnet I; Reff 1976: 19.
205. Bohrer 1998: 347.
206. Possible Assyrian elements that survive into the final painting are the thick wheels of the chariot and details of Semiramis' hair. The harness in the final painting does resemble some of those shown in seventh-century Assyrian reliefs (N. Tallis, pers. comm.), but the elaborate harness depicted in the study is far more diagnostic of Assyrian influence.
207. Mahon 1949: 223.
208. Ker Porter 1821–2. II: 355.
209. Mignan 1829: 199.

210. Schmid 1995: 23.
211. Arrian, *Anabasis* VII. 17.2
212. Strabo XVI 19.
213. Fraser 1842: 143–4.
214. Selby 1859: 4–5.
215. Rich 1839: 20–1.
216. Oelsner 1999/2000: 374.
217. Bergamini 1977: 111–52.
218. Rawlinson 1858 I: 526.
219. Rich 1839: 19.
220. Smith 1876.
221. Meissner 1901.
222. Scheil and Dieulafoy 1913.
223. Wetzel and Weissbach 1938.
224. Wetzel and Weissbach 1938.
225. Schmid 1995.
226. George 1992: 110.
227. See now J.-L. Monterro-Fenellós in André-Salvini 2008: 229–30.
228. 'Shinar' = Sumer, a very ancient name for an area equating to a large part of southern Iraq.
229. Genesis 11:1–9.
230. Josephus, *Jewish Antiquities* 1.119
231. Guinan 2002: 24 and ref.
232. For example, see Inowlocki 2006.
233. Josephus, *Jewish Antiquities* 1.113–18.
234. *Inferno* 31: 76–81.
235. A sculpture showing the Tower of Babel in the cathedral of Salerno is dated to the eleventh century; while twelfth-century examples are to be found in a fresco in the nave vault of the abbey church of St Savin-sur-Gartempe, France, and a mosaic at the cathedral of Monreale, Sicily. More famous is the thirteenth-century mosaic depiction in the Basilica di San Marco, Venice.
236. The *c*. 1000 AD *Caemon Manuscript* (Bodleian Library, Oxford, MS Junius 11) and the eleventh-century *Illustrated Hexateuch* (British Library, London, MS Cotton Claudius B.IV) contain the earliest surviving manuscript illustrations of the Tower of Babel known to the present author.
237. König 2007: 57–61, 90–4.
238. See Minkowski 1960; Wegener 1995.
239. Mansbach 1982: 46–9.
240. Most notably *The Massacre of the Innocents*, whose mundane, contemporary setting made (and still makes) the violence of its subject shockingly immediate to the viewer (see, e.g., De Vries 1991: 213).
241. Sullivan 1992: 155.
242. Bruegel is known to have associated with humanist intellectuals and thought privately to have opposed the harsh religious persecution associated with Spanish rule in the Netherlands, yet he benefited from the patronage of one of Philip II's closest advisers, Cardinal Antoine Perrenot de Granville, and in 1563 he chose to move from Antwerp to Brussels, where the Spanish government was based. Similarly there is almost no direct evidence for Bruegel's religious views. Perhaps the single most revealing piece of biographical information is the claim of Carel van Mander that on his deathbed he ordered his wife to burn

243. Mansbach 1982: 49.
244. See especially the surviving paintings of the Labours of the Months cycle: *Gloomy Day*, *Return of the Herd*, *Hunters in the Snow*, *Haymaking* and *The Harvesters*.
245. Herodotus 1 181. 'Zeus Belus' is Herodotus' term for Marduk, who was indeed the head of the Babylonian pantheon as Zeus was of the Greek. 'Belus', or rather Bel, simply means 'Lord', but by Late Babylonian times the title had become synonymous with the name of Marduk.
246. Pieter the Elder wrote his surname without an 'h' after 1559. Both sons retained the original spelling of 'Brueghel'.
247. The last volume of *Turris Babel* is particularly concerned with identifying the original language spoken before the Confusion of Tongues. This was a topic discussed by other scholars in the seventeenth century, although many tended towards the view that the Hebrew of the Pentateuch must be the original language (Bennett and Mandelbrote 1998: 104–5). The question of the origin and early forms of language is still an area of fascination for scholars today (two important recent examples are Mithen 2005 and Kenneally 2007). On Kircher and his work more generally see Findlen 2004.
248. Arab reaction to the creation of the state of Israel in 1948 included violence against Iraqi Jews, the vast majority of whom ultimately had to emigrate by means of airlifts to Israel in 1950–1. Further persecution in the later twentieth century forced almost all Jews to leave Iraq. See Rejwan 1985; Rakowitz 1997: 177–91.
249. Grayson 1975a: no. 5: rev. 11–13.
250. The prophet Ezekiel was among those taken away at this time.
251. A rival tradition attributes the destruction of the temple to the Edomites. The account in the apocryphal Book of 1 Esdras (4:45) is supported by Obadiah 1:11–14. Their actions were clearly neither forgotten nor forgiven. The famous Psalm 137, which begins: 'By the rivers of Babylon we sat and wept', goes on to say (verses 7–9): 'Remember, O Lord, what the Edomites did on the day Jerusalem fell. "Tear it down," they cried, "tear it down to its foundations!" O Daughter of Babylon, doomed to destruction, happy is he who repays you for what you have done to us – he who seizes your infants and dashes them against the rocks.'
252. 2 Kings 25:6–7; cf. Jeremiah 39:6–7.
253. Jeremiah 40–1.
254. The arrival of Sheshbazzar and the returning Jews soon led to friction between them and the Judeans whose predecessors had not been deported. The Book of Ezra relates intrigues leading to delays in the rebuilding of the temple, and subsequent drives for ethnic and religious purity, with marriages to non-Jewish wives broken up, and they and any children by them being driven away.
255. Parker and Dubberstein 1971: 27.
256. Parker and Dubberstein 1971: 25.
257. See Toomer 1984: 9–14.
258. The Babylonian practice was to count from the first full regnal year rather than the date of accession (e.g. 604 BC as the first

year of Nebuchadnezzar). Elsewhere in this book we have followed the modern practice of counting from date of accession (i.e. 605 BC for Nebuchadnezzar).

259. The British Museum, while using the dates given above, has engaged in correspondence with people on both sides of this particular discussion over the years and would recommend anyone interested to read the following two books, which represent the two sides of the argument: Furuli 2003 and Jonsson 1998.

260. Lipschits 2003.

261. Daniel 1:4–5.

262. A close copy of the same miniature exists in a later (1560) MS of al-Biruni held by the Bibliothèque nationale de France (Manuscrit Arabe 1489, f. 147v).

263. Larsen 1989: 189.

264. Psalms 137:1–4.

265. Finke 1974: 100.

266. Jobert 1997: 177–201.

267. Larsen 1995: 101–3l.

268. Delitzsch 1902; 1903; 1905; 1906. See also Larsen 1989; 1995: 95–106; Johanning 1988; Lehmann 1994; 1999; Bohrer 2003: 286–96.

269. Delitzsch 1920; 1921.

270. Daniel 11:2–4.

271. Van der Spek 2003: 311–24.

272. No mention is made of Nabonidus. Instead, immediately following Belshazzar's Feast, 'That very night Belshazzar, king of the Babylonians, was slain, and Darius the Mede took over the kingdom, at the age of sixty-two' (Daniel 5:30). Whether Darius the Mede is in fact Cyrus, or possibly the Median king Astyages, is unclear.

273. Collins 1998: 86–7.

274. Daniel 6:25–7.

275. Daniel 4:28–33.

276. See here Reiner 1985: I 8–10, with extensive discussion. This may be compared with an omen from the astrological series Enuma Anu Enlil XVII §VI 4: ?If an eclipse occurs in Ululu in the morning watch, Sin [will request] a high priestess? (see Rochberg-Halton 1988: 133). The name given to the new priestess upon her appointment reflects the circumstances; it translates as 'high priestess requested by the Moon god'.

277. Reiner 1985 I: 26–38.

278. Kinnier Wilson and Finkel 2007: 18–20.

279. Eichmann et al. 2006: 172.

280. Recognized as a source by Samuel Palmer (Lister 1973: 308). The Weiditz illustration depicts neither Nebuchadnezzar nor St John Chrysostom, but simply a man reduced to the state of a beast by his passions.

281. Butlin 1990: 91.

282. See Boime 1987: 326–30.

283. Wind 1937: 183.

284. *The Marriage of Heaven and Hell,* pl. 23.

285. In *The French Revolution* Blake supports the republican ideal (Richey 1992), but by 1795 Robespierre and the Reign of Terror seem to have cooled Blake's initial enthusiasm for the

286. Letter to William Hayley, 23 October 1804: 'thank God I was not altogether a beast as he was; but I was a slave in a mill bound among beasts and devils'; Keynes 1966: 850; Mitchell 1995: 449.

287. *The Marriage of Heaven and Hell*, plates 22–3.

288. The other versions are held by the Boston Museum of Fine Arts and the Minneapolis Institute of Arts.

289. After printing, the images were finished with watercolours and ink. For *Nebuchadnezzar* and other images Blake made multiple copies of a print without renewing the paint on the plate, and balancing the resulting weaker prints by using more ink and watercolour in the finishing (Butlin 1990: 83). Some (including the Tate Britain versions of *Nebuchadnezzar* and *Newton*) were reprinted *c*. 1805 (and are watermarked 'JWHATMAN/1804' – Butlin 1981–2: 101–3; 1983–4: 159; 1990: 83–4), when further additions were also made to some of the 1795 prints.

290. Lindsay 1989.

291. Bindman 1977: 98–101; Butlin 1981: 156–77.

292. It is in this spirit that *Newton* forms the model for the large bronze statue, designed by Eduardo Paolozzi, that stands outside the British Library today.

293. Daniel 5:1–4.

294. Beaulieu 1989: 186–8.

295. Beaulieu 1989: 192.

296. Isaiah 13:20–22.

297. Although separated by the reigns of three kings (Evil-Merodach, Neriglissar and Labashi-Marduk), the gap between the reigns of Nebuchadnezzar and Nabonidus was less than a decade.

298. Daniel 5:5–6.

299. Daniel 5:26–8.

300. Josephus, *Jewish Antiquities* 10 11 2; see also Sack 1991: 29.

301. Schama 1999: 418. For a summary of scientific analysis of the painting see Bomford et al. 2006: 110–17.

302. Panofsky 1969: 13–14; Bialostocki 1984: 14.

303. Goetz 1938: 287.

304. Of these figures it seems very likely that the costume of the woman on the right was inspired by Veronese's *Rape of Europa* (1580, Sala di Anticollegio, Palazzo Ducale, Venice) (Starcky 1990: 74), while the woman whose face is visible to the left of Belshazzar may be Saskia van Uylenburgh, whom Rembrandt had married in 1634.

305. Bialostocki 1984: 10. In this case the influence of Pieter Lastman (to whom Rembrandt was once apprentice) may be seen in the costume and pose of Belshazzar, which seem to derive specifically from Lastman's *Haman Begging Esther for Mercy* (1618, Museum Narodowe, Warsaw) (De Winkel 2006: 255–8).

306. See Zell 2002: 61–3; Alexander-Knotter 1999: 144–5.

307. Anonymous 1821: 8.

308. Bindman 1999: 268.

309. The image was engraved by William and Edwin Finden for Thomas Hartwell Horne's *Landscape Illustrations of the Bible, Consisting of Views of the most Remarkable Places Mentioned in the*

Old and New Testaments. From Original Sketches Taken on the Spot (London, 1838).

310. William Wordsworth, Ecclesiastical Sonnets 25, *Missions and Travels*.

311. And, indeed, the source of the name 'Apocalypse' for this genre (Collins 1998: 269).

312. Revelation 17:3–6.

313. Jeremiah 51:7.

314. Augustine's explicit identification of the earthly and heavenly cities with Babylon and Jerusalem respectively is made not in *De Civitate Dei* but in his commentary on Psalm 65 (Lancel 2002: 401).

315. *De Civitate Dei* XIV. i.

316. For a discussion of the tapestries and their production see Muel 1996.

317. See Henderson 1985 for detailed discussion of manuscript sources.

318. The luxurious costume of the Whore of Babylon is based on an earlier drawing by Dürer of a Venetian lady (Vienna, Albertina Inv. No. 3064 D37) (Carey 1999: 138, no. 4.19).

319. 'As a subject, the cycle established an iconographic standard on which all future printed interpretations of the Apocalypse were based; and indeed, the designs were copied not just in woodcuts and engravings, but also in paintings, reliefs, tapestries and enamels, both within Germany and in France, Italy and Russia' (Carey 1999: 130, no. 4.5).

320. Muel 1996: 69–70, no. 5. 64.

321. Revelation 17:1; Jeremiah 51:13.

322. 'Blake's entire aesthetic project can be described as a dramatization of the pre-apocalyptic condition. Among other things, this means that the Whore of Babylon has a strong, nearly ubiquitous presence in his work, both in her more explicit form (Rahab or the Female Will) and in her general symbolic function as that which must be eliminated before the Logos can ascend to his throne at the Last Judgement' (Goldsmith 1993: 140).

323. Hagstrum 1964: 78.

324. Daniel 7; Revelation 17:9.

325. Warner 1982: 225.

The Legacy
of Babylon

The Legacy of Babylon

Babylon is still with us. In appraising what this presence might consist of two discrete strands emerge, the one scarcely detectable, the other immensely visible. The first is the issue of what features embedded in our present world may be attributed one way or another to an origin within ancient Mesopotamian society: ideas, conventions and even scientific discoveries. Surprisingly enough such intangibles can be uncovered. Then there is the very name itself, living, evolving and ever the substance of image and icon. At the time of going to press an internet search for 'Babylon' brought up about 48,000,000 entries, a tally that speaks for itself. Babylon continues to inspire creativity, reaching from fine art to pop culture. The following pages address in outline these two legacies and bring the story, as far as we can, right up to date.

The Babylonian inheritance

Irving Finkel

Throughout its long and complex history the intellectual life of ancient Mesopotamia exerted huge influence on the contemporary cultures that surrounded it. Independently of political or military expansion the 'bookish' underpinning of Sumerian and Semitic civilization spread beyond the home boundaries to take root elsewhere. Itinerant scribal teachers set up schools far beyond Mesopotamia, exporting Babylonian learning and understanding. Despite its difficulties Babylonian in cuneiform script came to achieve widespread status as the international *lingua franca* in the second millennium BC. As a result cuneiform's systematic study of language, traditional literature and theoretical ideas about the gods and the world found fertile reception and had lasting effect.

Among these ideas divination was perhaps primary. The urge to predict the future was a major Mesopotamian preoccupation over some three thousand years. There can be no doubt that Babylonian extispicy (telling the future by examining the liver of a sheep for ominous marks) played a directly parental role in later Greek, Etruscan and Roman practice, as exemplified in the inscribed teaching liver model shown here (Fig. 176) on the one hand, and a famous Etruscan bronze liver from Vicenza on the other. Babylonian doctors, too, were famous, and more than one enquiry for expertise and prescriptions came from far-flung courts.

Here we concentrate on such elements from this major and hallowed canon of knowledge as have survived into our own time. Given that cuneiform writing, and the knowledge preserved in it, became totally extinct during the first few centuries AD, it is not surprising that the Western world has looked no further back for its cultural heritage than to the Greek and Latin authorities of classical Antiquity. The intellectual heritage from the classical authors was so great and so pervasive that – even after the decipherment of cuneiform in the nineteenth century – it was a long time before such acknowledgement was even considered with regard to the ancient Mesopotamian world.[326]

The problem persists. That there are links, influences and movable cultural goods has gradually become apparent through long and dedicated scholarship, but not in a way that has made headlines or led to a general reassessment of our own cultural inheritance. There are complex problems in searching for clear-cut examples. The evidence is there, but requires either vast learning in the researcher in terms of both ancient language and science or – rarer still – collaboration between such scholars with a shared purpose. The cases that have been painstakingly brought into the light principally concern the modern fields of mathematics, astronomy and medicine, not to mention astrology and divination in general, even though many writers would shrink from ceding to their Babylonian predecessors the conception of such clear-cut categories. Intrinsic to the problem is what has disparagingly been called the 'lukewarm Babylonian mind', a view that defines that same mind as sluggish, superstitious, obsessed with demonology and fortune-telling, and incapable of theoretical thinking.[327] Good marks, however, are always given the Babylonians for observation and recording of detail. Here we cannot reassess the temperature of that pre-Greek mind, but we can explore certain intellectual 'filaments' that survived the dust of Mesopotamia to the extent that we can still notice their flicker today.

Traceable elements of the best of Babylonian science have been preserved within Indian, Arabic and medieval European writings. The transmission of such material occurred at different times and involved processes that are far from understood, but certainly depend on host language shifts – such as Babylonian into Aramaic, or Babylonian into Greek. Much work remains to be done on all these elusive and far-reaching manifestations of our Babylonian inheritance, and only an outline of its nature can be given here.

E FIG. 177
Babylonian in Greek dress

Tablets and fragments such as this show us how Greek scholars in Babylon tried to master Babylonian wisdom in cuneiform writing. The first step was learning the cuneiform signs and studying the ancient word lists. Here terms for 'canal' are given, including the Sumerian and Babylonian words *palal* and *atappu*. The scribe then spells out this strange-sounding vocabulary in familiar Greek script.

Sumerian word	Greek spelling	Babylonian word	Greek spelling
(pa₅-lal)	φα-λαλ (pa-lal)	(a-tap-pi)	αθαφ atap

About 100 BC
Probably from Babylon
Clay, H 9.0 cm, W 7.0 cm
British Museum, BM 34797
Geller 1997: 68–9; Westenholz 2007: 263

FIG. 178
'Babylonian hours'

This sixteenth-century sundial shows several different systems for measuring time, including 'Babylonian hours'. The particular system is not really Babylonian, but this pocket instrument does use the Babylonian principle that hours can vary in length with daylight. Thus summer hours are longer than winter hours. At this time systems with variable hours were still common in Europe.

AD 1585–95
Workshop of Hans Tucher, Nuremberg
Ivory, brass and gold
Octavius Morgan bequest
L 11.7 cm, W 5.9 cm, Th. 1.6 cm
British Museum, 1888,1201.288
Ward 1981: 88

FIG. 179 *opposite below*

Babylonian Astronomical System B
Many fragments of this important astronomical manuscript have been gradually identified and put together in the British Museum during the last century, and new 'joins' are still being made. It covers the years 208–10 of the Seleucid era (104–102 BC), and exemplifies what is today called 'System B'. According to System B, lunar movement steadily accelerates and decelerates, whereas System A had assumed two alternating speeds.

Fig. 180 shows that documents such as this were copied into Greek, thus surviving into later astronomy.

103 BC
From Babylon, purchased 1879
Clay
H 10.2 cm, W 33.0 cm, Th. 4.0 cm
British Museum, BM 34580+
Neugebauer 1955: 144–6, no. 122; Britton and Walker 1996: 61

Mathematics, numbers and counting

Complex numbers appear right at the moment that writing first appears, probably well before 3200 BC. The earliest clay records employ a quite bewildering group of systems and symbols to express numerals.[328] From the Old Babylonian period of King Hammurapi, between 1800 and 1600 BC, teachers and schoolboys have bequeathed to us many documents that demonstrate familiarity with fractions, algebra, quadratic equations, cubic equations and even what was later known as the Pythagorean theorem.

The central numerical structure that underpinned three millennia of daily Mesopotamian calculation was the sexagesimal system (counting in 60s, as opposed to our decimal system of counting in 10s). A single upright cuneiform wedge can represent 1 or 6 (or powers of 60), two such wedges can represent 2 or 2 x 60 (and so on), and a single diagonal wedge can express 10 (or 10 x 60, or 10 x powers of 60). This coupled with the use of the sign *lá*, 'minus', meant that small, large and immense numbers could be easily expressed and manipulated: 60 x 60 = 3,600 became a catch-all to mean 'a very large number'. The same place-value system allowed fractions to be expressed. In modern transliteration commas and semicolons convey the difference. Thus a vertical wedge followed by a diagonal wedge can be understood as 1,10 (= 60 + 10) = 70 as well as 1;10 (= 1 + 10/60) = 1+1/6. Surprisingly enough, all this worked very comfortably, since 60 is divisible in many ways.

It is above all the underlying and characteristic '60-ness' of this scribal determination that has reached down right into our modern world. The division of the minute into 60 seconds, and of the hour into 60 minutes, as well as the division of the periphery of the circle into 360 degrees, is inherited from the counting with 60 as a base in ancient Mesopotamian mathematics, and from the Babylonian division of the circle of the ecliptic into 360 time-degrees. The Babylonian day was measured as 12 DANNA ('double hour') units, each of which was subdivided into 30 UŠ, and 12 x 30 = 360 UŠ. This system is attested in Greek astronomy by the mid-second century BC.

Mastery of numbers remained a persistent cultural feature among Mesopotamian thinkers charged with learning and tradition. By the first millennium BC mathematics was being applied to the prediction of astronomical phenomena, it having been established through observation that certain of those phenomena were periodic. Investigations of one type identified a whole number of cycles made by one heavenly body (such as the sun) with a whole number of cycles made by another (such as the moon), for example the calendrical cycle 19 (sidereal) years = 235 lunar (synodic) months. Thus adding a total of 7 additional (intercalary) months at intervals to the normal year of 12 lunar months kept the lunar and solar calendars in line over a cycle of 19 years. The use of the nineteen-year intercalation cycle by some astronomers may go back to the eighth century BC at Babylon. This fundamental cycle is embedded in late Antique and medieval Jewish and Christian liturgical calendars.

Astronomy

The study of Babylonian astronomy was pioneered in the late nineteenth century. Certain dry-looking archives from the Hellenistic Babylonian cities of Babylon and Uruk presented columns of numbers that understandably repelled early cuneiformists. Undeterred, the Jesuit fathers J. Epping, J.N. Strassmaier and F.X. Kugler conjured results from them that, from an intellectual standpoint, were nothing short of revolutionary.

These late-period texts proved to be astronomical ephemerides (mathematical tables predicting the movements of the moon and planets). The discovery was of fundamental importance not only for the history of Babylonian civilization and culture, but also for Western astronomy in general. Virtually in one stroke Epping's 1889 *Astronomisches aus Babylon* changed the narrative history of astronomy and gave meaning to the words 'Babylonian astronomy', which could now be seen as fully comparable to Greek astronomy. It was soon found that Babylonian astronomical ephemerides were the source of much knowledge transmitted to cultures beyond Mesopotamia, both west to Greece and east to India, where the following features all eventually found acceptance:

1. The sexagesimal number system (counting in 60s)
2. Values for a variety of astronomical constants, such as the length of the lunar month
3. Period relations such as the 18-year Saros cycle of lunar eclipses
4. The 3:2 ratio of longest to shortest daylight for Babylon
5. A scheme for calculating times for the risings of zodiacal signs.

In due course it was also discovered that these tables represented only a part of a much more extensive astronomical literature that included the results of regular nightly observations of the heavens made in Babylon from the eighth to the first century BC. More than a thousand of these 'non-mathematical' astronomical records survive,

E FIG. 180 *above*

Greek papyrus with Babylonian System B

This remarkable fragment of papyrus shows in the right-hand column part of the astronomical table found in the Babylonian System B, Column G (see Fig. 179). It literally exemplifies the transmission of Babylonian astronomical knowledge into Greek. This information for predicting planetary movement must be based on Babylonian sources.

1st century AD. Papyrus
H 17 cm, W 7 cm. Private collection, USA
Neugebauer 1988; Jones 1997

together with other studies that derived from them. Such writings embody a thousand-year tradition of astronomical enquiry.

Babylonian celestial sciences have given us omens, observational texts (such as the astronomical diaries of Babylon), texts dealing with lunar and planetary phenomena, horoscopes and other late astrological manuscripts (many of which remain unstudied and unpublished). On top of that are the works of truly mathematical astronomy which date to the Seleucid period (the last few centuries BC). These include several hundred ephemerides, and procedure texts for calculating astronomical phenomena.

In the Middle East, the Babylonian names of the months have survived intact and will be familiar to any speaker of modern Hebrew or Arabic.

E FIG. 181

The Babylonian zodiac list

This document equates the twelve months of the year with the constellations of the zodiac, and is an important stage in the development of the zodiac system as we know it today. It attributes both the Pleiades and Taurus to month 2, both Orion and Gemini to month 3, and both Pegasus and Pisces to month 12. The translations of the ancient month names and their modern equivalents are:

Babylonian month name	Translation of name	Constellation
1 Nisanu	The hired man	Aries
2 Ajaru	The stars	Pleiades
2 Ajaru	The bull of heaven	Taurus
3 Simanu	The true shepherd of Anu	Orion
3 Simanu	The great twins	Gemini
4 Du'uzu	The crab	Cancer
5 Abu	The lion	Leo
6 Ululu	The barley-stalk	Virgo
7 Tashritu	The balance	Libra
8 Arahsamna	The scorpion	Scorpio
9 Kislimu	Pabilsag (god)	Sagittarius
10 Tebetu	The goat-fish	Capricorn
11 Shabatu	The giant	Aquarius
12 Adaru	The field	Pegasus
12 Adaru	The tails	Pisces

Probably 5th century BC
Probably from Babylon
Clay
H 6.3 cm, W 2. 4.4. cm
British Museum, BM 77824
Kugler 1970: 228–32; Stephenson and Walker 1985: 17

Astrology

At the same time the Babylonians made equally serious researches into astrology. From a historical perspective the influence of Babylonian celestial divination and astrology was just as penetrating as that of the astronomical tradition. The following elements became fundamental to Greek, Greco-Roman and later European astrology, but they are all attested to originally in cuneiform and were invented in ancient Mesopotamia for purposes of Babylonian astrological divinatory science:

1. Celestial divinatory omens
2. The zodiac itself
3. The horoscope
4. The dodecatemoria (a twelfth part, an ancient term for the twelve divisions of the zodiac)
5. Trine aspect (concerning two astral bodies which are a third part of the zodiac, i.e. 120° distant from each other)

FIGS 182, 183, 184
Signs of the Babylonian zodiac

Among the few known cuneiform documents with line drawings are the two remarkable tablets illustrated in Figs 182–184, which include detailed drawings of certain constellations. They undoubtedly form part of a single large compilation. Certain 3rd–2nd century BC images of Babylonian zodiac signs occur already among divine symbols more than a thousand years earlier.

E FIG. 182
Zodiac Compilation Tablet 1
The obverse of this tablet opens with a lunar eclipse omen:

If there is an eclipse of the moon in the month of Ajaru in the middle watch and the south wind blows, and Venus is not present during the eclipse, Saturn broken *... [...] Jupiter is present during the eclipse,* broken *will grow old; ruin in Elam; Elam will be destroyed; its land will be plundered; the king of Elam will fall through weapons; he will never come back; the son of a nobody will take the throne of Elam.*

The drawings show, from left to right, with the first labelled in cuneiform:

The Pleiades (seven stars)
The moon (a bearded god in a circle, probably Marduk, killing a lion with his weapon)
Taurus (a prancing bull).

The reverse of this tablet (not illustrated here) shows part of a circle divided into twelve sections, of which 6, 7, 8 and 9 survive, which are combined with Pisces, Aries, Taurus and Gemini.

3rd–2nd century BC, reign of an Antiochus
Clay
H 10.0 cm, W 17.0 cm, Th. 3.0 cm
From Uruk
Staatliche Museen zu Berlin, Vorderasiatisches Museum, VAT 7851
Weidner 1967: 12–34

ⓔ FIGS 183, 184
Zodiac Compilation Tablet 2

This companion tablet to Fig 182 is much more complete, thanks to the fact that two large pieces, one now in Berlin (above) and the other in Paris (below), would make a spectacular international 'join'.

Fig. 83 (above) shows the obverse of the upper portion. Here the drawings, which are all labelled, show:

Jupiter (an eight-pointed star)
Hydra (a blend of the Babylonian dragon with a snake)
Leo (a lion).

Fig. 184 (below) shows the reverse of the lower portion. It depicts similarly Corvus (a crow biting the end of the snake), Virgo (a maiden holding a barley stalk) and Mercury (an eight-pointed star).

A great deal of information is crammed into Tablet 2. Both sides contain omens, images, hemerological predictions, and a curious tradition whereby a particular city, temple, wood plant and stone are united in tabular form and associated with a micro-zodiac system under the constellation Leo.

3rd–2nd century BC, reign of an Antiochus.
From Uruk
Clay
Fig. 183 (above) H 11.0 cm, W 19.0 cm
Staatliche Museen zu Berlin, Vorderasiatisches Museum, VAT 7487
Fig. 184 (below) H 11.5 cm, W 19.0 cm
Paris, Musée du Louvre, département des Antiquités orientales, AO 6448
Weidner 1967: 12–34

6. Exaltations (the place of a planet in the zodiac in which it was considered to exert its greatest influence)

7. Benefics and malefics (features of good/favourable and bad/unfavourable influence).

From the earliest recognition that movements in the heavens were periodic (second millennium BC) to the latest methods to predict them (sixth to fourth centuries BC), annually recurring phenomena were of central importance in Babylonian astronomy. Beginning with the dates of equinoxes and solstices, as in the work called MUL.APIN (Fig. 185), and the corresponding variation in daylight length over a year, Babylonian astronomy achieved a progressive understanding of the relationships between years, months and days and the determination of increasingly better values for the lengths of the (solar) year and the (lunar) month. Good time values were crucial for predicting phenomena – whether annual, such as equinoxes and solstices; or at greater intervals, such as first appearances of the planet Jupiter; or lesser, such as the first visibility of the moon each month. These relations have broad application to many astronomical problems. The behaviour of the moon with respect to the sun underlies Babylonian calendrical systems, but the calendar does not support all astronomical enquiry, and it is the unification of method for both lunar and planetary relations that constitutes the foundation of Babylonian astronomy.

It is evident that a substantial proportion of Babylonia's hard-won astronomical knowledge had become available to the Greeks by the first half of the second century BC. In the process the names of certain Babylonian masters survived the erosion of their script: Cidenas (Kidinnu), Naburianus (Nabu-rimanni) and Sudines. A good deal of this material was already available to

 FIG. 185
The Babylonian compilation known as MUL.APIN

MUL.APIN, 'The Plough Constellation', is a two-part astronomical compilation that lists the stars and constellations, as well as giving schemes for predicting risings and settings of the planets, and how to measure the lengths of daylight with a water-clock or sun-shadows. The text was compiled between 1000 and 700 BC, but this particular example dates to about 500 BC.

Some of this information was known in Babylon long before MUL.APIN. A much older tablet of about 1700 BC already contains a linear zigzag scheme applied to a water clock, involving the variation in the length of daylight over a solar year.

Later the Greek Anaximander (c. 610 – c. 546 BC), the student of Thales, claimed to have 'invented' the shadow-clock (gnomon), building a sundial in or near Sparta.

About 500 BC
From Babylon
Clay
H 15.0 cm, W 7.0 cm
British Museum, BM 42277
Hunger and Pingree 1989: pl. 14, source D

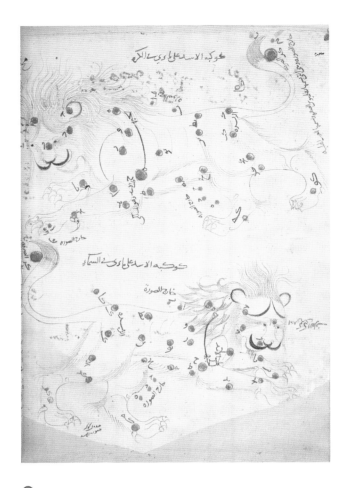

Hipparchus, who was working in the second half of the same century, while the crucial Babylonian component of Ptolemy's *Almagest* has been summarized as follows:

1. Many constellation names
2. The zodiacal reference system
3. The degree as the basis of angular measure
4. The 'finger' as the unit of eclipse magnitude
5. The use of sexagesimal fractions
6. Observations, especially of eclipses, going back to the reign of Nabonassar in 747 BC
7. Fundamental parameters including an excellent value for the length of the mean lunar month
8. Period relations for the moon and planets
9. The magnitude of the principal inequalities.

In conclusion, to quote Britton and Walker:

Even more fundamental and far-reaching, however, was the Babylonian discovery that it was possible to create mathematical models which would yield reliable numerical predictions of complex astronomical phenomena. For it was this outgrowth of the Babylonian compulsion to predict, which – recast into a more general and powerful mathematical format – motivated not only [Ptolemy's] *Almagest* but virtually all subsequent astronomy and science.[329]

E FIG. 186
The constellation Leo lives on

'Abd al-Rahman al-Sufi was a tenth-century AD Persian astronomer who translated Greek Hellenistic astronomical texts into Arabic, including Ptolemy's *Almagest*, with the movements of stars and planets. He also made the first recorded observation of the Andromeda galaxy. Indirectly, his work inherited a great deal from Babylonian astronomy, as the survival of much of the Babylonian zodiac into his *Suwar al-Kawakib* shows. Parts of Babylonian astronomy passed into Hellenistic Greek texts which al-Sufi knew. From medieval Arabic they were then transmitted to the modern world.

14th-century copy of 10th-century AD text
Illumination in 'Abd al-Rahman al-Sufi, *Suwar al-Kawakib* (*Picture of the Fixed Stars*)
H 39.0 cm, W 44.0 cm (open)
British Library, MS Or.5323 f. 45v
Wellesz 1959: 20–6; 1964.

E FIG. 187
Celestial globe

This thirteenth-century AD globe follows the constellations laid out by al-Sufi. The constellation Leo here closely resembles the lower image in Fig. 186, which is labelled as suitable for a globe.

The zodiac and constellations have changed over time, but a majority of signs in both this and our modern zodiac have recognizable parallels in Babylonian astrology.

AD 1275–6
Brass with inlaid silver
D 24.0 cm
From Mosul, made by Muhammad ibn Hilal
British Museum, 1871, 0301.1
Savage-Smith 1985: 219, no. 4

Healing and medicine

Herodotus claimed that Babylonians had no doctors, but medicine – if loosely described as a system of practical treatments for preventing and combating disease and infection – certainly existed in Mesopotamia. We have texts to refute Herodotus' criticisms from well before 2000 BC down to the end of the first millennium. Healing practice, as with mathematics and astronomy, was never broken down into synthesis or treatise, but tackled the problem of cure by several complementary strands. A broad pharmacology, primarily plant-based, was administered both externally and internally, supplemented where necessary or desirable by the use of spells, incantations, amulets and charms. Disease and illness, broadly speaking, were attributed to invasive evil forces that required driving out, although there were also other types of affliction. Anatomical knowledge was uneven and limited, and understanding of the workings of the body remained largely instinctive rather than the result of reasoned investigation.

A very great deal of attention was devoted to observing patients, describing their outer form, physical appearance and symptoms, and recording the findings. A parallel tradition linked such observations to the responsible element, whether demon, spirit or the 'hand' of some deity. Other compositions assembled recipes, indexing them from head to foot on multi-column tablets that were prized and recopied. These provided the practitioner with a reference library of many thousands of entries from which symptom, origin and treatment – vegetable or verbal – could be

E FIG. 188

Stars and constellations according to the Hindu system

This rare nineteenth-century AD Sanskrit treatise compares Indian, Islamic and European astronomical systems. All three systems have constellations and zodiacs, and in this sense the author of this work compares what are actually three different legacies of a single ancient Mesopotamian phenomenon.

AD 1840
Illumination in *Durgāshankara Pāthaka, Sarvasiddhāntatattvacūdāmani (Crest-jewel of the Essence of all Systems of Astronomy)*
H 22.0 cm, W 34.0 cm (open)
British Library, MS Or.5259, ff. 56v–5
Losty 1982: 154–5, no. 140

FIG. 189
A Babylonian gynaecological teaching compendium

The many recipes collected in this compendium cover medical complications in pregnant women and women in childbirth. It was evidently a teacher's handbook from which individual passages were dictated. It treats barrenness, spontaneous abortion and many other matters, and includes a pregnancy test. This involved urination on barley sprouts, a technique attested to also in Egyptian, Greek and later sources. In addition an otherwise unknown women's internal disease called *alluttu*, 'the Crab', is mentioned, perhaps the origin of the name 'cancer'.

About 500 BC.
Probably from Babylon; excavated by Hormuzd Rassam and acquired 1881
Clay. British Museum, BM 42313+

FIG. 190
Recipes against spontaneous abortion

This tablet is a student's copy from the same Babylon archive as Fig. 189. It includes recipes against sterility and spontaneous abortion. The first and third recipes rely on the mouse as embodying fertility:

*If a woman tends to lose her foetus in the first month, second month
or third month, dry a hulû-mouse,
crush and grind it up, (add) water
three times, and mix it with oil;
add alluharu. Give it to her to drink and she will not lose her foetus.*

*To make a barren woman pregnant,
you flay an edible mouse
open it up and fill it with murru;
dry it in the shade, crush and grind it up, and mix it with fat
you insert it in her vagina and she will get pregnant.*

About 500 BC
Probably from Babylon
Clay
British Museum, BM 42333
Finkel 2000: 171–3, text 17

established, juxtaposed and addressed. Tablets from this broad milieu, especially those with therapies rather than recitations, are rare enough from the third and second millennia BC, but become plentiful in the great libraries of Assyria during the seventh century BC. The later archives of Babylon and Uruk preserved the same range of writings, and reveal that the great wealth of traditional curative lore was cherished and used there too.

Medical survivals

The question here is whether elements within the long history of native Mesopotamian medicine can be shown to have had an afterlife. It is likely that hard-won knowledge of the relevant properties of local plants persisted on a local level, possibly even to be reflected in early twentieth-century Iraqi Bedouin traditions. As remarked above, the demise of cuneiform script meant that knowledge – including technical information about healing plants and minerals, medical recipes and procedures – could only survive later if translated into another language (e.g. Aramaic) or transmitted orally. This partly explains why medical information from late Antiquity preserved in Syriac, Aramaic and even Middle Persian all show extensive Greek influence, since Greek science dominated the scholarly world under Byzantium and beyond.

There is, accordingly, a Babylonian component within early Greek medicine, and comparisons can be revealing. In both systems anatomical knowledge was paltry, with the exception of two remarkable Greek physicians from Alexandria, Herophilus and Erasistratus, the only Greek scholars known to dissect human bodies. Babylonian and Greek healers had to make do with a very rudimentary knowledge of internal anatomy, with only a vague idea about the place and nature of organs within the body, and even less understanding of their function. The lungs were understood to be connected with respiration and the kidneys with urination, but little was known about digestion or how blood moves within the body. We have virtually no Babylonian data about surgery and only one late Hippocratic treatise deals with this crucial subject. What both systems had in common was an interest in prognosis, specifically in predicting how long the symptoms were likely to persist, or whether the patient was likely to live or die. It was on the basis of skill at prognosis that physicians earned their reputations, and it is likely that realistic prognoses were possible, given the careful noting of similar symptoms in countless patients. Diagnosis, on the other hand, was a much more difficult proposition since ancient physicians had neither instruments nor technology at their disposal. Babylonian and Greek physicians often classified diseases in similar terms, such as 'eye' disease, 'coughing' disease, or types of fever. As for drug treatments, Babylonian physicians mastered long lists of plants and minerals with descriptions of their properties, while the Greek Discorides later catalogued hundreds of different medicinal plants according to their usages. Knowledge about drugs was inevitably acquired empirically and, once established, carefully transmitted. Finally both Babylonian and Hippocratic would-be physicians underwent apprenticeship to a practising physician (often as a member of the family), and medical training was usually secret, not to be shared with a layman or even other physicians.

At the same time there are important differences between Greek and Babylonian medicine. Greeks looked to theory and to the four humours that became so influential in later European medicine as a way of explaining disease as the result of internal imbalances within the body, rather than of external forces such as demons. Babylonian medicine, on the other hand, contains no theoretical explanation of disease beyond the idea that disease reflected fate itself or divine intervention in human affairs. One remarkable exception comes from the site of Uruk, the so-called 'Proto-Humours' text; this does entail an attempt to locate the source of disease in one of four main body areas and is probably a response to Greek ideas. There is no matching concern in Babylon with the Greek focus on diet and regimen. While Greeks always favoured case histories in their medical compilations, the Babylonians record their findings in general terms of symptoms and disease.

Recent work has uncovered significant points of similarity between late Mesopotamian medical practice and the early Knidos – rather than Hippocrates' own Kos – component of the Greek Hippocratic corpus. Compare a sample passage from Babylonia (a) with its Greek counterpart (b):[330]

(a) *ninû*, *kukru*, juniper, … you use sufficient quantities, you grind, you sift, you mix with sheep's-kidney tallow, … you throw on glowing *ašagu*-coals. A *burzigallu* vessel … you seal off [its sides] with emmer-wheat dough; you put a reed tube into it, you put honey and ghee in his mouth, in the reed tube, steaming; [he will aspirate,] it will hit his lungs. You do this every day for seven (or: nine) days and … . He should eat regularly(?), drink good brewer's beer and he will recover.

(b) Then apply a vapour-bath of vinegar, soda cress seeds and marjoram: grind these fine, mix the vinegar into an equal amount of water, instil a little oil, and then dissolve the soda, cress seed and marjoram into it; pour into a pot, set on a lid that covers it completely, bore a hole through the lid, and insert a hollow reed. Then set the pot on coals to boil, and when vapour passes up through the reed, have the patient open his mouth wide and draw in the vapour, talking care not to burn his throat. Soak sponges in hot water, and have the patient apply these externally to his upper and lower jaws. Make a gargle for him of marjoram, rue, savory, celery, mint and a little soda; prepare dilute melicrat, and instil a little vinegar into it; grind the leaves and soda fine, and have the patient gargle.

Both internal evidence and explicit acknowledgement tell us that certain material in Hippocrates derives from the 'Ancients'; a good number of those same ancients were certainly the doctors of Babylon.

Babylonian lore lived on, too, among those Jewish scholars who remained in Babylon and ultimately founded the great academies in such places as Sura and Pumbeditha, in which the Babylonian Talmud came to be produced. A variety of traditions concerning divination, magic and medicine in Talmudic Aramaic writings certainly stem from the Babylonian cultural world and ultimately reflect familiarity with native Mesopotamian cuneiform.[331] Babylonian teaching methods had their effect, meanwhile; certain favoured devices in rabbinic textual explanation seem to echo the study and interpretation of revered ancient texts that once took place in classrooms by the rivers of Babylon.[332]

Babylon in Contemporary Art and Culture

Michael Seymour

One remarkable aspect of Babylon's survival into the present has been its gradual loss of identity as a specific place. Beginning with Rome's identification with Babylon in the Book of Revelation, the name became associated with a set of characteristics rather than a real city. This process continued through St Augustine's separation of earthly and heavenly cities that did not necessarily represent any one physical place,[333] and Babylon gradually evolved into the universal City of Sin. The story of the Tower of Babel, meanwhile, had always had qualities of myth that made its geographical and historical location almost irrelevant, 'Babylon' becoming 'Babel'. As the two traditions, City and Tower, developed, Babylon itself was to stay buried for two thousand years.[334] The born-again Babylon of later invention, despite the spectacular excavations of the early twentieth century, has remained far better known than Nebuchadnezzar's city itself.

The Tower of Babel in the twentieth century

Modern art has seen a revival of interest in the Tower of Babel, coupled with transformations in meaning. Paintings reflect increasingly the concerns of a multicultural and multilingual world, drawing on the confusion of tongues and the scattering of peoples and all but abandoning the old moral lessons on the overreach of humanity. Whether such representations suggest confusion, alienation or harmony, issues of pride and ambition no longer predominate. Many works embody a complex modern engagement with the idea of Babel; one striking example is Michael Lassel's *trompe-l'oeil* interpretation (Fig. 193), in which personal and modern historical associations enrich the traditional theme.

The dispersal of peoples and the confusion of tongues are integral to the Genesis account, but the way in which these themes have resonated with twentieth-century experience is entirely new. Anne Desmet's work on the Tower of Babel (Figs 194, 195) is rooted in an interest in architecture and in the Colosseum-like towers painted by Bruegel, but also incorporates other themes – the combination of architecture with volcanoes, the links between print media, typography and the confusion of tongues and, in the *Babel Flower* series, human and natural cycles of destruction, rebirth and regeneration.

In literature the most important reworkings of the Babel theme are those of Jorge Luis Borges. One story, 'The Lottery in Babylon', perhaps inspired by Herodotus' *Babylonian Marriage Market*, describes a society where, in the name of fairness, all aspects of life are determined by lottery. Most famous, however, is 'The Library of Babel', published in 1941. The story is set in a vast library containing every possible combination of 25 characters printed over 40 lines (each of 80 characters) and 410 pages. The overwhelming majority of books are undecipherable strings of characters throughout; the librarians spend their lives searching for occasional snatches of mean-

ⓔ FIG. 191
M.C. Escher, *Tower of Babel*

This image is partly an exercise in perspective and geometrical forms. The picture contains both darkness (the strangely modern vision of the looming tower and the rain – Escher's hint that we are witnessing the beginning of racial or ethnic divisions) and humour (in the animated gestures of the confused builders themselves). Escher himself wrote of the image:

Some of the builders are white and others black. The work is at a standstill because they are no longer able to understand one another. Seeing as the climax of the drama takes place at the summit of the tower which is under construction, the building has been shown from above as though from a bird's-eye view.

M.C. Escher

AD 1928
Woodcut
H 62.1 cm, W 38.6 cm
M.C. Escher Foundation, Netherlands
Locher 1992

ⓔ FIG. 192 *opposite*
Julee Holcombe, *Babel Revisited*

Surprising new ideas still emerge from the long-established theme of Babel. Julee Holcombe's digital artworks echo and update Old Masters. In this case the use of sixteenth-century Tower of Babel paintings in the basic composition is immediately apparent, but the modern iconography transforms the meaning.

Babel Revisited takes an allegorical gaze at history and modernity and how human beings, like nature, are doomed to the continual repetition of what has gone before.

Julee Holcombe

AD 2004
Iris print
H 107.5 cm, W 112.5 cm
Conner Contemporary Art, Washington, DC

ing, knowing that somewhere within the library are contained all possible books. The narrator of the story follows this information to its logical conclusion, realizing that:[335]

> There is no combination of characters one can make – *dhcmrlchtdj*, for example – that the divine Library has not foreseen and that in one or more of its secret tongues does not hide a terrible significance. There is no syllable one can speak that is not filled with tenderness and terror, that is not, in one of those languages, the mighty name of a god. To speak is to commit tautologies.

In this closed system, with no external reference, meaning dissolves. After a lifetime of wandering through identical rooms, the narrator (one of many 'librarians') has come to regard all the books and combinations as equally meaningful, mystical and divine. The confusion of tongues is complete.

E FIG. 193
Michael Lassel, *Tower of Babel*

With its puzzles and symbolism, *trompe l'oeil*
is a genre well suited to the theme of Babel.
Disarmingly, Lassel's image uses these normally
playful qualities to focus on the serious topics of
human displacement and loss, even destruction,
of identity.

*As I grew up under a dictatorship, I understand my
painting not only in its original sense as a symbol of
pride but also as a memorial for the countless
victims of any tyranny.*

*Using shoes to build the tower finds its explanation
in my memories of my father's rural shoemaker's
workshop. There I often watched him, working,
talking to his waiting customers. The conversation
always revolved around everyday life. Early on I
established a connection between every pair of
shoes and the story of its owner's life.*

Michael Lassel

AD 2001
Oil on canvas
H 110.0 cm, W 80.0 cm
Artist's own collection

ℰ FIGS 194, 195

Anne Desmet, Toppled Tower I
AD 2002
Collage on panel, H 38.2 cm, W 49.2 cm
London, Hart Gallery

Anne Desmet, Babel Flower: Dusk

AD 2005
Flexograph print, indented plywood print and collage on paper
D 79.4 cm
University of Manchester, The Whitworth Art Gallery

The Tower of Babel has been a long-term theme in Anne Desmet's work. *Toppled Tower* shows the influence of sixteenth-century Tower of Babel paintings, while other pictures link the tower to other architecture or even to volcanoes. The *Babel Flower* images, showing different times of day, seem to turn the tower inside out, enclosing the viewer. They involve a consideration not of destruction alone, but of cycles of destruction, rebirth and change, signified in the form of the flower and the passage of time.

Bruegel's setting of the tower in the prosperous merchant town of Antwerp has particular family associations. The biblical account of the Babel Tower is very moving and relevant to the 21st century in that it evokes a sense of the intense, grandiose, timeless beauty of mankind's most ambitious constructions – the vulnerable yet aspirational qualities of towers and, by extension, the ambition and fragility of human dreams.

Anne Desmet

FIG. 196
Edwin Long, *The Babylonian Marriage Market*

Edwin Long's depiction of the Babylonian Marriage Market epitomizes one approach to depicting Babylon in the modern era: the bringing to life of a well-known Greek or biblical text with the help of newly available archaeological material. The details of Long's painting were based on scrupulous study of the Assyrian reliefs and other objects at the British Museum. The scene itself, however, is pure Greek invention: Herodotus described an auction whereby marriageable girls of Babylon were lined up in order of beauty and sold off. The money raised in bride-prices for the most beautiful brides supposedly provided dowries for the plainer women.

AD 1875. Oil on canvas
H 125 cm, W 287 cm
Royal Holloway, University of London
Cowling 2004

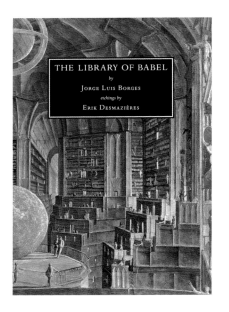

FIG. 197
The Library of Babel

Jorge Luis Borges' philosophical *Library of Babel* is as strange and hard to visualize as the Tower of Babel itself. In the cover illustration, Erik Desmazières does not follow literally the cellular structure described by Borges, but creates his own graphic vision of an infinitely large and endlessly puzzling library.

Erik Desmazières
AD 1997
Duotone etching
Cover artwork for Jorge Luis Borges, *The Library of Babel*, published in 2000 by David R. Godine, Boston

Babylon in music

There is a rich body of modern music on Babylonian themes, among them Verdi's epic opera *Nabucco*, shortened from *Nabuchodonosor* (= Nebuchadnezzar). First performed at Milan's Teatro alla Scala in 1842, *Nabucco* has achieved lasting fame on the subject of the Babylonian Captivity. The opera weaves together biblical, classical and new elements, and the king of the title is somewhat overshadowed by the fictional character Abigaille who plots to usurp his throne. Two famous oratorios focus on the last hours of Belshazzar: Handel's *Belshazzar*, first performed in 1745, and William Walton's *Belshazzar's Feast*, first performed in 1931; the latter remains one of the best-known English choral works. Semiramis has also been the subject of several musical treatments, most famously Rossini's *Sémiramide*. Rossini's opera had its premiere in Venice in 1823, and it has been suggested that a Parisian performance inspired Degas to study Assyrian reliefs at the Louvre and ultimately to produce *Sémiramis construisant Babylone*.

Partly in order to regain popularity after the disastrous 'Babel–Bibel' affair (see p. 154), the Deutsche Orient-Gesellschaft turned to recent archaeological discoveries in their own 1908 operatic production *Sardanapal: historische Pantomime*. By this time Sardanapalus was thought to be the Assyrian king Ashurbanipal of Nineveh.[336] The set designers used the most up-to-date information; the story, however, was not substantially different from that of Byron's play *Sardanapalus* of 1821, written before any major excavation in Mesopotamia had been conducted. In this way the production satisfied existing tastes, but failed in what had seemed at first to be its driving motive: to reflect the giant strides that had been made in the study of ancient Mesopotamia in the preceding eighty years. Today we also see a quite different phenomenon: the widespread currency of the name of Babylon throughout popular music.

Babylon in Hollywood

The most impressive attempt to represent ancient Babylon on screen is undoubtedly D.W. Griffith's *Intolerance: Love's Struggle through the Ages* (1916). Having made a fortune from *The Birth of a Nation*, a film remembered today primarily for its glorification of the Ku Klux Klan,[337] Griffith embarked upon a very different and supremely ambitious project: a three-hour epic whose explicit theme was love's struggle against intolerance.

The film followed four historical storylines, but the Babylonian chapters were far and away the most memorable. The spectacular sets, built to full scale and populated with huge crowds of extras, were researched by Griffith and his assistants in some detail and praised in the souvenir programme by the Oxford Assyriologist A.H. Sayce.[338] Equally apparent, however, is Griffith's reliance on paintings, specifically Edwin Long's *Babylonian Marriage Market*, John Martin's *Belshazzar's Feast* and *The Fall of Babylon* by George Rochegrosse. Although incorporating traditional aspects of all these stories, however, the plot of the Babylonian component in *Intolerance* is original. Most significantly the central figure is a new and thoroughly modern creation: Constance Talmadge plays a 'wild mountain girl' who demands independence, does not wish to be married off, and disguises herself as a soldier to battle alongside her beloved Belshazzar. In order to add drama to the production, in Griffith's version of events Babylon is besieged and assaulted by Cyrus (although the city eventually falls only through treachery).

FIG. 198
Sardanapal: historische Pantomime

Walter Andrae produced set designs for the 1908 Berlin production of the opera *Sardanapal* while still working on excavations in Iraq. In Berlin the designs were developed and reworked, with Professor Friedrich Delitzsch insisting on accurate rather than invented cuneiform inscriptions. The opera itself, however, did not reflect such attention to Mesopotamian archaeology: its roots were in ancient Greek myth and eighteenth- and nineteenth-century European romanticism.

AD 1908
Photograph originally published in *Die Woche* vol. 3, no. 36

E FIG. 199

Scene from *Intolerance,* dir. D.W. Griffith

Some of the most spectacular film scenery ever produced, the Babylon set for D.W. Griffith's silent epic *Intolerance* involved literally a cast of thousands. Griffith did all he could to research ancient Mesopotamian art, architecture and costume, employing assistants to help him piece together a great scrapbook of images and information about the city. This did not prevent him from employing fantastic visions of Babylon from art. Such blurring of the boundaries between history and fantasy remains the norm in representations of the ancient past in film and television today.

AD 1916
Film still
Bibliothèque du film (BIFI), Paris
Drew 2001

E FIG. 200
Scene from *Metropolis*, dir. Fritz Lang

The 1927 silent film *Metropolis* featured both the ancient and this, the New Tower of Babel, updating the story of the confusion of tongues for an age of factories and massive industrialization. Lang's film argues that Joh Frederson, the technocrat who rules the city Metropolis, must learn to respect his workers and to communicate with them as human beings.

AD 1927
Film still
Bibliothèque du film (BIFI), Paris
Elsässer 2000; Gunning 2008

A strikingly original use of ancient Babylon was made by Fritz Lang in the 1927 silent master-piece *Metropolis*. Like Griffith's, Lang's film came with an explicit moral message: 'The link between the head and the hands must be the heart.' In other words workers and rulers need to communicate and to empathize in order to build a better world. The biblical Tower of Babel is juxtaposed with a 'New Tower of Babel' at the top of which lives Joh Frederson (Alfred Abel), the ruler of Metropolis. In common with some twentieth-century art Lang's film takes the biblical theme of the confusion of tongues and uses it to address modern questions of alienation and failure to commu-nicate – an approach recently updated in Alejandro González Iñárritu's film *Babel* (2006).

Chant Down Babylon: Rastafari

One of the most common ways in which we encounter the name of Babylon today is through pop-ular music, a development in no small part attributable to Rastafarian culture and particularly the songs of Robert Nestor Marley. Bob Marley himself was intensely and vocally dedicated to Rastafarian religion and culture, and was viewed by Rastafarians (and others) even during his own lifetime as far more than a popular singer. His personal use of the name Babylon played a signifi-cant part in establishing its force in contemporary culture worldwide. Through songs such as 'Chant Down Babylon', 'Babylon System' and 'Exodus', Bob Marley brought a distinct Rastafarian view of the concepts of Babylon and Zion to an incredibly wide audience.

For Rastafarians Babylon stands for the establishment and white power structure in general, and insofar as it signifies any specific place America and Europe. By the same token Zion in

FIG. 201
Robert Nestor Marley (1945–1981)

Through the music of Bob Marley, Western popular culture became familiar with the Rastafarian use of Babylon to refer to white power structures and oppression. Today the name is used in this way by a huge variety of artists, writers and musicians.

Rastafarian belief signifies redemption and salvation, and is tied to the land of Ethiopia rather than to the city of Jerusalem. Emperor Haile Selassie represented the black African Messiah prophesied by the American activist Marcus Garvey, and his rise to power in Ethiopia signalled the emergence of a new Zion.

Babylon is everywhere

Today the name of Babylon pervades popular culture afresh, appearing in a huge range of contexts, and is recognized and understood even by audiences who are not necessarily sure if there ever was a real city of Babylon, or where in the world it might have been. Imperial Rome, *fin-de-siècle* Paris, Victorian London, and today's New York, Los Angeles, Las Vegas and Tokyo – all have been represented as modern incarnations of the city of Babylon. In other cases the name has been attached to whole industries: Kenneth Anger's *Hollywood Babylon* (Fig. 2) is the classic example, but today a series of exposés by Imogen Edwards-Jones on travel and fashion employ the same format. The name recurs regularly in music, sometimes even with the text of Psalm 137 ('By the rivers of Babylon we sat down and wept'), but reggae surely remains the genre in which its meaning is most powerful.

It has been more than one hundred years now since the beginning of Robert Koldewey's excavations at Babylon, but archaeology has not displaced other ways of engaging with Babylon. Nor should it. The rich traditions that have developed in art, literature and music have a life of their own, and are meaningful in different ways. It is true that archaeology offers us the only means of knowing Nebuchadnezzar's city as it was lived in and experienced two and a half thousand years ago, but the way in which the ancient world has been absorbed and even reinvented in later culture is important in its own right. As the case of Babylon shows, our enduring fascination with the human past is a gloriously varied and wide-ranging phenomenon. There is room in it for a little imagination yet.

The Site of Babylon Today

John Curtis

Since the end of the First World War, and the foundation of modern Iraq, Babylon has occupied an important place in the hearts and minds of Iraqi citizens, symbolizing as it does the glories of ancient Mesopotamia. Together with other cultural icons such as Assyrian winged bulls and the golden dome of the Ali el Hadi Mosque at Samarra (badly damaged in 2006), it has also come to be seen as one of the symbols of modern Iraq and has frequently been invoked in attempts to underpin Iraqi national identity. For this reason different aspects of Babylon – particularly the Lion of Babylon, the Ishtar Gate and general views across the ruins – have figured on postcards, stamps, coins and banknotes.

In spite of the fame and notoriety of Babylon, however, there was little to be seen at the site. There was, certainly, the famous Lion of Babylon, and the foundations of the Ishtar Gate with animal figures in plain, unglazed moulded bricks. However, the upper part of the gate with its brilliantly coloured bricks had been reconstructed in Berlin and the ruins of the ancient mudbrick buildings were, as they so often are, a disappointment for the average visitor. Even the half-size reconstruction of the Ishtar Gate near the entrance to the site could not compensate for the lack of an exciting visual experience. It is scarcely surprising, therefore, that the Baathist government of Saddam Hussein decided to embark on a major scheme of reconstruction. Consequently the 'Archaeological Restoration of Babylon Project' commenced on 14 February 1978, under the direction of the State Organization of Antiquities and Heritage, and continued all through the Iraq–Iran War, which started in September 1980. In 1982 a set of legal-tender coins was issued commemorating this restoration project. The seven coins each bear an image of Babylon. Four of them show the Ishtar Gate and panels of bulls and lions, one shows the Lion of Babylon, another shows the Stela of Hammurapi (now in the Louvre in Paris) and the last shows a reconstruction of the ziggurat. This set of coins, in a presentation case, was accompanied by a small bronze tablet with a modern cuneiform inscription which in the accompanying booklet is translated with the following outlandish text: 'Saddam Hussein the mighty hero, the beloved, the President of Iraq and the restorer of the city of Babylon, hero of the 17–30 July, 1968'.

In the course of the reconstruction project the Southern Palace of Nebuchadnezzar (605–562 BC) was extensively restored. This vast building contains five major courtyards and about 250 rooms, the grandest of which is the throne room of Nebuchadnezzar, the Al-'Arsh (Crown Hall). The main entrance to the palace is through a reconstructed arch 30 metres high and many of the walls have been rebuilt to a height of 18 metres. Bricks in the original construction were frequently stamped with cuneiform inscriptions of Nebuchadnezzar, and following this ancient tradition many of the new bricks used in the rebuilding were stamped with inscriptions in Arabic of Saddam Hussein. These bricks bear the pretentious legend: 'In the era of President Saddam Hussein of Iraq, the protector of Great Iraq and reproducer of its reawakening and the builder of its civilization' or 'In the era of Saddam Hussein, protector of Iraq, who rebuilt the royal palace'.

🇪 FIG. 202 *above*

British postcard showing the Lion of Babylon

About AD 1918
Private collection

🇪 FIG. 203 *top right*

Commemorative postage stamps

50 *fils*, Lion of Babylon
10 *fils*, Ishtar Gate

AD 1967
Private collection

FIG. 204 *centre*

Inscribed brick of Saddam Hussein

AD 2004
Photograph by the author

🇪 FIG. 205 *below left*

Babylon commemorative coin

One of a set of Babylon commemorative coins, this one showing the ziggurat, together with a modern cuneiform tablet with building inscription naming Saddam Hussein.

AD 1982
Private collection

🇪 FIG. 206 *below right*

***250-dinar* postage stamp showing dragon, bull and lion reliefs from Babylon**

2005, from a series commemorating ancient civilizations of Iraq.

Private collection

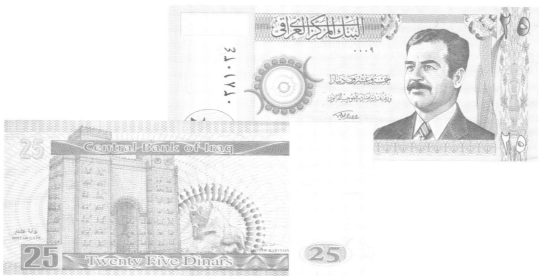

Restoration work was also focused on the Ishtar Gate and the Processional Way, on the temple of the goddess Ninmah, and on the Greek theatre that had been built in the Hellenistic period after Alexander's conquest of Babylon. Fifteen semicircular banks of seats were restored in the theatre, allowing it to accommodate 2,500 people.

The restoration of Babylon, or at least the first phase of it, was mostly finished in time for the first Babylon International Festival in September 1987, held while fighting in the war against Iran was still raging. This was an extravaganza that ran for a month and included companies performing music and dance from about thirty different countries. The official theme of the festival was 'From Nebuchadnezzar to Saddam Hussein, Babylon undergoes a renaissance', and the promotional literature issued by the festival committee unashamedly linked Saddam with the great historical figures of Hammurapi and Nebuchadnezzar, 'whose legacies transcended time and history to fuse with the great strides and magnificent splendour of H.E. President Saddam Hussein'. For this event a special medal was issued showing the portrait of Saddam alongside that of Nebuchadnezzar.

The 1988 festival, held while the war was drawing to a close, lasted only ten days but was even grander. In the words of Sir Terence Clark, then British ambassador to Iraq:

> The diplomatic corps was seated in the Processional Way, by then heavily restored, and we listened to hymns of praise to President Saddam Hussein for Iraq's victory over Iran and to a father recounting to his son the story of the greatness of Nebuchadnezzar, which he likened to the greatness of Saddam. We watched as rows of soldiers and girls dressed in Babylonian costumes marched before us down the Processional Way, accompanied by lit torches and music played on 'Babylonian' instruments, to the far end where two tall palm trees carried the profiled portraits of Nebuchadnezzar on one and the remarkably similar portrait of Saddam on the other.

Thereafter, with the exception of a break in 1990–1 because of the first Gulf War, festivals were held annually until 2002 with the restored Hellenistic theatre, the Al-'Arsh Hall and the Ninmah temple all being used for performances. As late as 2001–2 a new 25-dinar note was issued showing on the reverse the Ishtar Gate and the Lion of Babylon.

E FIG. 207 *above left*
500-fils postage stamp commemorating Babylon Festival

This stamp depicts a medal showing Saddam Hussein side by side with Nebuchadnezzar.

AD 1988, Private collection

E FIG. 208 *above right*
25-dinar banknote

The note shows both the Ishtar Gate and the Lion of Babylon.

AD 2001, Private collection

FIG. 209 *top*
Saddam Hussein's palace at Babylon

Photograph by the author

FIG. 210
**Nebuchadnezzar's Southern Palace in
modern hands**

Here can be seen Babylon reconstructions from
the time of Saddam Hussein, as well as the US
military accommodation known as the 'City of
Tents'.

2003
Photograph by Prof. J. Russell

It is impossible not to have some sympathy with the Iraqi desire to rebuild Babylon, but it was carried out in a manner and on a scale that most architectural conservators find completely unacceptable, even though Iraqi archaeologists did their best to be guided by the evidence from archaeology and cuneiform texts, and the descriptions of historians such as Herodotus. It is fortunate, then, that the second phase of the restoration programme, which included the re-creation of the Hanging Gardens – one of the Seven Wonders of the World – and rebuilding the ancient ziggurat, never took place. But while it may be possible to make excuses for the restoration work just described, there can be nothing but condemnation for some other works undertaken at Babylon during the same period. These included the creation of three artificial lakes on the site and the heaping up of three gigantic mounds, one on the old bed of the River Euphrates, on top of which a palace was built for Saddam. No expense was spared in the construction of this absurdly lavish palace, which provides a commanding view over the ancient site.

There can be no denying that what happened to Babylon in the Saddam era was bad, but what happened in the aftermath of the second Gulf War was inexcusable. In April 2003 a small military camp was established at Babylon by American forces. By June 2003 (when the writer visited Babylon with a group from the British Museum) the camp was still relatively small. Thereafter, however, it rapidly escalated in size so that by the summer of 2004 there was widespread concern about the potential damage that was being caused, with publication in newspapers and on the web of photographs showing the immense scale of the military activity at Babylon. The camp, 150 hectares in size, had been established right in the middle of the ancient city of Babylon, straddling the inner wall of the city, and at its height it was home to two thousand soldiers. Such was the strength of public opinion around the world that at the end of 2004 a decision was taken by the Polish army, which had taken over the camp in September 2003, to hand Babylon back to the Iraqi authorities. To mark this event a meeting was convened at Babylon in the period 11–13 December, for which the Polish military authorities commissioned a report from the archaeologists attached to the Polish forces. This lengthy and very useful document is entitled *Report Concerning the Condition of the Preservation of the Babylon Archaeological Site*. However, while not in any way detracting from the Polish report, the Iraqi minister of culture felt there would be benefit in having further reports, firstly by the Iraqi archaeologists working at Babylon and secondly by myself. Consequently I was invited to the meeting at Babylon and was privileged to be shown around the site together with other participants by Dr Maryam Umran Musah, the curator of Babylon, and her two assistants, Mr Haidar Abdul Wahid and Mr Raed Hamed.

It is impossible to overstress the insensitivity involved in establishing a military camp in the middle of one of the most famous sites of the ancient world – a site that is part of the cultural heritage of the whole world –

FIGS 211, 212
Damage to dragon reliefs at Babylon

2004
Photographs by the author

irrespective of what might have happened there before. This action has been compared with situating a military camp at Stonehenge or around the Great Pyramid – it should not have been allowed to happen. It was a further insult to the Iraqis then to ignore the well-established names of the site of Babylon and to use terms such as 'Ronson Gate', 'Reno Gate', 'Warsaw Gate', and so on. It is quite impossible, however well intentioned the military may have been, to build a military camp without causing extensive damage. The movement around the site of massive military vehicles, sometimes carrying concrete T-blocks, will inevitably have caused damage to the fragile archaeological deposits beneath, although in most cases it is not yet possible to quantify or qualify it. We do know, however, that heavy vehicles were driven along the famous Processional Way, breaking many of the ancient brick paving slabs in the process.

In the course of the tour of inspection we were shown numerous instances of recent damage. We saw about a dozen trenches of various sizes, some of them evidently cut through archaeological deposits. The largest of these, close to the site of the ancient ziggurat Etemenanki, was about 170 metres long, 2 metres deep and 1–1.5 metres wide. Piled up on the sides of the trench were earth mixed with ancient pottery, fragments of brick with inscriptions of Nebuchadnezzar, and ancient bones. This trench was said to have been dug as an anti-tank precaution, which seems excessively zealous given that the threat concerned was a civil insurrection. There were also about a dozen cuttings, evidently done with a mechanical shovel and aimed at removing topsoil to fill up sandbags and HESCO containers (large canvas cases filled with earth) or to create banks of earth for defence. Two of these were about 35 metres by 20 metres with a depth of 6 metres, and while sometimes these cuttings might have been into old spoil-tips remaining from the German excavations in the early twentieth century, on other occasions they are clearly dug into archaeological deposits. Around the camp there were literally thousands of sandbags and HESCO containers, often topped with barbed wire. At some stage it was pointed out that it was bad practice to fill these with earth obtained from ancient Babylon, and the decision was taken to bring in earth and

FIG. 213
**Heavy vehicle damage to Babylon's
Processional Way**

2004
Photograph by the author

FIG. 214 *above*
**HESCO containers filled with displaced
archaeological deposits**

Dr Maryam Musah of the Iraq State Board of
Antiquities on a tour of inspection at Babylon.

2004
Photograph by the author

FIG. 215 *left*
**Anti-tank trench through archaeological
deposits at Babylon**

2004
Photograph by the author

FIGS 216, 217
The helipad at Babylon

2004
Photographs by the author (left) and Prof. J. Russell (below).

sand from outside Babylon – but this is just as bad, if not worse. The bags are biodegradable, and when they disintegrate (as some already have) they will spill their contents, sometimes from archaeological sites outside Babylon, on to the surface of the site, contaminating the deposits and distorting the record at Babylon itself.

Before the war there was already a flattened area for helicopters to land. This helipad was greatly enlarged in size after the occupation and many other parts of the site were flattened and covered in gravel, sometimes compacted and chemically treated to keep down the dust. Apart from the helipad such spaces were then used for barracks, latrines, dining-halls and storehouses and for parking military vehicles and equipment. As in the case of the sandbags the gravel is foreign to Babylon and will again contaminate the archaeological deposits at the site.

In the area of the so-called 'Fuel Farm', where the military vehicles refuelled, there is extensive evidence of spillage that will have caused environmental pollution as well as contamination of the archaeological deposits beneath. Particularly distressing is the damage to ten of the dragon (or *mušhuššu*) figures in the foundations of the Ishtar Gate. These are formed out of moulded bricks, and the damage has obviously been caused by souvenir hunters trying to prise bricks out of the wall.

The disclosure of the full extent of the damage caused widespread outrage, not least at UNESCO, which has now set up a special Babylon committee as an offshoot of its International

Iraq Committee. After the handover Iraqi facility protection officers, 160 strong in the first instance, moved into Babylon to look after the ruins. The proposal was that they should be quartered in the former palace of Saddam. It would be good to report that since then there have been no further problems, but this is not entirely true. The strength of the insurgency in the Hillah area has naturally caused some difficulties, and there have been disagreements between the Antiquities Department and local civic officials, no doubt mirroring what is going on in many other parts of Iraq. On a more positive note, however, there have been some constructive developments. In particular a memorandum of understanding between the World Monuments Fund and the Getty Conservation Institute on one side and the State Board of Antiquities on the other was drawn up in February 2008, promising assistance to the State Board in the preparation of a conservation and management plan for the ancient city of Babylon. Also recent study of old plans and satellite images, chiefly by Elizabeth Stone of Stony Brook University, New York, suggests that the damage may not be quite as bad as first thought, in that some of the trenches, cuttings and flattened areas are in parts of the site that are not archaeologically sensitive. If this is indeed true, it is more by luck than judgement. We must now await the comprehensive report that is promised before a complete assessment of damage is possible.

Babylon is still not a World Heritage Site, but on 29 October 2003 (while it was still under military occupation) it was included by the Iraq government on their tentative list, a necessary preliminary to a formal aplication for inclusion in the World Heritage List. Elsewhere in Iraq, as at Babylon, there are cautious grounds for optimism. A recent survey by a joint Iraq – British Museum team, facilitated by the British Army, found that at eight important archaeological sites in the south of the country, including Larsa and Lagash, there was no evidence of fresh or ongoing looting. Of course, it would be dangerous to conclude that the same conditions prevail throughout the country, and the situation may well be much worse at sites further to the north, where the looting after the war is known to have been more intensive. However, it certainly seems as if the fever of looting that erupted during and after the coalition invasion has now abated. If this is indeed the case, and if the security situation continues to improve as it has done in recent months, it will not be long before the Iraq State Board for Antiquities and Heritage is able to make serious advances towards the further protection and promotion of the Iraqi cultural heritage.

Above all, it is to be hoped that in the future Babylon will be accorded the respect it deserves not only as one of the most important archaeological sites in the world, but as a place that has played a significant role in the development of world civilization.

Notes: The Legacy of Babylon

326. For a wide-ranging treatment of these issues see Dalley 1998.
327. Larsen 1987; Rochberg 2004: 268–9.
328. Nissen et al. 1993: 25–9, and see generally Robson 1999.
329. Summary and quotation here are after Britton and Walker 1996: 66–7.
330. Adapted from Stol 2004: 72–3.
331. See especially Geller 2004.
332. Lieberman 1987.
333. In one sense Rome was both cities: Augustine's work was in part a response to Alaric's recent sacking of Christian Rome (Kaufman 1995: 75–7).

334. Though it was never wholly forgotten; one mound was always known as Babil, and many of the early European visitors to Mesopotamia recognized or were guided to the correct site.
335. Borges 1998: 117.
336. More recently it has been argued that Sardanapalus is a conflation of the names of Ashurbanipal and Esarhaddon.
337. Kirby 1978: 121; Gallagher 1982: 69.
338. Hanson 1972: 498.

List of Exhibits

Concordance of British Museum Object Numbers

Illustration Acknowledgements

All photographs of British Museum objects are taken by members of the British Museum Imaging and Photographic Department and are copyright the Trustees of the British Museum. Numbers given in this list are figure numbers.

Photo © akg images: 117

Ancient Wonders, Inc., Brighton, Michigan USA: 84

© Bibliothèque nationale de France: 16, 21, 121, 122, 144

The Bodleian Library, University of Oxford: 131

Reproduced by kind permission of the Board of Trinity College, Dublin: 57

bpk:
  © bpk 14
  © bpk/Kupferstichkabinett, SMB/ Volker-H. Schneider: 98
  © bpk/SMB-Vorderasiatisches Museum Berlin/Olaf M. Teßmer: 26, 31, 32, 34, 38, 39, 63, 41, 46, 72, 76, 77, 78, 79, 81, 107, 108, 130, 182, 183
  © bpk/SBB: 198
  © bpk/SBB/Ruth Schacht: 5; 25, 40
  © bpk/Vorderasiatisches Museum, Berlin; SMB: 24
  © bpk/Vorderasiatisches Museum, Berlin; SMB/Klaus Göken: 35
  © bpk/Vorderasiatisches Museum, Berlin; SMB/R. Jessen: 22
  © bpk/Vorderasiatisches Museum, Berlin; SMB/Jürgen Liepe: 30, 33, 60

Bridgeman Art Library:
  © Bibliothèque Municipale, Dijon, France/ The Bridgeman Art Library: 11
  © Bibliothèque nationale de France, Paris/The Bridgeman Art Library: 137
  © British Library, London, UK/ British Library Board. All Rights Reserved/The Bridgeman Art Library: 112
  Photo © Castello della Manta, Saluzzo, Italy, Alinari/The Bridgeman Art Library: 95
  Photo ©Galleria degli Uffizi, Florence, Italy/The Bridgeman Art Library: 96
  © Held Collection/The Bridgeman Art Library: 10;
  © Kunsthistorisches Museum, Vienna, Austria/The Bridgeman Art Library: 116
  © Musée des Tapisseries, Angers, France, Lauros, Giraudon/The Bridgeman Art Library: 171
  © Musée d'Orsay, Paris, France, Giraudon/The Bridgeman Art Library: 101
  Photo © Museo Archeologico Nazionale, Naples, Italy/The Bridgeman Art Library: 86
  Photo © National Gallery, London, UK/The Bridgeman Art Library: 94
  © National Gallery, London, UK/The Bridgeman Art Library: 164
  © Royal Holloway and Bedford New College, Surrey, UK/The Bridgeman Art Library: 196
  © Whitford and Hughes, London, UK/The Bridgeman Art Library: 6

© The British Library Board: 105, 111, 123, 124, 141, 142, 143, 163, 186, 188

Broelmuseum, Kortrijk: 120

Courtesy of Cinemathêque Française 200

Photo © City and County of Swansea: Swansea Museum Collection: 58

Conner Contemporary Art, Washington, DC: 192

CORBIS:
  © Richard Ashworth/Robert Harding World Imagery/CORBIS: 113
  © Mick Wheeler/CORBIS: 12
  © Lynn Goldsmith/CORBIS: 201

J.E. Curtis: 209, 211, 212, 213, 214, 215, 216

The De Morgan Centre for the Study of 19th Century Art and Society: 139

© Erik Desmazieres/David R. Godine publisher: 197

M.C. Escher Foundation, Netherlands: 191

© Fotoarchiv /SMB- Vorderasiatisches Museum: 23

© Georg Gerster/Panos: 8

Germany, Mittelrhein-Museum Koblenz: 118

Paul Goodhead: maps and diagrams in figs 3, 4, 21, 28, 29, 45, 85, 88, 93, 125, 148.

Photo © Hart Gallery, Copyright Anne Desmet: 194, 195

Arnulf Hausleiter/Deutsches Archäologisches Institut: 153

Israel Antiquities Authority: 150

© Michael Lassel: 193

Mittelrhein-Museum, Koblenz: 118

© 2007 Musée du Louvre/Raphaël Chipault: 52, 67, 68, 80, 147, 184

© 2008 National Gallery of Art, Washington DC: 146

National Museums Liverpool, Walker Art Gallery: 145

Newcastle City Council, The Laing Art Gallery, Tyne and Wear Museums: 167

© Photograph reproduced by kind permission of the Bethlem Art and History Collection Trust: 169

Photo © 2008 Museum of Fine Arts, Boston: 100

Photo © Photo12com-ARJ: 135

Private collection: 83

Private collection: 180

© Rheinisches Bildarchiv Koeln: 136

RMN:
  Photo RMN/© Michèle Bellot: 102
  Photo RMN/© Gérard Blot: 134
  Photo RMN/© Jérôme Galland: 75
  Photo RMN/© Christian Jean/Jean Schormans: 109
  Photo RMN/© Hervé Lewandowski: 51, 103, 104
  Photo RMN/© Franck Raux: 1, 26, 36, 54, 65

© Roger Viollet/Getty Images: 15

Dr. J. Russell: 210, 217

SMB-Vorderasiatisches Museum Inv: 1

Straight Arrow Books, NY: 2

Su concessione del Ministero per I Beni e le attivita culturali. Soprintendenza di Siena e Grosseto: 119.

© Tate, London 2006: 154, 158

© Triangle Film Corporation/Wark Producing, courtesy the Kobal Collection: 199

V&A Images/Victoria and Albert Museum: 170

© Venezia, Biblioteca Nazionale Marciana: 114

University of Edinburgh Library: 133

Bibliography

BABYLON EXHIBITION CATALOGUES

Many of the objects featured in this volume have also been included in the corresponding French and German exhibition catalogues. These publications include additional bibliography:

André-Salvini 2008:
B. André-Salvini (ed.), *Babylone. Catalogue de l'exposition « Babylone »* Paris, musée du Louvre, 14 Mars–2 Juin 2008. Paris.
Marzahn 2008:
J. Marzahn (ed.), *Babylon: Wahrheit*. Berlin.
Wullen 2008:
M. Wullen (ed.), *Babylon: Mythos*. Berlin.

CLASSICAL RESOURCES

Editions used in this catalogue are as follows:

Arian, *Anabasis*
1976, 1983, trans. P.A. Brunt and E.I. Robson, *Anabasis of Alexander*. Loeb Classical Library. 2 vols London.
St Augustine, *City of God*
1957-72, trans. G. E. McCracken, W. M. Green, D. S. Wiesen, P. Levine, E. M. Sanford and W. C. Greene. *Saint Augustine,* The City of God Against the Pagans. Loeb Classical Library. 7 vols. London.
al-Biruni, *Chronology of Ancient Nations*
1879, trans. C. E. Sachau, *The Chronology of Ancient Nations. An English Version of the Arabic Text of the Athâr-ul-Bâkiya of Albîrûnî, or Vestiges of the Past Collected and Reduced to Writing by the Author in AH 390-1, AD 1000*. London.
Dante, *Inferno*
1996, trans. P. Dale. *The Divine Comedy*. London.
Diodorus Siculus
1933-, trans. C. H. Oldfather, C. L. Sherman, C. B. Welles, R. M. Geer and F. R. Walton *Diodorus Siculus,* Library of History. Loeb Classical Library. 12 vols. London.
Eusebius *Chronicle*:
1913-26, 1984, trans. R. Helm, *Eusebius, Werke. Vol. VII, Die Chronik des Hieronymus*. Berlin.
Eusebius *Praeparatio Evangelica*
1903, trans. E. H. Gifford, *Eusebius of Caesarea,* Praeparatio Evangelica (Preparation for the Gospel*)*. 5 vols. London.
Herodotus, *Histories*:
2003, trans. A. de Selincourt, ed. J. Marincola, *Herodotus,* The Histories. London.

Josephus, *Jewish Antiquities*:
1930-65; 1967-81, trans. H. St J. Thackeray, R. Marcus, A. Wikgren and L. H. Feldman, *Josephus,* Jewish Antiquities. Loeb Classical Library. 5 vols (vols. IV-IX in *Josephus*). London.
Josephus, *Against Apion*:
1926, H. St J. Thackeray trans. *Josephus, Vol. I:* The Life*;* Against Apion. Loeb Classical Library. London.
Philo of Byzantium
Trans. D. Oates, in Finkel 1988.
Quintus Curtius Rufus, *History of Alexander*:
1984, trans. J. Yardley, *Quintus Curtius Rufus,* The History of Alexander. Harmondsworth.
Strabo, *Geography*
1917-32, trans. H. L. Jones, *Strabo,* Geography. Loeb Classical Library. 8 vols. London.
Valerius Maximus, *Memorable Doings and Sayings*
2000, trans. D. R. S. Bailey, *Valerius Maximus,* Memorable Doings and Sayings. Loeb Classical Library. 2 vols. London.
Yaqut
Cited in C. Janssen 1995, *Babil, the City of Witchcraft and Wine. The Name and Fame of Babylon in Medieval Arabic Geographical Texts*. Mesopotamian History and Environment Series 2. Ghent.

For biblical quotations the New International Version (NIV) is used throughout.

BIBLIOGRAPHY

Adler 1930:
E.K. Adler (ed.), *Jewish Travellers*. London.
Ainsworth 1888:
W.F. Ainsworth, *A Personal Narrative of the Euphrates Expedition*. 2 vols. London.
Alexander 1928:
C.M. Alexander, *Baghdad in Bygone Days*. London.
Alexander-Knotter 1999:
M. Alexander-Knotter, 'An Ingenious Device: Rembrandt's use of Hebrew inscriptions,' *Studia Rosenthaliana* 33: 131–59.
Andrae 1952:
W. Andrae, *Babylon, die Versunkene Weltstadt und ihr Ausgräber, Robert Koldewey*. Berlin.
Andrae 1961:
W. Andrae, *Lebenserrinerungen eines Ausbgräbers*. K. Bittel and E. Heinrich eds. Stuttgart.
Andrae and Boehmer 1992:
E.W. Andrae and R.M. Boehmer, *Bilder eines Ausgräbers: Die Orientbilder von Walter Andrae*

1898–1919 / Sketches by an Excavator: Walter Andrae's Oriental Sketches (2nd edn). Berlin.
André-Salvini: 2003:
B. André-Salvini: *Le Code de Hammurabi*. Paris.
André and Ziegler 1982:
B. André and C. Ziegler, *Naissance de l'écriture. Cuneiformes et hiéroglyphes*. Paris.
Anonymous 1780:
Anonymous comment in *Critical Review*, June 1780: 405.
Anonymous 1803:
Anonymous, *An Inscription of the size of the original, copied from a stone lately found among the ruins of ancient Babylon and sent as a present to Sir Hugh Inglis, baronet, by Harford Jones Esq., the Hon. the East India Company's Resident at Bagdad, and now deposited in the Company's Library in Leadenhall Street, London*. London.
Anonymous 1821:
Anonymous, *A Description of the Pictures Belshazzar's Feast and Joshua, painted by Mr Martin, lately exhibited at the British Institution, and now at no. 343, Strand* (2nd edn) London.
Anonymous 1878:
Anonymous, *Handbook for Travellers in Turkey in Asia including Constantinople* (4th edn). London.
Armstrong 1990:
C.M. Armstrong, *The Moralizing Prints of Cornelis Anthonisz*. Princeton.
Asher 1840:
A. Asher (ed.), *The Itinerary of Rabbi Benjamin of Tudela*. London and Berlin.
Baine and Baine 1975:
R.M. Baine and M.R. Baine, 'Blake's Other Tigers, and "The Tyger",' *Studies in English Literature, 1500–1900* 15: 563–78.
Barnett 1974:
R.D. Barnett, 'Charles Bellino and the Beginnings of Assyriology,' *Iraq* 36: 5–28.
Barnett 1976:
R.D. Barnett, *Sculptures from the North Palace of Ashurbanipal at Nineveh (668–627 BC)*. London.
Bartsch 1803–21:
A. von Bartsch, *Le Peintre-Graveur*. 21 vols. Vienna.
Bartsch 1987:
A. von Bartsch, *The Illustrated Bartsch* [vol. 56]. New York.
Beaulieu 1989:
P.-A. Beaulieu, *The Reign of Nabonidus King of Babylon 556–539 B.C.* Yale Near Eastern Researches 10. Yale.
Belaiew 1927–8:
N.T. Belaiew, 'On the Sumerian "Mina," its Origin

and Probable Value,' *Transactions of the Newcomen Society* 8: 120–53.

Bennett and Mandelbrote 1998:
J. Bennett and S. Mandelbrote, *The Garden, the Ark, the Tower, the Temple: Biblical Metaphors of Knowledge in Early Modern Europe*. Oxford.

Bergamini 1977:
G. Bergamini, 'Levels of Babylon reconsidered,' *Mesopotamia* 12: 111–52.

Bergamini 1988:
G. Bergamini, 'Excavations in Shu-Anna, Babylon 1987,' *Mesopotamia* 23: 5–17.

Berger 1973:
P.-R. Berger, *Die neubabylonischen Königsinschriften: Königsinschriften des ausgehenden babylonischen Reiches (626–539 a. Chr.)*. Alter Orient und Altes Testament 4 (1). Neukirchen.

Berger 1975:
P.-R. Berger, 'Der Kyros-Zylinder mit den Zusatzfragment BIN II Nr. 32 und die akkadischen Personennamen im Danielbuch,' *Zeitschrift für Assyriologie* 54: 192–234.

Bergmann 1953:
E. Bergmann, *Codex Hammurabi Textus Primigenius* (3rd edn). Rome.

Bewsher 1867:
J.B. Bewsher, 'On Part of Mesopotamia Contained Between Sheriat-el-Beytha, on the Tigris, and Tell Ibrahim,' *Journal of the Royal Geographical Society* 11 (4): 155–9.

Bialostocki 1984:
J. Bialostocki, 'A New Look at Rembrandt Iconography,' *Artibus et Historiae* 5: 9–19.

Bindman 1977:
D. Bindman, *Blake as an Artist*. Oxford.

Bindman 1978:
D. Bindman, *The Complete Graphic Works of William Blake*. London.

Bindman 1999:
D. Bindman, 'The English Apocalypse,' in F. Carey (ed.), *Apocalypse and the Shape of Things to Come*. London.

Bindman 2001:
D. Bindman, *William Blake: The Complete Illuminated Books*. London.

Binyon 1898:
L. Binyon, *Catalogue of Drawings by British Artists, and Artists of Foreign Origin Working in Great Britain*, 4 vols. London.

Bohrer 1998:
F.N. Bohrer, 'Inventing Assyria: Exoticism and reception in nineteenth-century England and France,' *The Art Bulletin* 80: 336–56.

Bohrer 2003:
F.N. Bohrer, *Orientalism and Visual Culture: Imagining Mesopotamia in Nineteenth-century Europe*. Cambridge.

Boime 1987:
A. Boime. *Art in an Age of Revolution, 1750–1800*. Chicago and London.

Bomford et al. 2006:
D. Bomford, J. Kirby, A. Roy, A. Rüger and R. White, *Art in the Making: Rembrandt*. London.

Borger 1975:
R. Borger (ed.), *Die Welt des Alten Orients, zum 200. Geburtstag Georg Friedrich Grotefends. Keilschrift, Grabungen, Gelehrte*. Göttingen.

Borges 1998:
J. L. Borges, *Collected Fictions*, Translated by Andrew Huxley. London.

Börker-Klähn 1982:
J. Börker-Klähn, *Altvorderasiatische Bildstelen und vergleichbare Felsreliefs*. Baghdader Forschungen 4. Mainz.

Brinkman 1964:
J.A. Brinkman, 'Merodach–Baladan,' in R.D. Biggs and J.A. Brinkman (eds), *Studies Presented to A. Leo Oppenheim, June 7, 1964*. Chicago.

Britton and Walker 1996:
J. Britton and C.B.F. Walker, 'Astronomy and Astrology in Mesopotamia,' in C.B.F. Walker (ed.), *Astronomy before the Telescope*: 42–67. London.

Buckingham 1827:
J.S. Buckingham, *Travels in Mesopotamia*. London.

Budge 1920:
E.A.W. Budge, *By Nile and Tigris*. 2 vols. London.

Butlin 1981:
M. Butlin, *The Paintings and Drawings of William Blake*. 2 vols. London and New Haven.

Butlin 1981–2:
M. Butlin, 'A Newly Discovered Watermark and a Visionary's Way with Dates,' *Blake: An Illustrated Quarterly* 15 (1981–2): 101–3.

Butlin 1983–4:
M. Butlin, '*Paintings and Drawings of William Blake (1981)*: Some minor additions,' *Blake: An Illustrated Quarterly* 17 (1983–4): 159.

Butlin 1990:
M. Butlin, *William Blake, 1757–1827*. London.

Campbell 1992:
M.J. Campbell, *John Martin: Visionary Printmaker*. York.

Campbell Thompson 1902:
R. Campbell Thompson, *Cuneiform Texts from Babylonian Tablets in the British Museum*. Vol. 14. London.

Carey 1999:
F. Carey (ed.), *The Apocalypse and the Shape of Things to Come*. London.

Carruthers 1929:
D. Carruthers (ed.), *The Desert Route to India*. Hakluyt Society, Second Series, No. 63. London.

Clayton and Price 1988:
P.A. Clayton and M.J. Price, 'Introduction,' in P.A. Clayton and M.J. Price (eds) *The Seven Wonders of the Ancient World*: xvi–12. London and New York.

Collins 1998:
J. J. Collins, *The Apocalyptic Imagination: An Introduction to Jewish Apocalyptic Literature*. (2nd edn) Grand Rapids and Cambridge.

Contenau 1929:
G. Contenau, *Contrats néo-babyloniens II: Achéménides et séleucides*. Textes cunéiformes du Louvre 13. Paris.

Cowling 2004:
M. Cowling, 'Archaeology and Aestheticism: *The Babylonian Marriage Market* and High Victorian taste,' in *The Price of Beauty: Edwin Long's* Babylonian Marriage Market *(1875)*: 14–23. London.

Cowper 1894:
H.S. Cooper, *Through Turkish Arabia*. London.

Crüsemann et al. 2000:
N. Crüsemann, U. von Eickstedt, E. Klengel-Brandt, L. Martin, J. Marzahn and R.-B. Wartke, *Vorderasiatisches Museum Berlin. Geschichte und Geschichten zum hundertjährigen Bestehen*. Berlin.

Dalley 1994:
S.M. Dalley, 'Nineveh, Babylon and the Hanging Gardens: Cuneiform and classical sources reconciled,' *Iraq* 56: 45–58.

Dalley 1998:
S.M. Dalley (ed.), *The Legacy of Mesopotamia*. Oxford.

Dalley 2002:
S.M. Dalley, 'More about the Hanging Gardens', in L. al-Gailani-Werr, J.E. Curtis, H. Martin, A. McMahon, J. Oates and J.E. Reade (eds), *Of Pots and Pans: Papers on the Archaeology and History of Mesopotamia and Syria as presented to David Oates on his 75th Birthday*: 67–73. London.

Dalley 2003:
S.M. Dalley, 'Why did Herodotus not Mention the Hanging Gardens of Babylon?' in P. Derow and R. Parker (eds), *Herodotus and his World: Essays from a Conference in Memory of George Forrest*: 171–89. Oxford.

Dalley 2005:
S.M. Dalley, 'Semiramis in History and Legend,' in E.S. Gruen (ed.), *Cultural Borrowings and Ethnic Appropriations in Antiquity*. Oriens et Occidens 8: 11–22. Stuttgart.

De Chancel 1987:
B. de Chancel, 'Les manuscrits de la Bouquechardière de Jean de Courcy,' *Revue d'histoire des textes* 17 : 219–90.

Delaporte 1920:
L. Delaporte, *Catalogue des cylindres orientaux, cachets et pierres gravées de style oriental du Musée du Louvre I, Fouilles et missions*. Paris.

Delaporte 1923:
L. Delaporte, *Catalogue des cylindres orientaux, cachets et pierres gravées de style oriental du Musée du Louvre, II, Acquisitions*. Paris.

Delitzsch 1902:
F. Delitzsch, *Babel und Bibel: Ein Vortrag*. Leipzig.

Delitzsch 1903:
F. Delitzsch, *Zweiter Vortrag über Babel und Bibel*. Stuttgart.

Delitzsch 1905:
F. Delitzsch, *Babel und Bibel. Dritter (Schluss-)*

Vortrag. Stuttgart.

Delitzsch 1906:
F. Delitzsch, *Babel and Bible: Three Lectures on the Significance of Assyriological Research for Religion, Embodying the Most Important Criticisms and the Author's Replies*. Chicago.

Delitzsch 1920:
F. Delitzsch, *Die Grosse Täuschung (Teil I)*. Stuttgart.

Delitzsch 1921:
F. Delitzsch, *Die Grosse Täuschung (Teil II)*. Württemberg.

De Vries 1991:
L. De Vries, 'The Changing Face of Realism,' in D. Freedberg and J. de Vries (eds), *Art in History / History in Art: Studies in Seventeenth-century Dutch Culture*: 209–44. Santa Monica.

De Winkel 2006:
M. De Winkel, *Fashion and Fancy: Dress and Meaning in Rembrandt's Paintings*. Amsterdam.

Dhorme 1911:
E. Dhorme, 'Tablette rituelle néo-babylonienne,' *Revue d'Assyriologique et d'Archéologie Orientale* 8: 41–63.

Dodgson 1903:
C. Dodgson, *Catalogue of Early German and Flemish Woodcuts Preserved in the Department of Prints and Drawings in the British Museum (vol. 1)*. London.

Dodgson 1911:
C. Dodgson, *Catalogue of Early German and Flemish Woodcuts Preserved in the Department of Prints and Drawings in the British Museum (vol. 2)*. London.

Dodgson 1926:
C. Dodgson, *Albrecht Dürer*. London.

Donbaz 1990:
V. Donbaz, 'Two Neo-Assyrian Stelae in the Antakya and Kahrammarafl Museums,' *Annual Review of the Royal Inscriptions of Mesopotamia Project* 8: 5-24.

Don-Yehiya 1998:
E. Don-Yehiya, 'Zionism in Retrospective,' *Modern Judaism* 18(3): 267-76.

Drew 2001:
W.M. Drew, *D.W. Griffith's* Intolerance: *Its Genesis and Vision*. Jefferson and London.

Eichmann et al. 2006:
R. Eichmann, H. Schaudig and A. Hausleiter, 'Archaeology and Epigraphy at Tayma (Saudi Arabia),' *Arabian Archaeology and Epigraphy* 17: 163–76.

Ellis 1881:
T.J. Ellis, *On a Raft, and through the Desert*. 2 vols. London and New York.

Elsässer 2000:
T. Elsässer, *Metropolis*. London.

Esposito 2006:
D. Esposito, '*Dalziel's Bible Gallery* (1881): Assyria and the biblical illustration in nineteenth-century Britain,' in S.W. Holloway (ed.), *Orientalism, Assyriology and the Bible*. Hebrew Bible Monographs 10: 267–96. Sheffield.

Feaver 1975:
W. Feaver, *The Art of John Martin*. Oxford.

Findlen 2004:
P. Findlen (ed.), *Athanasius Kircher: The Last Man Who Knew Everything*. London and New York.

Finet 1973:
A. Finet, *Le Code de Hammurapi*. Littératures anciennes du Proche-Orient 6. Paris.

Finke 1974:
U. Finke, *German Painting from Romanticism to Expressionism*. London.

Finkel 1988:
I.L. Finkel, 'The Hanging Gardens of Babylon,' in P.A. Clayton and M.J. Price (eds), *The Seven Wonders of the Ancient World*: 38–58. London and New York.

Finkel 1998:
I.L. Finkel, 'A Babylonian ABC,' *British Museum Magazine* 31: 20–2.

Finkel 1999:
I.L. Finkel, 'The Lament of Nabû-šuma-ukin,' in J. Renger (ed.), *Babylon: Focus Mesopotamischer Geschicte, Wiege früher Gelehramskeit, Mythos in der Moderne*. Saarbrücken.

Finkel 2000:
I.L.Finkel, 'On Late Babylonian Medical Training,' in A.R. George and I.L. Finkel (eds), *Wisdom, Gods and Literature. Studies in Assyriology in Honour of W.G. Lambert*: 137–223.

Fisher and Ryland 1803:
T. Fisher, with J. Ryland (engraver), *An Inscription of the Size of the Original, Copied from a Stone lately Found among the Ruins of Ancient Babylon and Sent as a Present to Sir Hugh Inglis Bart. by Harford Jones Esq., the Honorable East India Company's Resident at Baghdad*. London.

Fitz 1991:
S. Fitz, 'Die Farbglasuren auf neubabylonischer Baukeramik,' in R. Wartke (ed.), *Handwerk und Technologie im Alten Orient. Ein Beitrug zur Geschichte der Teknik im Altertum*: 27–9. Mainz.

Fossey 1904:
C. Fossey, *Manuel d'Assyriologie*, tome I: *explorations et fouilles, déchiffrement des cunéiformes, origine et histoire de l'écriture*. Paris.

Foster 2004:
K.P. Foster, 'The Hanging Gardens of Nineveh,' *Iraq* 66: 207–20.

Foster 2005:
B.R. Foster, *Before the Muses: An Anthology of Akkadian Literature* (3rd edn). Maryland.

Frame 1995:
G. Frame, *Rulers of Babylonia from the Second Dynasty of Isin to the End of Assyrian Domination (1157–612 BC)*. Royal Inscriptions of Mesopotamia, Babylonian Periods 2. Toronto.

Frankfort 1996:
H. Frankfort, *The Art and Architecture of the Ancient Orient* (5th edn). New Haven and London.

Fraser 1842:
J.B. Fraser, *Mesopotamia and Assyria, from the*

Earliest Ages to the Present Time; With Illustrations of their Natural History. Edinburgh.

Fraser 1910:
D. Fraser, *Persia and Turkey in Revolt*. Edinburgh and London.

Furuli 2003:
R. Furuli, *Persian Chronology and the Length of the Babylonian Exile of the Jews*. Oslo.

Gadd 1936:
C.J. Gadd, *The Stones of Assyria*. London.

Gall 1994:
L. Gall (ed.), *FFM 1200. Traditionen und Perspektiven einer Stadt. Kat. Ausstellung Bockenheimer Depot Frankfurt/Main*. Sigmaringen.

Gallagher 1982:
B. Gallagher, 'Racist Ideology and Black Abnormality in *The Birth of a Nation*,' *Phylon* 43(1): 68–76.

Gasche et al. 1987:
H. Gasche, R.G. Killick, J.A. Black, et al., *Habl as-Sahr 1983–85: Nebuchadnezzar's Cross-country Wall north of Sippar*. Northern Akkad Project Reports 1. Ghent.

Gaster 1899:
M. Gaster, *The Chronicles of Jerahmeel; or the Hebrew Bible Historiale. Being a Collection of Apocryphal and Pseudo-epigraphical Books (by Various Authors: Collected by Eleazar ben Asher, the Levite) Dealing with the History of the World from the Creation to the Death of Judas Maccabeus*. Oriental Translation Fund. New series 4. London.

Geller 1997:
M.J. Geller, 'The Last Wedge,' *Zeitschrift für Assyriologie* 87: 43–95.

Geller 1997–2000:
M.J. Geller, 'The Aramaic Incantation in Cuneiform Script (AO 6489 = TCL 6, 58),' *Jaarbericht 'Ex Oriente Lux'* 35–6: 127–43.

Geller 2004:
M.J. Geller, 'West Meets East: Early Greek and Babylonian diagnosis,' in H.F.J. Horstmanshoff and M. Stol (eds), *Magic and Rationality in Ancient Near Eastern and Graeco-Roman Medicine*: 11–61. Leiden.

George 1992:
A.R. George, *Babylonian Topographical Texts*. Orientalia Lovaniensia Analecta 40. Leuven.

Gibson 1972:
M. Gibson, *The City and Area of Kish*. Field Research Projects. Miami.

Gibson 1989:
W.S. Gibson, '*Mirror of the Earth': World Landscape in Sixteenth-century Flemish Painting*, Princeton.

Glassner 1993:
J.-J. Glassner, *Chroniques mésopotamiennes*. Paris.

Godwin 1979:
J. Godwin, *Athanasius Kircher: A Renaissance Man and the Quest for Lost Knowledge*. London.

Goetz 1938:
H. Goetz, 'Persians and Persian Costumes in Dutch Painting of the Seventeenth Century,' *The Art Bulletin* 20 (3): 280–90.

Goldsmith 1993:
S. Goldsmith, *Unbuilding Jerusalem: Apocalypse and Romantic Representation*. Ithaca.

Grayson 1975a:
A.K. Grayson, *Assyrian and Babylonian Chronicles*. Texts from Cuneiform Sources 5. Locust Valley.

Grayson 1975b:
A.K. Grayson, *Babylonian Historical-literary Texts*. Toronto and Buffalo.

Guinan 2002:
A. Guinan, 'A Severed Head Laughed: Stories of divinatory interpretation,' in L. Ciraolo and J. Seidel (eds), *Magic and Divination in the Ancient World*. Ancient Magic and Divination 2: 7–40. Leiden.

Gunning 2008:
T. Gunning, *The Films of Fritz Lang: Allegories of Vision and Modernity*. London.

Hager 1801:
J. Hager, *A Dissertation on the Newly Discovered Babylonian Inscriptions*. London.

Hagstrum 1964:
J.H. Hagstrum, *William Blake: Poet and Painter*. Chicago.

Hanson 1972:
B. Hanson, 'D.W. Griffith: Some sources,' *Art Bulletin* 5: 493–515.

Henderson 1985:
G. Henderson, 'The Manuscript Model of the Angers "Apocalypse" Tapestries,' *The Burlington Magazine* 127: 208–19.

Heuzey 1906:
L. Heuzey, 'Les Deux Dragons sacrés de Babylone et leur prototype chaldéen,' *Revue d'Assyriologie et d'Archéologie Orientale* 6 (3): 95–104.

Hilprecht 1903:
H.V. Hilprecht, *Explorations in Bible Lands during the Nineteenth Century*. Edinburgh.

Hind 1923:
A.M. Hind, *A Catalogue of Rembrandt's Etchings; Chronologically Arranged and Completely Illustrated*. 2 vols. London.

Hollstein 1953:
F.W.H. Hollstein, *Dutch & Flemish Etchings, Engravings and Woodcuts, ca. 1450–1700* [vol. 8]. Amsterdam.

Hollstein 1954:
F.W.H. Hollstein, *German Engravings, Etchings and Woodcuts, c. 1400–1700* [vol. 2]. Amsterdam.

Hollstein 1986:
F.W.H. Hollstein, *Dutch & Flemish Etchings, Engravings and Woodcuts, ca. 1450–1700* [vol. 30]. Amsterdam.

Hollstein 1993–4:
F.W.H. Hollstein, *The New Hollstein Dutch & Flemish Etchings, Engravings and Woodcuts, 1450–1700: M. van Heemskerck*. 2 vols. Amsterdam.

Hollstein 2001:
F.W.H. Hollstein, *The New Hollstein Dutch & Flemish Etchings, Engravings and Woodcuts, 1450–1700: P. Galle*. 4 vols. Amsterdam.

Horne 1836:
T.H. Horne, *Landscape Illustrations of the Bible, Consisting of Views of the most Remarkable Places Mentioned in the Old and New Testaments. From Original Sketches Taken on the Spot*. 2 vols. London.

Horowitz 1998:
W. Horowitz, *Mesopotamian Cosmic Geography*. Winona Lake.

Hunger and Pingree 1989:
H. Hunger and D. Pingree, *MUL.APIN. An Astronomical Compendium in Cuneiform*. Archiv für Orientforschung Beiheft 24. Horn.

Inowlocki 2006:
S. Inowlocki, 'Josephus' Rewriting of the Babel Narrative (Gen. 11:1–9),' *Journal for the Study of Judaism* 37: 169–91.

Invernizzi 2000:
A. Invernizzi, 'Discovering Babylon with Pietro della Valle,' in P. Matthiae et al. (eds), *Proceedings of the First International Congress on the Archaeology of the Ancient Near East* (Rome, May 18th–23rd 1998) 1: 643–9. Rome.

Ishaq 1979–81:
D. Ishaq, 'The Excavations at the Southern Part of the Processions-street and Nabu sha Hare Temple,' *Sumer* 41: 30–3, 49–54.

Ives 1773:
E. Ives, *A Voyage from England to India in the Year 1754*. London.

Jakob-Rost 1997:
L. Jakob-Rost, *Die Stempelsiegel im Vorderasiatischen Museum Berlin* (2nd edn). Mainz.

Jamot 1924:
P. Jamot, *Degas*. Paris.

Jobert 1997:
B. Jobert, *Delacroix*. Paris

Johanning 1988:
K. Johanning, *Der Babel-Bibel-Streit. Eine forschungsgeschichtliche Studie*. Frankfurt am Main.

Johnson 1989:
L. Johnson, *The Paintings of Eugène Delacroix: A Critical Catalogue (Vols 5 and 6: The Public Decorations and their Sketches)*. 2 vols. Oxford.

Johnson and Grant 1979:
M.L. Johnson and J.E. Grant, *Blake's Poetry and Designs*. London.

Jones 1997:
A. Jones, 'A Greek Papyrus Containing Babylonian Lunar Theory,' *Zeitschrift für Papyrologie und Epigraphik* 119: 167–72.

Jonsson 1998:
C.O. Jonsson, *The Gentile Times Reconsidered: Chronology and Christ's Return*. (3rd edn). Atlanta.

Jursa 2008:
M. Jursa, 'Nabû-šarrūssu-ukîn, rab-ša-reši, und Nebusarsekim' (Jer. 39:3), *NABU* 2008/5: 9–10.

Kaufman 1995:
P.I. Kaufman, 'Redeeming Politics: Augustine's Cities of God,' in. D.F. Donnelly (ed.), *The City of God: A Collection of Critical Essays*: 75–92. New York.

Kenneally 2007:
C. Kenneally, *The First Word: The Search for the Origins of Language*. New York: Viking.

Keppel 1827:
G. Keppel, *Personal Narrative of a Journey from India to England*. 2 vols. London.

Kerrich 1829:
T. Kerrich, *A Catalogue of the Prints, which have been Engraved by Martin Heemskerck; Or Rather an Essay Towards such a Catalogue*. Cambridge.

Ker Porter 1821–2:
R. Ker Porter, *Travels in Georgia, Persia, Armenia, Ancient Babylonia, &c. &c. During the Years 1817, 1818, 18819 and 1820*. 2 vols. London.

Keynes 1966:
G. Keynes (ed.), *The Complete Writings of William Blake*. Oxford.

King 1908:
L.W. King, *Cuneiform Texts from Babylonian Tablets in the British Museum*. Vol. 24. London.

Kinnier Wilson 2007
J.V. Kinnier Wilson, *Studia Etanaica. New Texts and Discussions*. Alter Orient und Altes Testament 338. Münster.

Kinnier Wilson and Finkel 2007:
J.V. Kinnier Wilson and I.L. Finkel, 'On *būšānu* and *di'u*, or why Nabonidus went to Tema,' *Le Journal des Médecines* 9: 17–22.

Kirby 1978:
J.T. Kirby. 'Griffith's Racial Portraiture,' *Phylon* 39(2): 118–27.

Klengel-Brandt and Cholidis 2006:
E. Klengel-Brandt and N. Cholidis, *Die Terakotten von Babylon im Vorderasiatischen Museum in Berlin. Teil I, Die Anthropomorphen Figuren*. Wissenschaftliche Veröffentlichung der Deutschen Orient-Gesellschaft (WVDOG) 115. Saarwellingen.

Klein 1996:
P.K. Klein, 'Review of Williams, J. *The Illustrated Beatus* vols I and II,' *The Burlington Magazine* 138 (1115): 130–1.

Koldewey 1900:
R. Koldewey, 'Die Götter Adad und Marduk,' *Mitteilungen der Deutschen Orient-Gesellschaft* 5: 11–15

Koldewey 1911:
R. Koldewey, *Die Tempel von Babylon und Borsippa*. Wissenschaftliche Veröffentlichung der Deutschen Orient-Gesellschaft 15. Leipzig.

Koldewey 1913:
R. Koldewey, *Das Wiedererstehende Babylon*. Leipzig.

Koldewey 1914:
R. Koldewey, *The Excavations at Babylon*. London.

Koldewey 1918:
R. Koldewey, *Das Ischtar-Tor in Babylon*. Wissenschaftliche Veröffentlichung der Deutschen Orient-Gesellschaft 32. Leipzig.

Koldewey 1990:
R. Koldewey, *Das Wiedererstehende Babylon* (5th revised edn, B. Hrouda, ed.). Berlin and Munich.

Koldewey and Wetzel 1931:
R. Koldewey and F. Wetzel, *Die Königsburgen von Babylon I, Die Südburg*. Wissenschaftliche Veröffentlichung der Deutschen Orient-Gesellschaft 54. Leipzig.

Koldewey and Wetzel 1932:
R. Koldewey and F. Wetzel, *Die Königsburgen von Babylon II, Die Hauptburg und der Sommerpalast Nebukadnezars im Hügel Babil*. Wissenschaftliche Veröffentlichung der Deutschen Orient-Gesellschaft 55. Leipzig.

Kohlmeyer, Strommenger and Schmid 1991:
K. Kohlmeyer, E. Strommenger and H. Schmid, *Wierererstehendes Babylon. Eine antike Weltstadt im Blick der Forschung*. Berlin.

König 2007:
E. König, *The Bedford Hours: The Making of a Medieval Masterpiece*. London.

Kramp 2005:
M. Kramp (ed.), *Eine Gemälgalerie für Koblenz. 170 Jahre Mittelrhein-Museum. 250. Geburtstag des Stifters Joseph Gregor Lang*. Koblenz.

Kugler 1907:
F.X. Kugler, *Entwicklung der Babylonischen Planetenkunde von ihren Anfängen bis auf Christus*. Münster.

Kunoth 1956:
G. Kunoth, *Die Historische Architektur Fischers von Erlach*. Düsseldorf.

Lademann 2007:
D. Lademann, *Larrinaga: Seven Wonders of the Ancient World: The Story*. Privately printed by Ancient Wonders, Inc.

Lambert 1964:
W.G. Lambert, 'The Reign of Nebuchadnezzar I: A turning point in the history of ancient Mesopotamian religion,' in W.S. McCullough (ed.), *The Seed of Wisdom. Essays in Honor of T.J. Meek*: 3–13. Toronto

Lambert 1965:
W.G. Lambert, 'Nebuchadnezzar King of Justice,' *Iraq* 27: 1–11.

Lambert 1984:
W.G. Lambert, 'The History of the muš-huš in Ancient Mesopotamia,' in P. Borgeaud, Y. Christe and I. Urio (eds), *l'Animal, l'Homme, le Dieu dans le Proche-Orient Ancien*. Actes du Colloque de Catigny 1981: 87–94. Leuven.

Lancel 2002:
S. Lancel, *St Augustine*. London.

Langdon 1912:
S. Langdon, *Die Neubabylonischen Keilinschriften*. Vorderasiatische Bibliothek 4. Leipzig.

Larsen 1987:
M.T. Larsen, 'The Mesopotamian Lukewarm Mind: Reflections on science, divination and literacy,' in F. Rochberg-Halton (ed.), *Language, Literature and History: Philological and Historical Studies Presented to Erica Reiner*: 203–25. New Haven.

Larsen 1989:
M.T. Larsen, 'Orientalism and the Ancient Near East,' in M. Harbsmeier and M.T. Larsen (eds), *The Humanities between Art and Science: Intellectual Developments 1880–1914*: 181–202. Copenhagen.

Larsen 1995:
M.T. Larsen, 'The 'Babel/Bible Controversy and its Aftermath,' in J.M. Sasson (ed.), *Civilizations of the Ancient Near East*. 4 vols. Vol. 1: 95–106. New York.

Larsen 1996:
M.T. Larsen, *The Conquest of Assyria: Excavations in an Antique Land 1840–1860*. London and New York.

Layard 1895:
A. Layard (ed.), *The Marvellous Adventures of Sir John Maundeville Kt*. Westminster.

Layard 1849:
A. H. Layard, *Nineveh and its Remains*. 2 vols. London.

Layard 1853:
A.H. Layard, *Discoveries in the Ruins of Nineveh and Babylon*. London.

Lehmann 1994:
R.G. Lehmann, *Friedrich Delitzsch und der Babel-Bibel-Streit*. Fribourg.

Lehmann 1999:
R.G. Lehmann, 'Der Babel-Bibel-Streit. Ein kulturpolitisches Wetterleuchten,' in J. Renger, J. (ed.), *Babylon: Focus mesopotamischer Geschichte, Wiege früher Gelehrsamkeit, Mythos in der Moderne. 2. Internationales Colloquium der Deutschen Orient-Gesellschaft 24.–26. März 1998 in Berlin*: 505–21. Saarbrücken.

Lemoisne 1946:
P.-A. Lemoisne, *Degas et son œuvre*. 2 vols, Paris.

Lieberman 1987:
S. Lieberman, 'A Mesopotamian Background for the So-called Aggadic 'Measures' of Biblical Hermeneutics?,' *Hebrew Union College Annual* 58: 157–225.

Lindsay 1989:
D.W. Lindsay, 'The Order of Blake's Large Colour Prints,' *The Huntington Library Quarterly* 52(1): 19–41.

Lipschits 2003:
O. Lipschits, 'Demographic Changes in Judah between the Seventh and the Fifth Centuries BCE,' in O. Lipschits and J. Blenkinsopp (eds), *Judah and the Judeans in the Neo-Babylonian Period*: 323–76. Winona Lake.

Lister 1973:
R. Lister, 'References to Blake in Samuel Palmer's Letters,' in M.D. Paley and M. Phillips (eds), *William Blake: Essays in Honour of Sir Geoffrey Keynes*: 305–9. Oxford.

Lloyd 1980:
S. Lloyd, *Foundations in the Dust: The Story of Mesopotamian Excavation* (2nd edn). London.

Locher 1992:
J.L. Locher, *Escher: The Complete Graphic Works* (2nd edn). London.

Loftus 1857:
W.K. Loftus, *Travels and Researches in Chaldaea and Susiana*. London.

Losty 1982:
J.P. Losty, *The Art of the Book in India*. London.

Louvre 1997:
Des mécènes par milliers. Un siècle de dons par les Amis du Louvre. Paris.

Macdonald Kinneir 1813:
J. Macdonald Kinneir, *A Geographical Memoir of the Persian Empire*. London.

Madonna 1976:
M.L. Madonna, '*Septem Mundi Miracula* come templi delle virtu. Pirro Ligorio e l'interpretazione cinquescentesca delle mervaiglie del Mondo,' *Psicon. Rivista internazionale di architettura* 7(3): 24–63.

Mahon 1949:
D. Mahon, 'Guercino's Paintings of Semiramis,' *The Art Bulletin* 31(3): 217–23.

Mansbach 1982:
S.A. Mansbach, 'Pieter Bruegel's Towers of Babel,' *Zeitschrift für Kunstgeschichte* 45(1): 43–56.

Martin-Jaquemier 1999:
M. Martin-Jaquemier, *l'Âge d'or du mythe de Babel 1480–1600. De la conscience de l'altérité à la naissance de la modernité*. Mont-de-Marsan.

Marzahn 1994:
J. Marzahn, *The Ishtar Gate. The Processional Way. The New Year Festival at Babylon*. Berlin.

Marzahn et al. 1992:
J. Marzahn, L. Jakob-Rost, E. Klengel-Brandt, R.-B. Wartke, *Das Vorderasiatisches Museum, Kataloghandbuch*. Mainz.

Matthews 2003:
R.J. Matthews, *The Archaeology of Mesopotamia: Theories and Approaches*. London.

McCall and Tubb 2003:
H. McCall and J.N. Tubb, *I am the Bull of Nineveh: Victorian Design in the Assyrian Style*. [Privately printed to accompany an exhibition in the Department of the Ancient Near East, British Museum, July 2003]. London.

Meder 1932:
J. Meder, *Dürer-Katalog: ein Handbuch über Albrecht Dürers Stiche, Radierungen, Holzschnitte, deren Zustände, Ausgaben und Wasserzeichen*. Vienna.

Meissner 1891:
B. Meissner, 'Babylonischen Pflanzennamen,' *Zeitschrift für Assyriologie* 6: 289–98.

Meissner 1901:
B. Meissner, *Von Babylon nach den Ruinen von Hira und Huarnaq*. Leipzig.

Meyer 1961:
G.R. Meyer, 'Ein Onyx-Zepter aus Babylon,' *Forschungen und Berichte* 5: 7–9.

Michalski 2003:
S. Michalski, 'Venus as Semiramis: A new interpretation of the central figure of Botticelli's "Primavera",' *Artibus et Historiae* 24(48): 213–22.

Michaux 1800:
A. Michaux, 'Cabinet des Antiques de la Bibliothèque nationale,' *Magasin Encyclopédique ou Journal des Sciences, des Lettres et des Arts* (rédigé par A.L. Millin) 6(3): 86–7.

Mignan 1829:
R. Mignan, *Travels in Chaldaea Including a Journey from Bussorah to Bagdad, Hillah, and Babylon, performed on foot* … London.

Millard 1964:
A.R. Millard, 'Another Babylonian Chronicle Text,' *Iraq* 26: 14–35.

Millin 1802:
A.-L. Millin, *Monuments inédits*. 2 vols. Paris.

Minkowski 1960:
H. Minkowski, *Aus dem Nebel der Vergangenheit steigt der Turm zu Babel: Bilder aus 1000 Jahren*. Berlin.

Minkowski 1991:
H. Minkowski, *Vermutungen über den Turm zu Babel*. Freren.

Mitchell 1988:
T.C. Mitchell, *The Bible in the British Museum. Interpreting the Evidence*. London.

Mitchell 1995:
W.J.T. Mitchell, 'Chaosthetics: Blake's sense of form,' *The Huntington Library Quarterly* 58(3): 441–58.

Mithen 2005:
S.J. Mithen, *The Singing Neanderthals: The Origins of Music, Language, Mind and Body*. London.

Monnier 1978:
G. Monnier, 'La genese d'une oeuvre de Degas. 'Semiramis construisant une ville',' *Revue du Louvre et des Musées de France* 28(5–6): 407–26.

Muel 1996:
F. Muel, *Tenture de l'Apocalypse d'Angers, l'Envers et l'Endroit*. Nantes.

Müller-Kessler 2002:
C. Müller-Kessler, 'Die aramäische Beschwörung und ihre Rezeption in den Mandäisch-magischen Texten,' *Res Orientales* 14: 193–208.

Muther 1972:
R. Muther, *German Book Illustration of the Gothic Period and the Early Renaissance (1460–1530)*. Metuchen.

Myers 1874
P.V.N. Myers, *Remains of Lost Empires*. New York.

Myrone 2008:
M. Myrone, *The Blake Book*. London.

Nathan 1930:
E. Nathan, *Jewish Travellers*, reprint 2004. London.

Nagel 1979:
W. Nagel, 'Where were the "Hanging Gardens" Located in Babylon?' *Sumer* 35: 242–41.

Nagler 1860:
G.K. Nagler, *Die Monogrammisten*. Vol 2. Munich.

Nesselrath 1999:
H.-G. Nesselrath, 'Herodot und Babylon: die Hauptort Mesopotamiens in den Augen eines

Griechen des 5. Jhs v. Chr,' in J. Renger (ed.), *Babylon: Focus mesopotamischer Geschichte, Wiege früher Gelehrsamkeit, Mythos in der Moderne; 24–26 März 1998 in Berlin, im Auftrag des Vorstands der Deutschen Orient-Gesellschaft (Internationales Colloquium der Deutschen Orient-Gesellschaft, 2)*: 189–206. Saarbrücken.

Neugebauer 1955:
O. Neugebauer, *Astronomical Cuneiform Texts. Babylonian Ephemerides of the Seleucid Period for the Motion of the Sun, the Moon, and the Planets*. Princeton and London.

Neugebauer 1988:
O. Neugebauer, 'A Babylonian Lunar Ephemeris from Roman Egypt,' in E. Leichty, M. deJ. Ellis and P. Gerardi (eds), *A Scientific Humanist: Studies in Memory of Abraham Sachs*. Occasional Publications of the Samuel Noah Kramer Fund 9: 301–4. Philadelphia.

Niebuhr 1774–8:
C. Niebuhr, *Reisebeschreibung nach Arabien und andern umliegenden Ländern...*, 2 vols. Copenhagen.

Nijhoff 1933–9:
W. Nijhoff, *Nederlandsche houtsneden 1500–1550*. The Hague.

Nissen et al 1993:
H. Nissen, P. Damerow and R.K. Englund, *Archaic Bookkeeping. Writing and Techniques of Economic Administration in the Ancient Near East*. Translated by P. Larsen. Chicago.

Oates 1986:
J. Oates, *Babylon* (2nd edn). London.

Oelsner 1999/2000:
J. Oelsner, Review of R. Rollinger, *Herodots babylonischer Logos*, Innsbruck 1993. *Archiv für Orientforschung* 46/47: 373–80.

Omer 1981:
M. Omer, *Turner and the Bible*. Oxford.

Ooghe 2007:
B. Ooghe, 'The Rediscovery of Babylonia: European travellers and the development of knowledge on Lower Mesopotamia, sixteenth to early nineteenth century,' *Journal of the Royal Asiatic Society* (3rd series) 17(3): 231–52.

Oppert 1863:
J. Oppert, *Expédition scientifique en Mésopotamie executée par ordre du gouvernement de 1851 à 1854, par MM. Fulgence Fresnel, Félix Thomas, Jules Oppert*. 2 vols. Paris.

Otter 1748:
J. Otter, *Voyage en Turquie et en Perse*. 2 vols. Paris.

Panofsky 1969:
E. Panofsky, 'Comments on Art and the Reformation,' in C. Harbison (ed.), *Symbols in Transformation: Iconographic Themes at the Time of the Reformation*. Princeton.

Parker and Dubberstein 1971:
R.A. Parker and W.H. Dubberstein, *Babylonian Chronology 626 B.C.–A.D. 75*. Reprint, Providence.

Parpola 1995:
S. Parpola, 'The Assyrian Cabinet,' in M. Dietrich

and O. Loretz (eds), *Vom Alten Orient zum Alten Testament. Festschrift fur Wolfram Freiherrn van Soden*. Alter Orient und Altes Testament 240: 379–401. Neukirchen-Vluyn.

Passavant 1862:
J.D. Passavant, *Le Peintre-graveur* [vol. 3]. Leipzig.

Paterson 1895:
J.G. Paterson, *From Bombay through Babylonia*. Glasgow.

Pearce 1996:
L.E. Pearce, 'The Number Syllabary Texts,' *Journal of the American Oriental Society* 116(3): 453–74.

Pedersén 2005a:
O. Pedersén, *Archive und Bibliotheken in Babylon: Die Tontafeln der Grabung Robert Koldeweys 1899–1917*. Abhandlungen der Deutschen Orient-Gesellschaft 25. Saarbrücken.

Pedersén 2005b:
O. Pedersén, 'Foreign Professionals in Babylon: Evidence from the archive in the palace of Nebuchadnezzar II,' in W.H. van Soldt (ed.), *Ethnicity in Ancient Mesopotamia: Papers Read at the 48th Rencontre Assyriologique Internationale, Leiden, 1–4 July 2002*: 267–72. Leiden.

Peters 1897:
J.P. Peters, *Nippur, or Explorations and Adventures on the Euphrates: the Narrative of the University of Pennsylvania Expedition to Babylonia in the Years 1888–1890*. 2 vols. New York and London.

Pinches 1882:
T.G. Pinches, 'On a Cuneiform Inscription Relating to the Capture of Babylon by Cyrus,' *Transactions of the Society of Biblical Archaeology* 7: 139–76.

Pinches 1883:
T.G. Pinches, 'Comment,' in *Proceedings of the Society of Biblical Archaeology* 5: 103–7.

Pinches 1896:
T.G. Pinches, 'The Religious Ideas of the Babylonians,' *Journal of the Transactions of the Victoria Institute* 28: 1–3

Pingree 1998:
D. Pingree, 'Legacies in Astronomy and Celestial Omens,' in S. Dalley (ed.), *The Legacy of Mesopotamia*: 125–37. Oxford.

Pollock 1999:
S.M. Pollock, *Ancient Mesopotamia: The Eden that never Was*. Cambridge.

Powell 1987–90:
M.A. Powell, 'Masse und Gewichte,' *Reallexicon der Assyriologie* 7: 457–530.

Pritchard 1969a:
J.B. Pritchard (ed.), *Ancient Near Eastern Texts Relating to the Old Testament* (3rd edn). Princeton.

Pritchard 1969b:
J.B. Pritchard (ed.), *The Ancient Near Eastern in Pictures Relating to the Old Testament* (2nd edn). Princeton.

Rakowitz 1997:
R.N. Rakowitz, 'Exodus from the Babylonian Captivity: The Jews of modern Iraq,' *International Journal of Group Tensions* 27: 177–91.

Rassam 1897:
H. Rassam, *Asshur and the Land of Nimrod*. New York and Cincinnati.

Rawlinson 1858:
G. Rawlinson, *The History of Herodotus*. 4 vols. London.

Rawlinson 1861:
H.C. Rawlinson, 'On the Birs Nimrud, or the Great Temple of Borsippa,' Journal *of the Royal Asiatic Society* 18: 1–34.

Rawlinson 1862–7:
G. Rawlinson, *The Five Great Monarchies of the Ancient Eastern World*. 4 vols. London.

Rawlinson and Norris 1861:
H.C. Rawlinson and E. Norris, *A Selection from the Historical Inscriptions of Chaldaea, Assyria, and Babylonia. The Cuneiform Inscriptions of Western Asia*. Vol. 1. London.

Ray 1693:
J. Ray, *A Collection of Curious Travels and Voyages*. London.

Reade 1964:
J.E. Reade, 'More Drawings of Ashurbanipal Sculptures,' *Iraq* 26 (1): 1–13.

Reade 1986:
J.E. Reade, 'Rassam's Babylonian Collection: The excavations and the archives.' Introduction to E. Leichty, *Catalogue of the Babylonian Tablets in the British Museum*, vol. VI: xii–xxxvi. London.

Reade 1993:
J.E. Reade, 'Hormuzd Rassam and his Discoveries,' *Iraq* 55: 39–62.

Reade 1999:
J.E. Reade, 'Early British Excavations at Babylon,' in J. Renger (ed.), *Babylon: Focus mesopotamischer Geschichte, Wiege früher Gelehrsamkeit, Mythos in der Moderne; 24–26 März 1998 in Berlin, im Auftrag des Vorstands der Deutschen Orient-Gesellschaft (Internationales Colloquium der Deutschen Orient-Gesellschaft, 2)*: 47–65. Saarbrücken.

Reade 2000:
J.E. Reade, 'Alexander the Great and the Hanging Gardens of Babylon,' *Iraq* 62: 195–217.

Reade 2002:
J.E. Reade, 'Early Monuments in Gulf Stone at the British Museum, with observations on some Gudea statues and the location of Agade,' *Zeitschrift für Assyriologie* 92: 258–95.

Reade and Safadi 1986:
J.E. Reade and Y. Safadi, *Claudius James Rich: Diplomat, Archaeologist and Collector* [4-page exhibition brochure]. London.

Reff 1976:
T. Reff, *The Notebooks of Edgar Degas. A Catalogue of the Thirty-eight Notebooks in the Bibliothèque Nationale and Other Collections*. 2 vols. Oxford.

Reiner 1985:
E. Reiner, *Your Thwarts in Pieces, your Mooring Rope Cut: Poetry from Babylonia and Assyria*. Michigan Studies in the Humanities 5. Ann Arbor.

Rejwan 1985:
N. Rejwan. *The Jews of Iraq: 3000 Years of History and Culture*. London.

Reuther 1926:
O. Reuther, *Die Innenstadt von Babylon (Merkes)*. Wissenschaftliche Veröffentlichung der Deutschen Orient-Gesellschaft 47. Leipzig.

Rich 1815:
C.J. Rich, *Memoir on the Ruins of Babylon*. London.

Rich 1839:
C.J. Rich, *Narrative of a Journey to the Site of Babylon ... edited by his Widow*. London.

Richey 1992:
W. Richey, 'The French Revolution: Blake's epic dialogue with Edmund Burke,' *English Literary History* 59: 817–37.

Robson 1999:
E. Robson, *Mesopotamian Mathematics, 2100–1600 BC*. Technical Constants in Bureaucracy and Education. Oxford Editions of Cuneiform Texts 14. Oxford.

Rochberg 2004:
F. Rochberg, *The Heavenly Writing. Divination, Horoscopy, and Astronomy in Mesopotamian Culture*. Cambridge.

Rochberg-Halton 1988:
F. Rochberg-Halton, *Aspects of Babylonian Celestial Divination: The Lunar Eclipse Tablets of Enûma Anu Enlil*. Archiv für Orientforschung Beiheft 22. Horn.

Rogers 1900:
R.W. Rogers, *A History of Babylonia and Assyria*. 2 vols. New York and Cincinnati.

Roth 1995:
M. Roth, *Law Collections from Mesopotamia and Asia Minor*. Society of Biblical Literature Writings from the Ancient World, Series 6. Atlanta.

Rutten 1936:
M. Rutten, *Encyclopédie photographique de l'art*. Vol. I. Paris.

Sack 1991:
R.H. Sack, *Images of Nebuchadnezzar: The Emergence of a Legend*. London and Toronto.

Saleh 1966:
Z. Saleh, *Britain and Mesopotamia (Iraq to 1914): A Study in British Foreign Affairs*. Baghdad.

Savage-Smith 1985:
E. Savage-Smith, *Islamicate Celestial Globes: Their History, Construction and Use*. Washington, DC.

Schama 1999:
S. Schama, *Rembrandt's Eyes*. London.

Schaudig 2001:
H. Schaudig, *Die Inschriften Nabonids von Babylon und Kyros' des Großen samt den in ihrem Umfeld entstandenen Tendenzschriften. Textausgabe und Grammatik*. Alter Orient und Altes Testament 256. Münster.

Scheil 1902:
V.Scheil, *Code des lois d'Hammurabi (Droit privé) roi de Babylone, vers l'an 2000 av. J.-C.* Mémoires de la Délégation en Perse vol. 4. Textes élamites sémitiques, Second Series: 11–162. Paris.

Scheil and Dieulefoy 1913:
V. Scheil and M. Dieulafoy, 'Esagil ou le temple de Bêl-Marduk à Babylone'. *Mémoires de l'Institut National de France, Académie des Inscriptions et Belles-Lettres* 39: 293–372.

Schmid 1995:
H. Schmidt, *Der tempelturm Etemenanki in Babylon*. Baghdader Forschungen, Band 17. Mainz am Rhein.

Seidel 1968:
U. Seidel, 'Die Babylonischen Kudurru-Reliefs,' *Baghdader Mitteillungen* 4: 7–220.

Seipel 2003:
W. Seipel, *Der Turmbau zu Babel. Ursprung und Vielfalt von Sprache und Schrift. Eine Ausstellung des Kunsthistorisches Museums Wien für die Europäische Kulturhaupstadt Graz 2003*. 4 vols. Graz and Milan.

Seipel and Wieczorek 1999:
W. Seipel and A. Wieczorek, *Von Babylon bis Jerusalem. Die Welt altorientalischen Königsstädte*. 2 vols. Mannheim, Vienna and Jersualem.

Selby 1859:
W.B. Selby, *Memoir on the Ruins of Babylon*. Selections from the Memoirs of the Bombay Government, New Series, vol. 51. Bombay.

Sérrulaz 1984:
M. Sérullaz, *Dessins d'Eugène Delacroix*. Musée du Louvre, Inventaire général des dessins. 2 vols. Paris.

Smith 1876:
G. Smith, [article in] *The Athenaeum* 2520 (12th Feb. 1876): 232–3 [republished in Koldewey 1914: 192–3].

Smith 1924:
S. Smith, *Babylonian Historical Texts relating to the Capture and Downfall of Babylon*. London.

Smith 2002:
E. Smith, *Evelyn Pickering De Morgan and the Allegorical Body*. Fairleigh.

Soucek 1975:
P.P. Soucek, 'An Illustrated Manuscript of al-Bīrunī's *Chronology of Ancient Nations*.' In P. J. Chelkowski (ed.), *The Scholar and the Saint: Studies in Commemoration of Abu `l-Raihan al-Bīrunī and Jalal al-Din al-Rūmī*': 103–68. New York:

Starcky 1990:
E. Starcky, *Rembrandt: The Masterworks*. London.

Steinmetzer 1922:
F.X. Steinmetzer, *Die Babylonischen Kudurru (Grentzsteine) als Urkundenform*. Parderborn.

Stevenson and Walker 1985:
F.R. Stephenson and C.B.F. Walker (eds), *Halley's Comet in History*. London.

Streck 1916:
M. Streck, *Assurbanipal und die letzten Assyrischen Könige bis zum Untergange Nineveh's*. Part 2. Leipzig.

Stol 2004:
M. Stol, 'An Assyriologist reads Hippocrates,' in H.F.J. Horstmanshoff and M. Stol (eds), *Magic and Rationality in Ancient Near Eastern and Graeco-*

Roman Medicine: 63–78. Leiden.

Stolper 1999:

M.W. Stolper, 'Achaemenid legal texts from the Kasr: interim observations,' in J. Renger (ed.), *Babylon: Focus mesopotamischer Geschichte, Wiege früher Gelehrsamkeit, Mythos in der Moderne; 24–26 März 1998 in Berlin, im Auftrag des Vorstands der Deutschen Orient-Gesellschaft (Internationales Colloquium der Deutschen Orient-Gesellschaft, 2)*: 365–75. Saarbrücken.

Stutenbrock 1997:

C. Stutenbrock, *Niederländische Gemälde des 16. und 17. Jahrhunderts*. Mainz.

Sullivan 1992 :

M.A. Sullivan, 'Bruegel's "Misanthrope": Renaissance art for a humanist audience.' *Artibus et Historiae* 13 (26): 143–62.

Tavernier 1678:

J.B. Tavernier, *Les six voyages de Jean Baptiste Tavernier, Ecuyer Baron d'Aubonne, en Turquie, en Perse, et aux Indes*. 2 vols. [copied from the Paris edition]. Amsterdam.

Thomas 1956:

L. Thomas, *Seven Wonders of the World*. Garden City.

Thomason 2001:

A.K. Thomason, 'Representations of the North Syrian Landscape in Neo-Assyrian Art,' *Bulletin of the American Schools of Oriental Research* 323: 63–96.

Thureau-Dangin 1921:

F. Thureau-Dangin, *Rituels accadiens*. Paris.

Thureau-Dangin 1922:

F. Thureau-Dangin, *Tablettes d'Uruk à l'usage des prêtres du temple d'Anu au temps des Séleucides*. Textes cunéiformes du Louvre, Vol. 6. Paris.

Toomer 1984:

G.J. Toomer, *Ptolemy's Almagest*. London.

Torriti 1978:

P. Torriti, *La Pinacoteca nazionale di Siena. I dipinti dal XV al XVIII secolo*. Siena.

Torriti 1990:

P. Torriti, *La Pinacoteca di Siena. I dipinti*. Siena.

Townsend 2003:

J. Townsend, *William Blake: The Painter at Work*. Princeton and London.

Unger 1930:

E. Unger, *Zur Topographie von Babylon nach der keilinschriftlichen Überlieferung*,' in F. Wetzel, *Die Stadtmauern von Babylon*. Wissenschaftliche Veröffentlichung der Deutschen Orient-Gesellschaft 48: 84–112. Berlin.

Unger 1931:

E. Unger, *Babylon. Die Heilige Stadt nach der Beschreibung der Babylonier*. Berlin and Leipzig.

Van de Mieroop 2004:

M. Van de Mieroop, *A History of the Ancient Near East, ca. 3000–323 BC*. Oxford.

Van der Spek 2003:

R.J. van der Spek, 'Darius III, Alexander the Great and Babylonian Scholarship,' in W. Henkelman

and A. Kuhrt (eds), *A Persian Perspective. Essays in Memory of Heleen-Sancisi-Weerdenburg*. Achaemenid History 13: 289–346. Leiden.

Van der Spek 2008:

R. Van der Spek, 'Berossus as Babylonian Chronicler and Greek Historian,' in R.J. van der Spek (ed.) with the assistance of G. Haayer, F.A.M. Wiggermann, M. Prins and J. Bilbija, *Studies in Ancient Near Eastern World View and Society presented to Marten Stol on the Occasion of his 65th Birthday, 10 November 2005, and his Retirement from the Vrije Universiteit Amsterdam*: 277–318. Bethesda, Maryland.

Van Rymsdyck and van Rymsdyck 1778:

J. and A. van Rymsdyck, *Museum Britannicum*. London.

Vattioni 1970:

F. Vattioni, 'Epigrafia Aramaica,' *Augustinianum* 10: 493–532.

Walker 1972:

C.B.F. Walker, 'A Recently Identified Fragment of the Cyrus Cylinder,' *Iran* 10: 158–9.

Wallenfels 2008:

R. Wallenfels, 'A New Stone Inscription of Nebuchadnezzar II,' in M. Ross (ed.), *From the Banks of the Euphrates: Studies in Honour of Alice Louise Slotsky*: 267–94. Winona Lake.

Ward 1981:

F.A.B. Ward, *A Catalogue of Scientific Instruments in the Department of Medieval and Later Antiquities of the British Museum*. London.

Warner 1982:

N.O. Warner, The Iconic Mode of William Blake,' *Rocky Mountain Review of Language and Literature* 36: 219–34.

Webb 1870:

F.C. Webb, *Up the Tigris to Baghdad*. London

Wegener 1995:

U. Wegener, *Die Faszination des Masslosen. Der Turmbau zu Babel von Pieter Bruegel bis Athanasius Kircher*. Hildesheim, Zurich and New York.

Weidner 1939:

E.F. Weidner, 'Jojachin, König von Juda, in babylonischen Keilschrifttexten,' in *Mélanges syriens offerts à Monsieur René Dussaud*. Vol 2. Bibliothèque Archéologique et Historique 30: 923–35. Paris.

Weidner 1954–6:

E.F. Weidner, 'Hochverrat gegen Nebukadnezar II,' in *Archiv für Orientforschung* 17: 1–9.

Weidner 1967:

E. Weidner, *Gestirn-Darstellungen auf Babylonsichen Tontafeln*. Österreichische Akademie der Wissenschaften Philosophisch-Historische Klasse Sitzungsberichte, 254. Band, 2 Abhandlung. Vienna.

Weinfeld 1991:

M. Weinfeld, 'Semiramis: Her name and her origin,' in M. Cogan, M. and I. Eph'al (eds), *Ah, Assyria: Studies in Assyrian History and Ancient Near Eastern Historiography Presented to Hayim Tadmor*.

Scripta Hierosolymitana, Publications of the Hebrew University of Jerusalem 32: 99–103. Jerusalem.

Wellesz 1959:

E. Wellesz, 'An Early al-Sufi Manuscript,' *Ars Orientalis* 3: 1–27.

Wellesz 1964:

E. Wellesz, 'Islamic Astronomical Imagery,' *Oriental Art* New Series 10 (2): 85–91

Westenholz 1996:

J.G. Westenholz (ed.), *Royal Cities of the Biblical World. Issued in Conjunction with a Special Exhibition held at the Bible Lands Museum, Jerusalem: Jerusalem, a Capital for All Times, Royal Cities of the Biblical World, January 17, 1996 – December 31, 1996*. Jerusalem.

Westenholz 2007:

A. Westenholz, 'The Graeco-Babyloniaca once again,' *Zeitschrift für Assyriologie* 97: 262–313.

Wetzel 1930:

F. Wetzel, *Die Stadtmauern von Babylon*. Wissenschaftliche Veröffentlichung der Deutschen Orient-Gesellschaft 48. Berlin.

Wetzel, Schmidt and Mallwitz 1957:

F. Wetzel, E. Schmidt and A. Mallwitz, *Das Babylon der Spätzeit*, Wissenschaftliche Veröffentlichung der Deutschen Orient-Gesellschaft 62. Berlin.

Wetzel and Weissbach 1938:

F. Wetzel and F.H. Weissbach, *Das Haupttheiligtum des Marduk in Babylon, Esagila und Etemenanki*. Wissenschaftliche Veröffentlichung der Deutschen Orient-Gesellschaft 59. Berlin.

White and Boon 1969:

C. White and K.G. Boon, *Rembrandt's Etchings: An Illustrated Critical Catalogue*. 2 vols. Amsterdam.

Wied 1990:

A. Wied, *Lucas and Marten van Valckenborch (1535–1597 und 1534–1612). Das Gesamtwerk mit kritischem Œuvrekatalog*. Freren.

Williams, J. 1994–2001.

The Illustrated Beatus: A Corpus of Illustrations of the Commentary on the Apocalypse. 4 vols. London.

Wind 1937:

E. Wind, 'The Saint as Monster,' *Journal of the Warburg Institute* 1(2): 183.

Wiseman 1956:

D.J. Wiseman, *Chronicles of Chaldean Kings (626–556 BC) in the British Museum*. London.

Wiseman 1966:

D.J. Wiseman, 'Some Egyptians in Babylonia,' *Iraq* 28: 154–8.

Wiseman 1972:

D.J. Wiseman, 'A Babylonian Architect,' *Anatolian Studies* 22: 141–7.

Wiseman 1983:

D.J. Wiseman, 'Mesopotamian Gardens,' *Anatolian Studies* 33: 137–44.

Zell 2002:

M. Zell, *Reframing Rembrandt: Jews and the Christian Image in Seventeenth-century Amsterdam*. Berkeley and London.

Index